SIMPLY COMPUTING FOR SENIORS

by Linda Clark

A John Wiley and Sons, Ltd, Publication

This edition first published 2011.

©2011. John Wiley & Sons, Ltd.

Registered office
John Wiley & Sons Ltd, The Atrium, Southern Gate, Chichester, West Sussex, PO19 8SQ, United Kingdom

For details of our global editorial offices, for customer services and for information about how to apply for permission to reuse the copyright material in this book please see our website at www.wiley.com.

The right of the author to be identified as the author of this work has been asserted in accordance with the Copyright, Designs and Patents Act 1988.

All rights reserved. No part of this publication may be reproduced, stored in a retrieval system, or transmitted, in any form or by any means, electronic, mechanical, photocopying, recording or otherwise, except as permitted by the UK Copyright, Designs and Patents Act 1988, without the prior permission of the publisher.

Wiley also publishes its books in a variety of electronic formats. Some content that appears in print may not be available in electronic books.

Designations used by companies to distinguish their products are often claimed as trademarks. All brand names and product names used in this book are trade names, service marks, trademarks or registered trademarks of their respective owners. The publisher is not associated with any product or vendor mentioned in this book. This publication is designed to provide accurate and authoritative information in regard to the subject matter covered. It is sold on the understanding that the publisher is not engaged in rendering professional services. If professional advice or other expert assistance is required, the services of a competent professional should be sought.

All website information, including prices and privacy settings, was correct at time of going to press. Websites do constantly update their privacy settings and policies. Please check the appropriate website for current details.

Wiley and the Wiley logo are trademarks or registered trademarks of John Wiley and Sons, Ltd. and/or its affiliates in the United States and/or other countries, and may not be used without written permission. iPhone, iPad and iPod are trademarks of Apple Computer, Inc. All other trademarks are the property of their respective owners. John Wiley and Sons, Ltd. is not associated with any product or vendor mentioned in the book. This book is not endorsed by Apple Computer, Inc.

Microsoft product screenshots reprinted with permission from Microsoft Corporation. ©2011 Microsoft

ISBN 978-1-119-97196-2

A catalogue record for this book is available from the British Library.

Set in Gill Sans Std

Printed in Italy by Printer Trento

Publisher's Acknowledgements

Some of the people who helped bring this book to market include the following:

Editorial and Production

VP Consumer and Technology Publishing Director: Michelle Leete

Associate Director – Book Content Management: Martin Tribe

Executive Commissioning Editor: Birgit Gruber

Assistant Editor: Ellie Scott

Development Editor: Shena Deuchars

Senior Project Editor: Sara Shlaer

Editorial Manager: Jodi Jensen

Editorial Assistant: Leslie Saxman

Marketing

Associate Marketing Director: Louise Breinholt

Marketing Executive: Kate Parrett

Composition Services

Layout: Indianapolis Composition Services

Compositor: Indianapolis Composition Services

Proof Reader: Susan Hobbs

Indexer: Potomac Indexing, LLC

Series Designer: Patrick Cunningham

About the Author

Linda Clark has run workshops and created learning materials designed to pass on knowledge of computing in clear, concise and simple language throughout her career. Linda's fascination for computers started around 1985 when she was training to become a college lecturer. She has taught computing skills to many students in further education and, more recently, to librarians throughout the Highlands and Islands of Scotland. On retirement, she joined Inverness & Black Isle U3A and formed two computing groups. In July 2007, Linda joined a steering group determined to set up a virtual U3A based entirely on the Internet. Now fully operational, this proved to be an exciting and stimulating challenge. She professes to be a computer user not an IT specialist and believes that she is learning something new every day. Her philosophy is "if I can do it so can you".

Author's Acknowledgments

I hope that you enjoy this book as much as I have enjoyed writing it. It has given me immense satisfaction to have the opportunity to write for beginners in a way that I hope will be accessible and will result in a growth in ability and confidence. My thanks therefore must go to Wiley for the wonderful help and support I have been given during the writing process: Birgit Gruber for inviting me to write the book and believing I could do it; Ellie Scott for her continuing support, encouragement and help; and Sara Shlaer for pointing me in the right direction from Chapter 1. In fact, I wish to record my thanks to all at Wiley for the professional way in which they dealt with me, a novice writer. I have learnt a lot. There is no way I could have completed this book without the assistance of Shena Deuchars, Mitcham Editorial Services who has made my writing and ideas come alive and sparkle. Finally, my thanks to Graham for being there, listening, encouraging and keeping me on track, almost.

Visit my website, lindasimplycomputing.com, for additional information and help.

How to Use This Book

Who Needs This Book
SIMPLY Computing for Seniors teaches you not only all you need to know about working with a computer, but also how to make real-world use of it. The simple, yet elegant, design features a multitude of images as well as tips and tricks to make this a perfect reference for the over 50s – just follow the instructions on your own computer.

Chapter Organisation
This book consists of sections, all listed in the book's table of contents. A *section* is a set of steps that show you how to complete a specific computer task.

Each section, usually contained on two facing pages, has an introduction to the task at hand, a set of full-colour screen shots and steps that walk you through the task and a set of tips. This format allows you to quickly look at a topic of interest and learn it instantly.

Chapters group together sections with a common theme. A chapter may also contain pages that give you the background information needed to understand the sections in a chapter.

Using the Mouse
This book uses the following conventions to describe the actions you perform when using the mouse:

Click
Press your left mouse button once. You generally click your mouse on something to select something on the screen.

Double-click
Press your left mouse button twice. Double-clicking something on the computer screen generally opens whatever item you have double-clicked.

Right-click
Press your right mouse button. When you right-click on anything on the computer screen, the program displays a shortcut menu containing commands specific to the selected item.

Click, Drag and Release the Mouse
Move your mouse pointer and hover it over an item on the screen. Press and hold down the left mouse button. Now, move the mouse to where you want to place the item and then release the button. You use this method to move an item from one area of the computer screen to another.

The Conventions in This Book
A number of typographic and layout styles have been used throughout *SIMPLY Computing for Seniors* to distinguish different types of information.

Bold
Bold type represents the names of commands and options that you interact with. Bold type also indicates text and numbers that you must type into a dialog box.

Italics
Italic words introduce a new term, which is then defined.

Numbered Steps
You must perform the instructions in numbered steps in order to successfully complete a section and achieve the final results.

Bulleted Steps
These steps point out various optional features. You do not have to perform these steps; they simply give additional information about a feature.

Indented Text
Indented text tells you what the program does in response to your following a numbered step. For example, if you click a certain menu command, a dialog box may open or a window may open. Indented text may also tell you what the final result is when you follow a set of numbered steps.

Notes
Notes give additional information. They may describe special conditions that may occur during an operation. They may warn you of a situation that you want to avoid – for example, the loss of data. A note may also cross-reference a related area of the book. A cross-reference may guide you to another chapter or to another section within the current chapter.

Icons and Buttons
Icons and buttons are graphical representations within the text. They show you exactly what you need to click to perform a step.

You can easily identify the tips in any section by looking for the tip icon. Tips offer additional information, including hints, warnings and tricks. You can use the tip information to go beyond what you have learned in the steps.

Operating System Differences
The screenshots were captured using Windows 7. The features shown in the tasks may differ if you are using an earlier operating system. For example, the default folder for saving photos in Windows 7 is named "Pictures"; in Windows XP, it is named "My Pictures".

Microsoft Office Starter contains cut-down versions of Word and Excel, so you may see some differences between your version and the screenshots and instructions in this book.

Table of Contents

1 GETTING STARTED — 3

- 4   Start Up and Shut Down Your Computer
- 6   The Keyboard
- 8   Use the Mouse or Touchpad
- 10   The Windows 7 Screen
- 12   Change the Look of the Desktop
- 14   Password Protection
- 16   Lock and Unlock Your Computer
- 17   Health and Safety

2 WORKING WITH WINDOWS 7 — 19

- 20   The Start Menu
- 22   Fill the Screen
- 24   Icons and Windows
- 26   Get Help
- 28   Use Accessories
- 30   Fast Access to Files

3 WRITING A LETTER — 33

- **34** Start and Explore Word 2010
- **36** Start a Document and Move Around
- **37** Correct Mistakes
- **38** Check Spelling and Grammar
- **40** Save and Close a Document
- **42** Open a Saved Document
- **44** Create Labels

4 MAKING A POSTER — 49

- **50** Create a Document and Add Text
- **52** Choose the Text Style, Size and Colour
- **54** Align and Number Paragraphs
- **56** Change the Margins and Page Size
- **57** Add a Picture
- **58** Modify a Picture

5 USING A PRINTER AND SCANNER — 61

- **62** Use Print Preview
- **64** Print a Document
- **66** Print a Picture
- **68** Copy Documents and Pictures
- **70** Scan Documents and Pictures

6 GETTING CONNECTED 73

- 74 Choose an ISP
- 75 Connection Types
- 76 Get Started on the Internet
- 78 Keep Safe
- 80 Windows Live Essentials
- 82 Social Networking

7 DISCOVERING THE INTERNET 85

- 86 Explore Internet Explorer
- 88 Change Your Home Page
- 90 Search the Internet
- 92 Save Your Favourite Pages
- 94 Print a Web Page
- 96 Save Text and Pictures

8 USING THE INTERNET 99

- 100 Shop Online
- 104 Explore Travel Sites
- 106 Book Tickets and Holidays
- 108 Buy and Sell on eBay
- 110 Use Online Banking
- 113 Add Skype to Your Computer
- 114 Use Skype

CONTENTS

9 SETTING UP AND USING EMAIL — 117

- 118 Choose and Set Up an Email Account
- 120 Access Your Email Account
- 122 Read and Respond to an Email
- 124 Write and Send an Email
- 126 Delete an Email
- 127 Deal with Junk Mail

10 ORGANISING EMAIL — 129

- 130 Open Email Attachments
- 132 Save Attachments
- 134 Send Attachments
- 136 Store Messages in Folders
- 138 Add People to a Contact List
- 140 Find People in a Contact List

11 MANAGING PICTURES — 143

- 144 Get Pictures from Camera to Computer
- 146 Open and View Pictures
- 148 Organise and Find Pictures
- 150 Improve the Appearance of Pictures
- 152 Save Pictures to a CD or Flash Drive
- 154 Share Pictures on the Internet

12 KEEPING RECORDS — 157

- 158 Start and Explore Excel 2010
- 160 Start Using Excel 2010
- 162 Set Up Columns and Rows
- 164 Add Information and Enhance Cells
- 166 Keep Accounts
- 171 Preview and Print

13 ORGANISING FILES AND FOLDERS — 173

- 174 Get Started with Windows Explorer
- 176 Find Files and Folders
- 179 Rename a File or Folder
- 180 Create Folders
- 182 Move and Copy Files
- 184 Delete and Recover Files
- 186 Keep Copies of Files

14 ENTERTAINMENT 189

- **190** Play a Game
- **192** Watch a Film
- **194** Watch TV
- **196** Listen to Music
- **198** Use Playlists
- **200** Download Music
- **203** Listen to Internet Radio

INDEX 204

CONTENTS

4 Start Up and Shut Down Your Computer

6 The Keyboard

8 Use the Mouse or Touchpad

10 The Windows 7 Screen

12 Change the Look of the Desktop

14 Password Protection

16 Lock and Unlock Your Computer

17 Health and Safety

GETTING STARTED

This chapter teaches you how to get started on your computer and how to protect your work. You learn how to use the keyboard and mouse or touchpad and where to find things in Windows 7. The chapter also focuses on the new additions to Windows that allow you to make changes to the Windows 7 screen so it looks the way you want it to. Finally, you'll learn a little bit about health and safety issues. Mostly, you find out just how amazingly helpful Windows 7 can be once you know which buttons to click.

START UP AND SHUT DOWN YOUR COMPUTER

Windows 7 starts when you turn on your computer. You will probably see the Welcome screen and will need to log in by typing in the password that you have from when the computer was first set up.

Start Up

1. Turn on your computer.

   The Windows 7 Welcome screen appears.

Note: *If your computer has been set up just for you, with no password, you will bypass the Welcome screen and go directly to the Desktop.*

2. Click on the icon for your user account name.

   You will be prompted to enter your password.

Note: *If you are the only user, you will be asked for your password straight away.*

3. Type in your password.

   As you type the characters they appear as asterisks to keep your password secret.

4. Click the **Go** arrow ( ) or press **Enter**.

✓ *If you forget your password, click on the Go arrow ( ) and OK to see the hint – a word or phrase to jog your memory.*

CHAPTER 1 GETTING STARTED

Shut Down

① Shut down any programs and documents you have open, saving your work.

② Click **Start** ().

The Start menu appears.

③ Click **Shut Down**.

Windows 7 shuts down and turns off the computer.

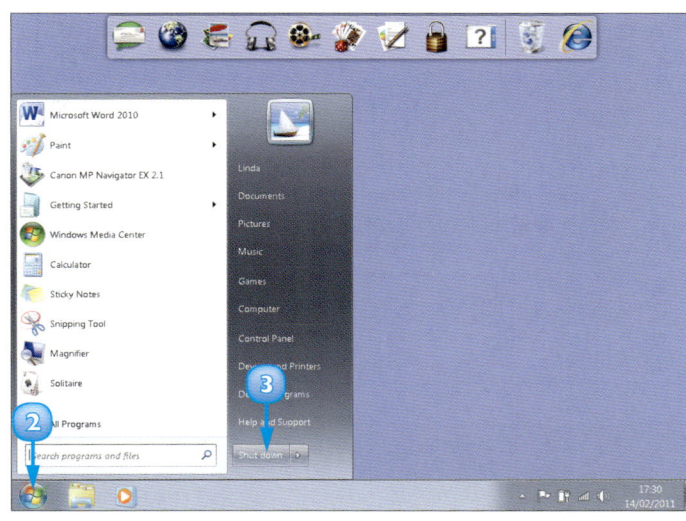

④ Click on the power button arrow () and click **Sleep** if you would like to return to the same documents and programs later.

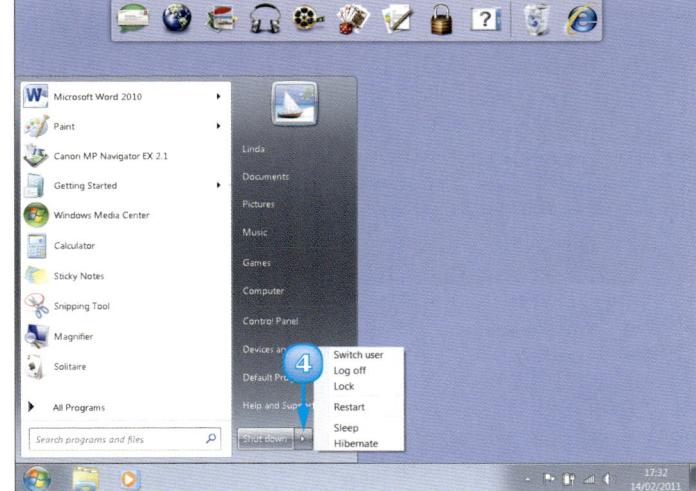

*If you are having problems with your computer, save your work and shut down all programs. Click **Start** and then the power button arrow () and click **Restart**. Your computer will shut down and start up again.*

Turning the power off without properly shutting down can cause problems and make your system unstable.

CHAPTER 1 GETTING STARTED

THE KEYBOARD

As well as letter and number keys, the computer keyboard has a lot of other keys which perform various tasks. You can refer back to this guide at any time if you are unsure about how to use a specific key. The keys on these two pages are the ones you will find most useful to start with.

A **Letter keys**

Press a letter key to type a letter in lower case.

B **Number keys**

Press a number key to type a number.

C **Symbol keys**

Press a symbol key to type a symbol.

D **Space bar (Spacebar)**

Press this bar once to make a space between two words.

E **Tab key (Tab)**

Press the Tab key to make a larger space.

F **Enter key (Enter)**

Press this key to move to the next line.

CHAPTER 1 GETTING STARTED

Shift keys (Shift)

Hold down a Shift key and press a letter key to type a capital letter or a symbol from the top row above the numbers and symbols.

Caps Lock key (Caps lock)

Press this key to type in capital letters and press again to turn it off.

Backspace key (Backspace)

Press this key to remove unwanted letters, words or spaces.

Arrow keys (◄, ►, ▲ and ▼)

Press the arrow keys to move around the text you have created.

Escape key (Esc)

If you get in a mess, pressing this key may take you back a step.

F1 (F1)

Press this key to see the Help menu.

CHAPTER 1 GETTING STARTED

USE THE MOUSE OR TOUCHPAD

Your desktop computer is likely to have a mouse. A laptop usually has a built-in touchpad. You can purchase a mouse for your laptop at an extra cost.

There are a lot of different types of mouse devices but most have left and right buttons. The mouse moves the cursor around the screen. The cursor changes shape depending on what you are doing: an arrow (⇖) selects and moves things; a hand (☝) clicks links on the Internet. It may take a little practice to be able to click on the correct icon.

Click the Mouse

1. Move the mouse so that the cursor (⇖) is over the Start button (⊞).

2. Click (press) the left mouse button and release it.

   Windows 7 displays the Start menu.

3. Move the mouse so that the cursor (⇖) is over a program.

4. Click the left mouse button.

   Windows 7 opens the program you clicked.

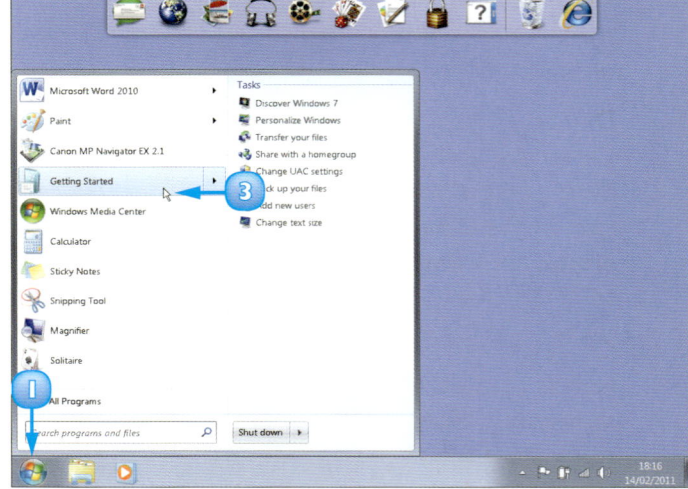

 You can also open a program by hovering over its desktop icon and double-clicking the mouse.

CHAPTER 1 GETTING STARTED

Drag and Drop

1. Move the mouse so that the cursor (👆) is over an item you would like to move.

2. Click and hold down the left mouse button.

3. Keep the left mouse button held down and drag the object.

4. Release the mouse button when the object is where you want it.

A Laptop Touchpad

 A touchpad works on the same principle as a mouse. It has left and right buttons. To move the cursor around on the screen, move your finger around on the touchpad.

 Left handed? Click Start, click Control Panel, click Hardware and Sound and then click Mouse to open the Mouse Properties dialog box. Click the Buttons tab, then click Switch primary and secondary buttons (☐ changes to ☑).

 Double-clicking a problem? Open the Mouse Properties dialog box. Click the Buttons tab. In the Double-click Speed group, click and drag the slider towards Slow.

🛑 **Clicking the right mouse button results in another menu appearing. Move the cursor away from the menu and press the Escape button (Esc) to delete it.**

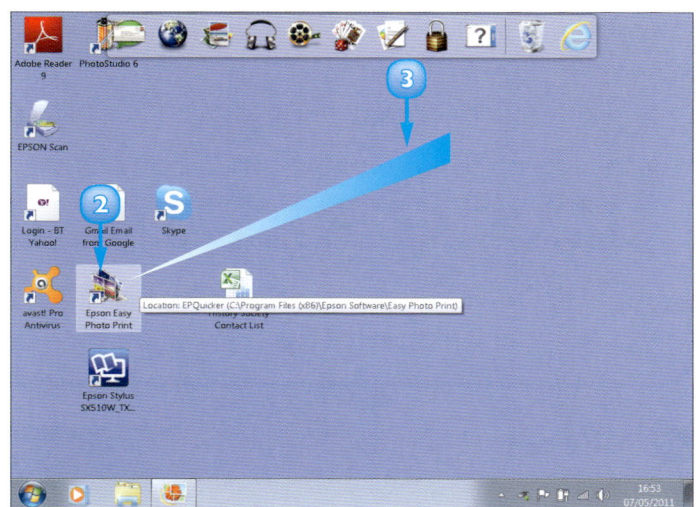

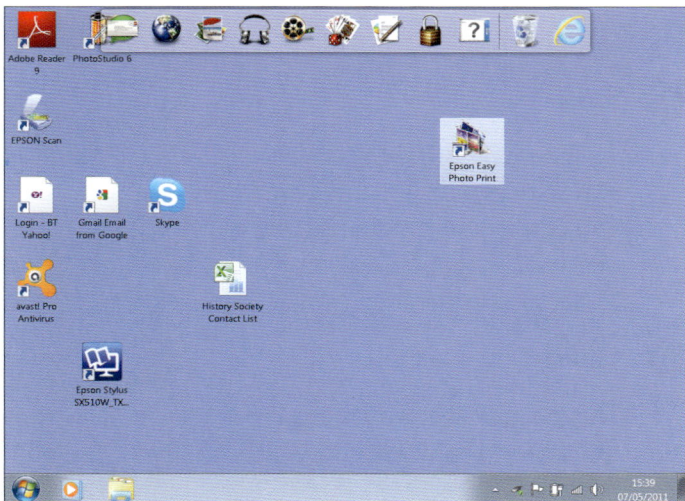

CHAPTER 1 GETTING STARTED

THE WINDOWS 7 SCREEN

After you log on, the next thing to appear is the Windows 7 screen, usually called the 'Desktop', which allows you to access all the other programs on your computer. You will probably need to refer back to this section but it will soon become automatic.

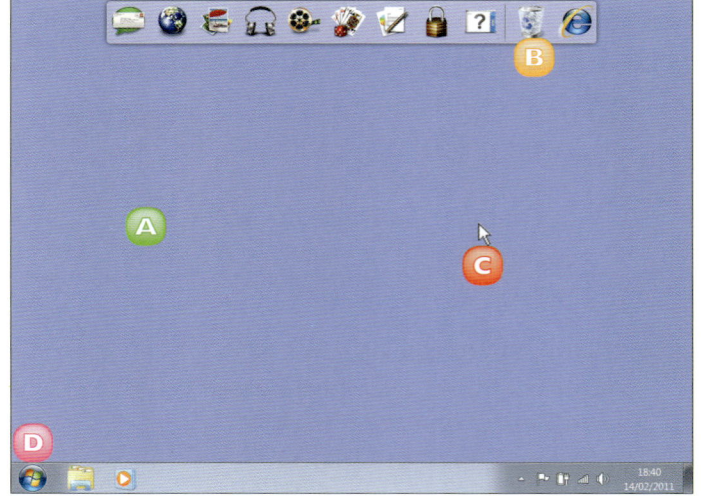

A **Desktop**

The Windows 7 screen gives you access to all other programs and features on your computer.

B **Icon**

A little image (📄) with an explanatory title appears when you add a new program to your desktop. You double-click an icon to access a program.

C **Cursor**

This pointer (▶) moves around the screen when you move your mouse.

D **Start Button**

Click on this button (⊞) to start programs and complete many tasks (see Chapter 2).

CHAPTER 1 GETTING STARTED

E **Taskbar**

You can see here which programs are running.

F **Taskbar Icons**

These icons give one-click access to various features.

G **Notification Area**

The icons displayed here let you know when things are happening or need to be updated. Run your cursor slowly across each one to see its title.

H **Time and Date**

Click on the time to change it and the date.

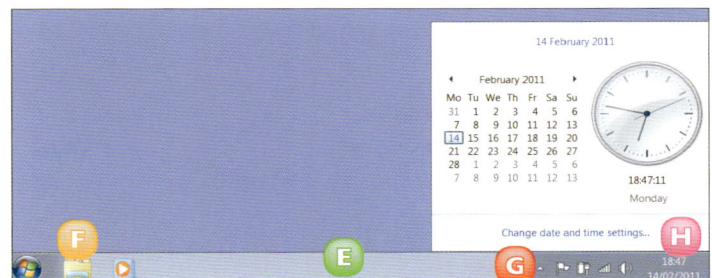

CHANGE THE LOOK OF THE DESKTOP

You can make many changes to personalise the desktop and many other aspects of Windows 7 — change the background, choose a new colour scheme, set up a screen saver (this appears if you leave your computer running for a long time without using it). We look at just a few of the many changes you can make and you can then explore for yourself.

1. Click **Start** ().
2. Click **Control Panel**.

   The Control Panel window appears.

3. Click **Appearance and Personalization**.

   The Personalization window appears.

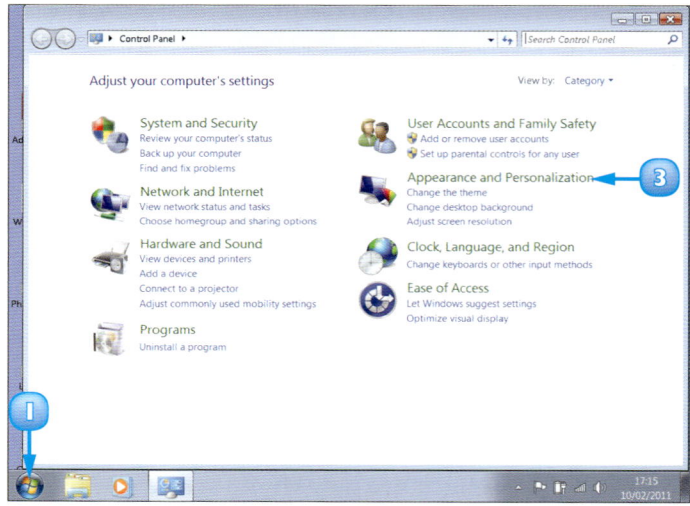

Select a Theme

1. Click **Change the theme**.
2. Point the cursor at the slider, hold down the left mouse button and move the slider up and down to see the themes that are available.
3. Try out the different themes before choosing one.

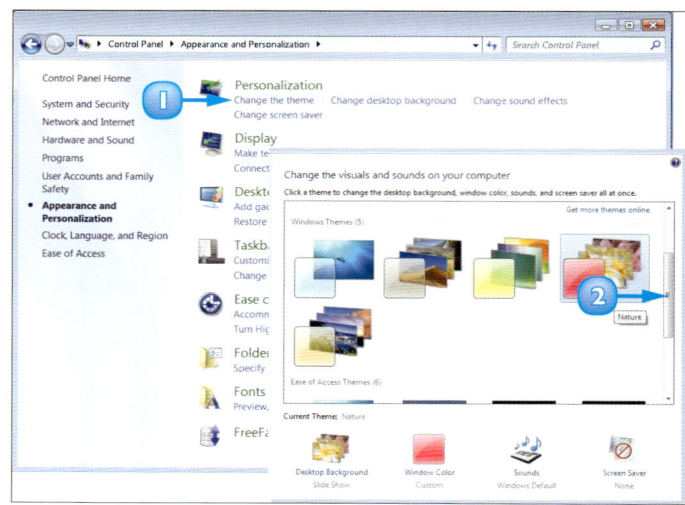

Select a Screen Saver

1. Click on the **Screen Saver** icon.

   The screen saver dialog appears.

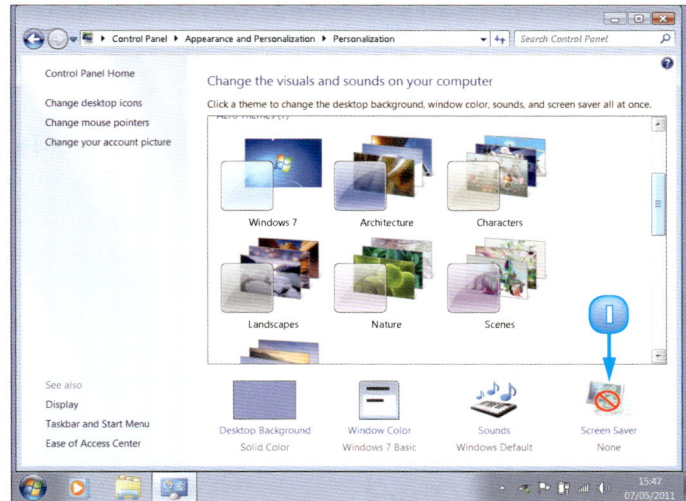

2. Click the Screen saver ▾ and click to choose a screen saver.

   A preview appears on the small screen in the dialog.

3. Click the Wait spinner (⬍) to set the number of minutes the computer will remain idle before the screen saver appears.

4. Click to tick the **On resume, display logon screen** to ensure that only those who know the password can see your work.

5. Click **OK**.

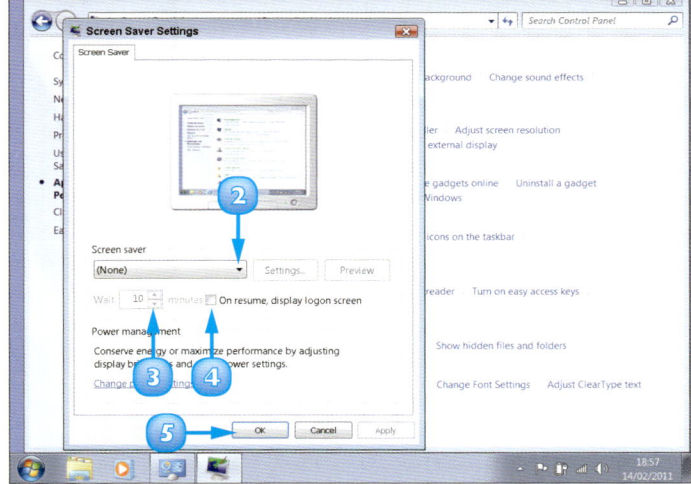

*You can choose a different background picture. Click **Change desktop background** in the Control Panel window and choose a new picture.*

Not got a password? See the next section to set one up.

CHAPTER 1 GETTING STARTED

PASSWORD PROTECTION

It is a good idea to protect Windows 7 with a password so that nobody else can access your files. If you have not already created a password, follow these steps.

① Click **Start** (⊞).

② Click **Control Panel**.

The Control Panel window appears.

③ Click **Add or remove user accounts**.

The Manage Accounts window appears.

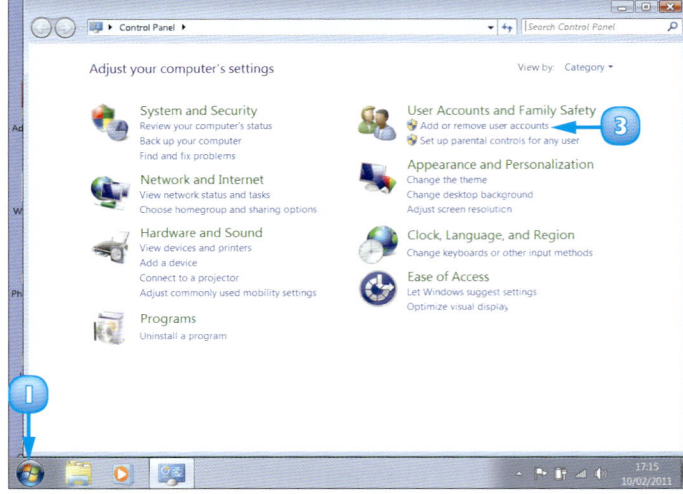

④ Click the user account to be changed.

The Change an Account window appears.

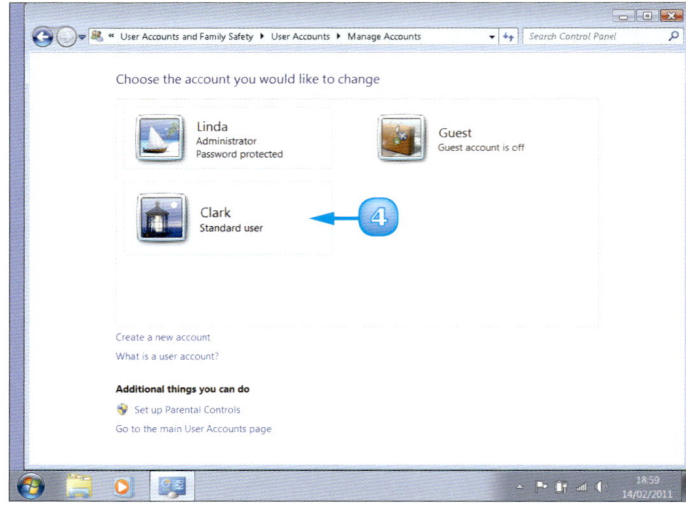

CHAPTER 1 GETTING STARTED

5 Click **Create a password**.

The Create a password window appears.

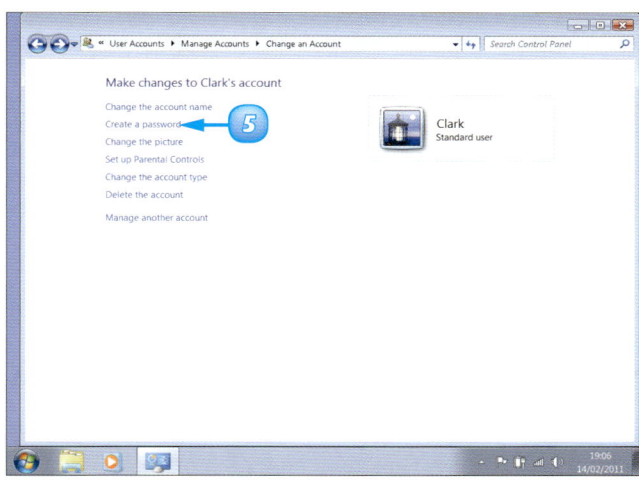

6 Type the password in the box.

7 Type the password in the box.

8 Type a word or phrase to use as a hint in case you forget the password.

9 Click **Create password**.

Note: *If you have made a mistake or can think of a better password, click* **Cancel** *and start again.*

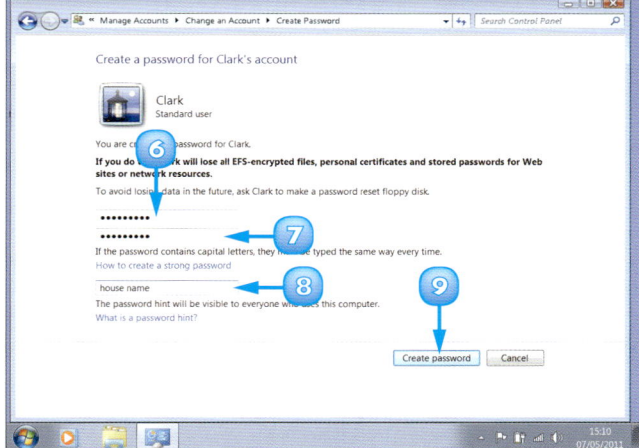

10 To change a password repeat Steps 1–4 and then click **Change the password**. Type your existing password, follow Steps 6–7 and click **Change password**.

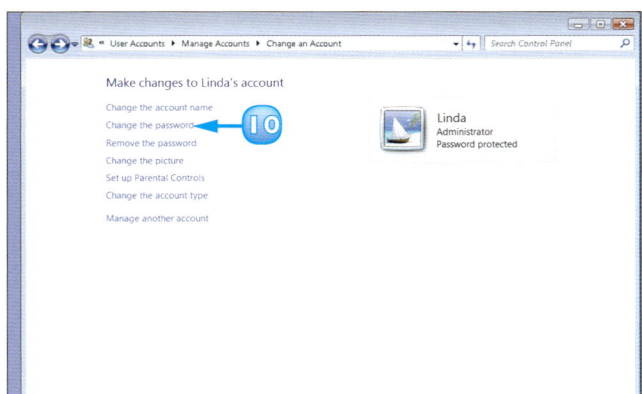

 *To be secure, your password should be at least 8 characters long and should contain capital and small letters and numbers. Do not use your first name or birthday.*

CHAPTER 1 GETTING STARTED

LOCK AND UNLOCK YOUR COMPUTER

With a password in place, you can lock your work so that it cannot be seen or changed by others if you need to leave your desk but do not want to close what you are working on.

Lock your Computer

1. Click **Start** ().
2. Click the power button arrow ().
3. Click **Lock**.

   The word 'Locked' appears under your user name.

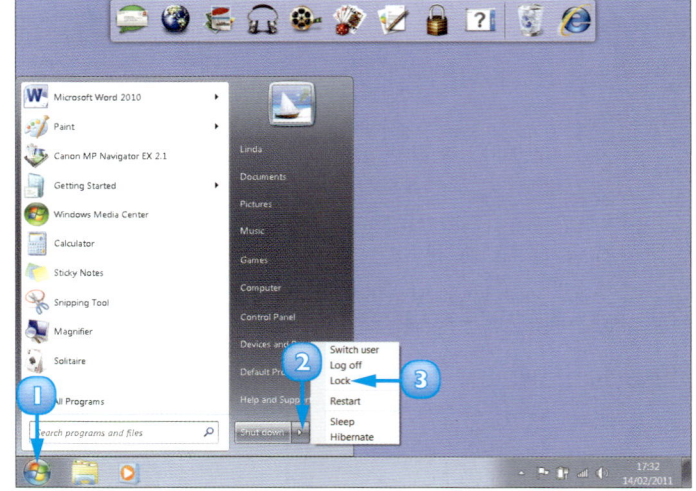

Unlock your Computer

1. Click in the password text box and type your password.
2. Click **Go** ().

   The desktop is restored.

 *If you have forgotten your password, click on the arrow () and **OK** the message to view your reminder phrase or word.*

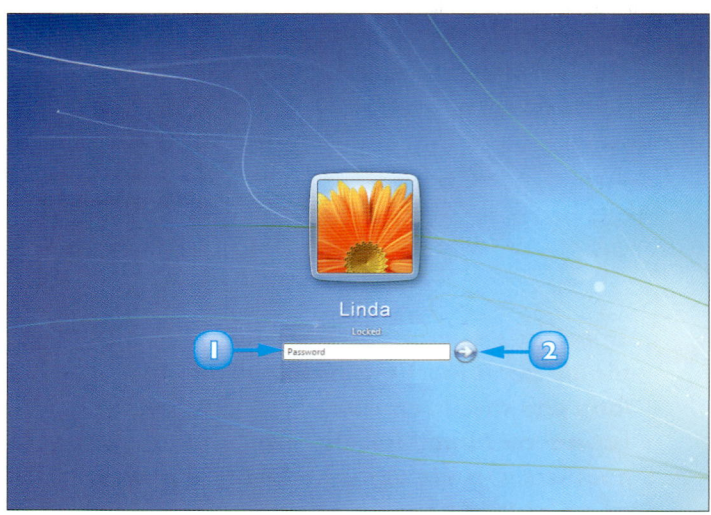

CHAPTER 1 GETTING STARTED

HEALTH AND SAFETY

You may be tempted to sit for a long time finding out about your computer and how it works but there are some simple rules that should be followed to remain healthy and keep safe. It is important to ensure that your computer is set up correctly and that you are not taking unnecessary risks.

Shutterstock® Images LLC

A The screen of your computer should be at the right height—the top should be in line with your eyes. The screen should not face a window and should be at the correct brightness to suit the room you are in.

B The chair should be at the correct height so that your feet are on the floor (or on a footrest).

C The keyboard and mouse should be within easy reach.

D Cables should not clutter the desk or floor under the desk.

E You should take regular breaks from looking at the screen to protect your eyes and so that you are not in the same position for long periods of time.

 Anybody who uses a computer for several hours a day should get their eyes checked regularly by an optician.

CHAPTER 1 GETTING STARTED

CONTENTS

20 The Start Menu
22 Fill the Screen
24 Icons and Windows
26 Get Help
28 Use Accessories
30 Fast Access to Files

2

WORKING WITH WINDOWS 7

This chapter contains additional information about useful features of Windows 7. We begin with the Start button, which provides access to all programs and tools, and move on to improving the visibility and layout of the screen. Help menus and how to make use of some handy accessories are explained. Finally, we look at some new features of Windows 7 – Jump Lists and Aero Peek for quick access to files and programs and Snap and Aero Shake for organising open windows on your desktop.

THE START MENU

So you have switched on and logged on to your computer. Now what? In Chapter 1, you learned how to change the look of your desktop, screen saver and password using the Start button ( ) and its menu. Now we investigate the Start menus to find out where they lead.

Left Menu

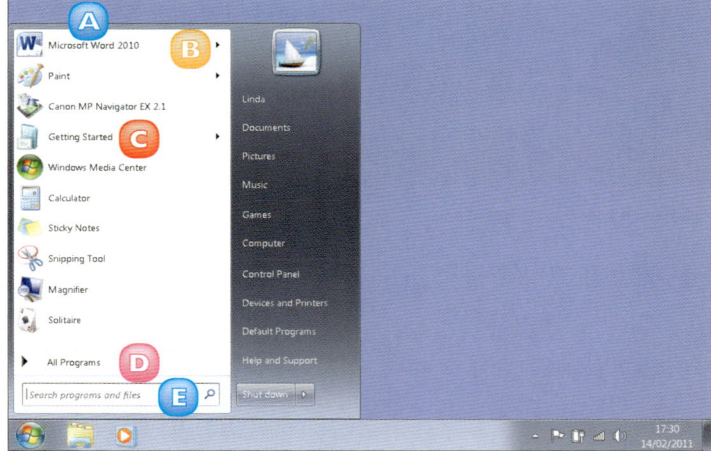

A *This menu lists programs already loaded on to your computer.*

B *Clicking an arrow to the right (▶) takes you to a menu that shows documents recently opened in that program.*

C *If you have an Internet connection,* **Getting Started** *opens a list of helpful Windows 7 videos.*

D **All Programs** *takes you to a list of the programs on your computer.*

E *Typing the name of a file or program in this box gives you a choice of possible solutions.*

 To close a program, click the Close button ( ) at the top of the screen.

CHAPTER 2 WORKING WITH WINDOWS 7

Right Menu

- **(F)** Click on your name to open your personal folder.
- **(G) Documents** – view and organise letters, notes, reports and other kinds of documents.
- **(H) Pictures** – view and organise digital pictures.
- **(I) Music** – play music and other audio files.
- **(J) Games** – play games on your computer.
- **(K) Computer** – see the disk drives and other hardware connected to your computer.
- **(L) Control Panel** – change settings and functions.
- **(M) Devices and Printers** – view and manage devices, printers and print jobs.
- **(N) Default Programs** – choose the programs that open, for example, when you want to play music or edit pictures.
- **(O) Help and Support** – find help topics, tutorials, troubleshooting and other support services.
- **(P) Shut down** – see Chapter 1.

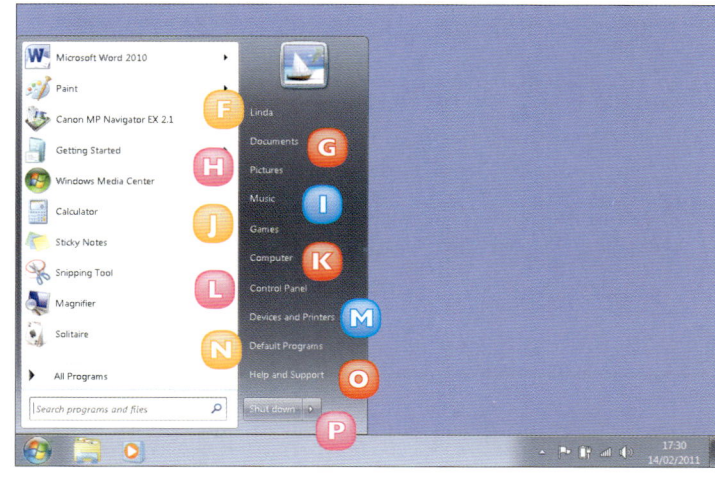

 Hardware *is a term used to describe the physical pieces of computer equipment, e.g. keyboard and printer.* **Software** *describes the programs and operating systems inside your computer.*

FILL THE SCREEN

The screen is where you view all the data and images on your computer. In Chapter 1, you learned how to change the look of your desktop. Here you find out what else you can do to enhance your viewing experience. We use Windows Help and Support to learn about resizing and moving Windows around.

Open a Program

① Click **Start**.

② Click **Help and Support**.

Windows Help and Support opens.

Work with a Program Window

① Hover over the outline of the window (⬚ changes to ↔).

② Hold down the left mouse button and drag in or out until the window is the size required.

③ Release the mouse button.

④ Click the blue band at the top of the window.

⑤ Hold down the left mouse button and drag the window to its new position.

⑥ Release the mouse button.

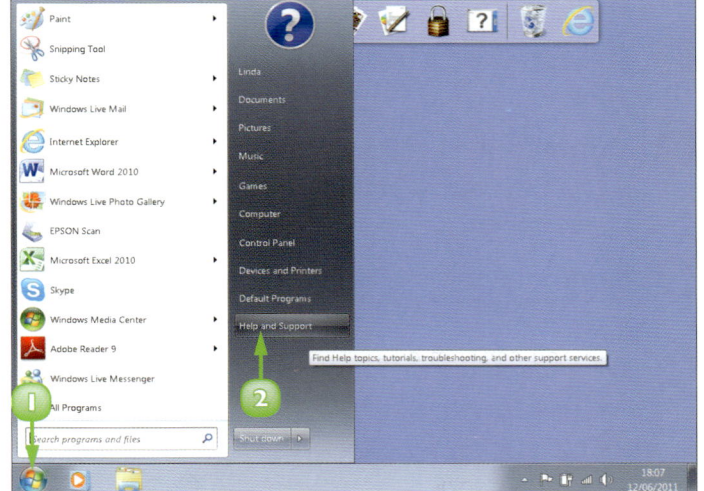

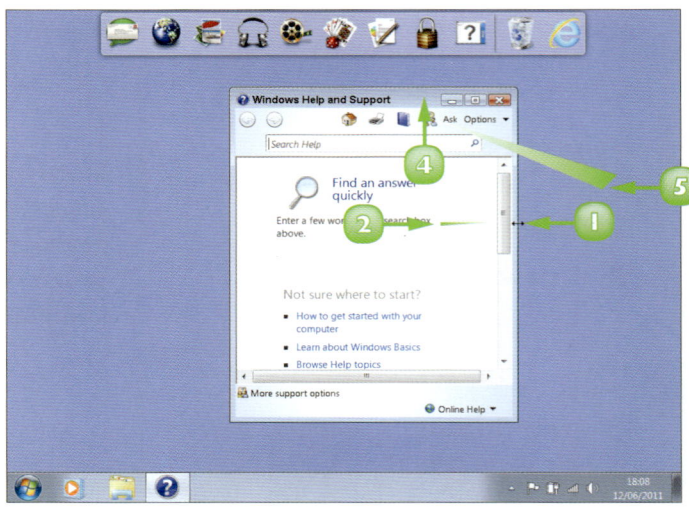

 To bring another window to the front, click anywhere on it.

CHAPTER 2 WORKING WITH WINDOWS 7

Optimise the Visual Display

1. Click **Start.**
2. Click **Control Panel.**
3. Click **Optimise Visual Display**

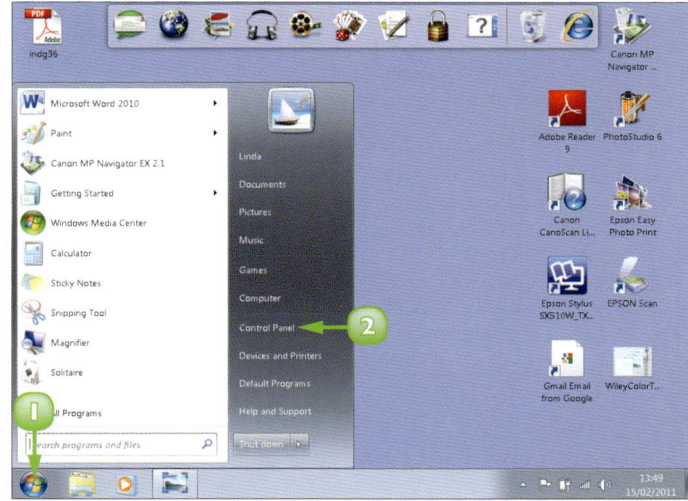

4. Click options to make it easier to see items on your computer's screen.

   A *You can use the scroll bar to move through the list.*

   B *You can turn on a magnifying tool.*

   C *You can change the thickness of the cursor.*

   D *You can choose to see fewer animations.*

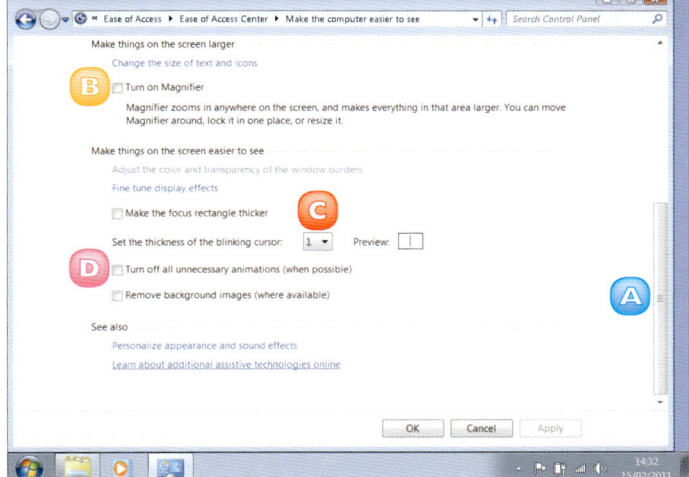

 If you click **Let Windows Suggest Settings,** *Windows makes suggestions for suitable changes.*

CHAPTER 2 WORKING WITH WINDOWS 7

ICONS AND WINDOWS

An icon is a small picture representing a file, a folder or a program. By clicking an icon on your desktop, you can open the file, folder or program. A window is a file or program that is open. You can have several windows open at the same time. This is useful if you want to refer to other documents while working on a new one. The taskbar shows all the folders and programs you have open. To move to another window, click on it or on its icon on the taskbar.

Rearrange Icons on the Taskbar

1. Point to an icon on the taskbar.
2. Hold down the left mouse button and drag the icon along the taskbar.
3. Release the mouse button.

   The icon moves to its new position on the taskbar.

Rearrange Icons on the Desktop

1. Point to an icon on the desktop.
2. Hold down the left mouse button and drag the icon to its new position.
3. Release the mouse button.

   The icon moves to its new position on the desktop.

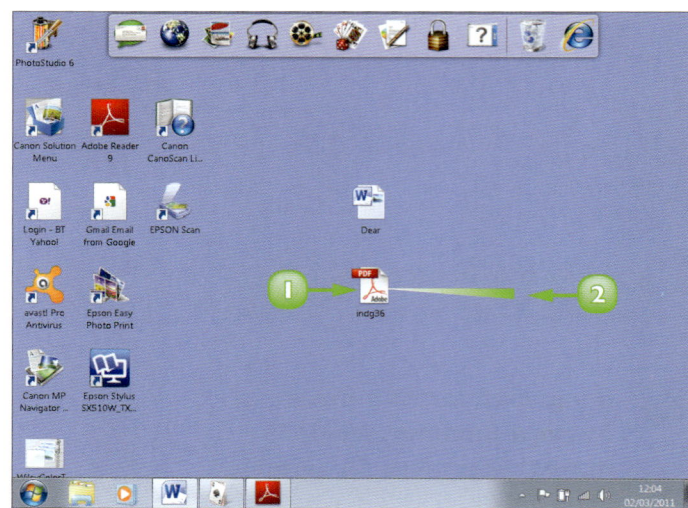

Minimise, Maximise and Close a Window

1. Click **Windows Explorer** (📁) in the Taskbar.
2. Click **Pictures**.
3. Double-click a picture.
4. Click **Restore Down** (🗗).

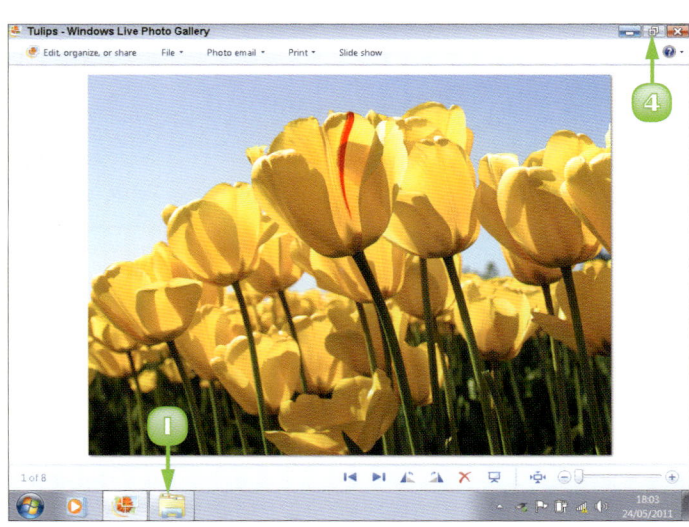

The window takes up only part of the screen.

5. Click **Minimize** (➖).

The window is reduced to an icon on the taskbar.

- **A** *You can click **Maximize** (🗖) to use the full screen again.*
- **B** *You can click **Close** (❌) to shut down the program and close the window.*

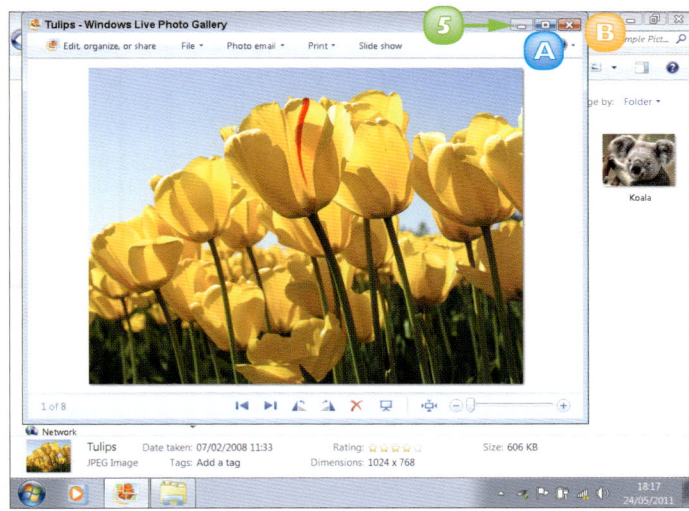

6. Click the taskbar icon to re-open the window.

✓ *If the title bar icons are not visible, click the title bar before clicking an icon.*

✓ *Snap and Aero Shake help you manage windows (see "Fast Access to Files" at the end of this chapter).*

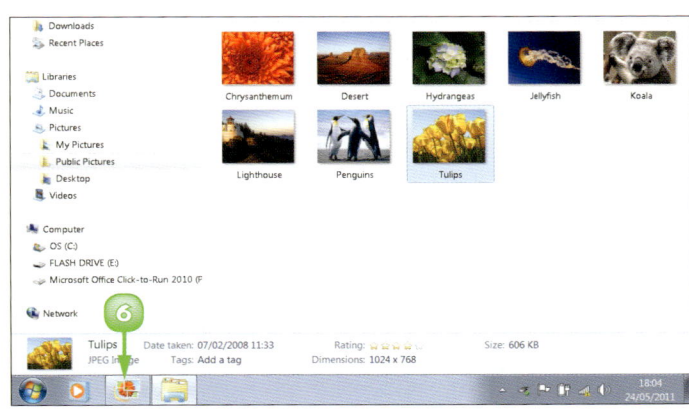

CHAPTER 2 WORKING WITH WINDOWS 7

GET HELP

There are several ways you can get help with Windows 7 and Office 2010. This section runs through a few of them. The Start menu is a good place to begin.

Start Menu – Getting Started

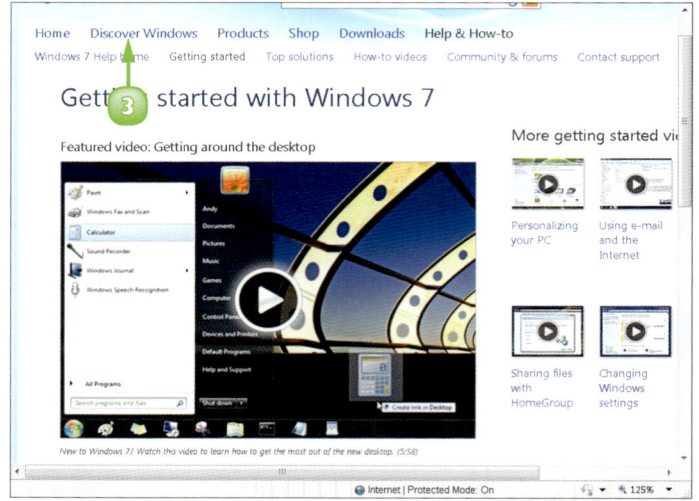

1. Click **Start**.
2. Click **Getting Started**.

   A list of help topics appears.

3. Click **Discover Windows**.

   If you are connected to the Internet, you can watch videos on the Windows 7 website.

   For information on how to get connected to the Internet, see Chapter 7.

Start Menu – Help and Support

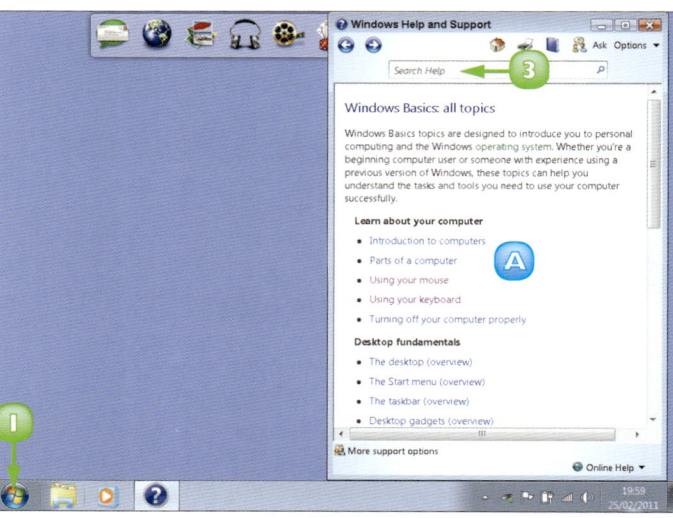

1. Click **Start**.
2. Click **Help and Support**.

   The Help and Support menu appears.

3. Type a question into the **Search Help** box at the top of the menu.

    You can also click on a topic.

   Click ⬅ or ➡ to move from page to page. Click ❌ to close Help and Support.

CHAPTER 2 WORKING WITH WINDOWS 7

Word 2010 Help

1. Open Microsoft Word (see Chapter 3).
2. Click ❓.
   - **A** The Help menu appears.
   - **B** You can click a topic.
   - **C** You can type a question in the box and click **Search** to see a list of possible solutions.
3. Click 📖 to open the table of contents.
4. Scroll down the list to find what you need help with.
5. Click on a title.

   A list of topics appears. Some of them are Microsoft videos of how to perform specific tasks.

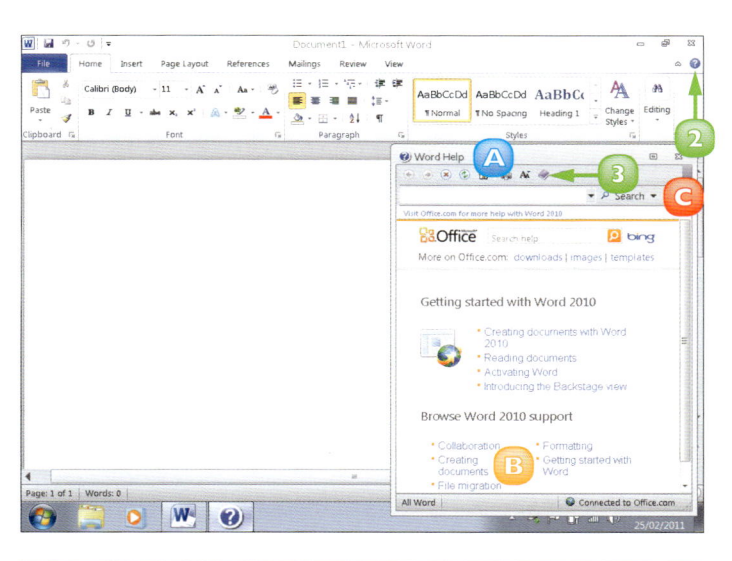

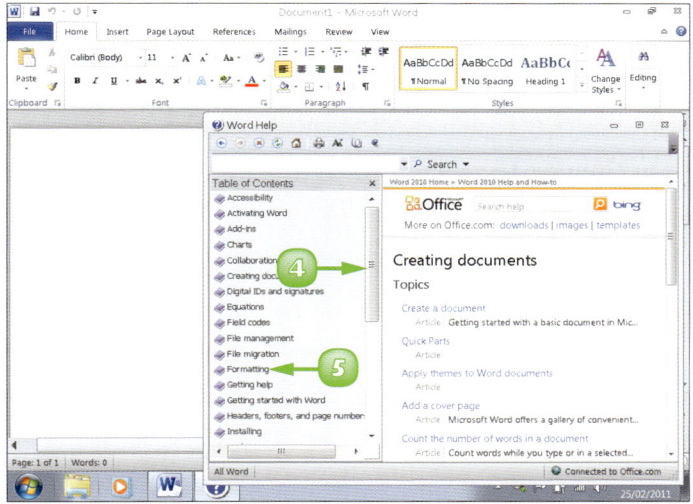

You can also get help from within the program for Excel (Chapter 12) and all other Office 2010 programs.

You need to be connected to the Internet (see Chapter 7) before you can access the full Help for Word and watch the videos.

CHAPTER 2 WORKING WITH WINDOWS 7

USE ACCESSORIES

Windows 7 has some very useful tools in Accessories. You can post reminders on your desktop, enlarge tiny text to make it easier to read, access a calculator and take a cutting, for example, of a book review that you want to keep or pass on to a friend.

Sticky Notes

1. Click **Start**.
2. Click **Sticky Notes**.
3. Type in the text for your note.
4. Click **+** to add another note.
5. Click **×** to delete the note.
6. Click outside the note to continue working.

Magnifier

1. Open a file to read.
2. Click **Start**.
3. Click **Magnifier**.

   A. *A window opens at the top of the screen. Move the cursor around to magnify other areas.*

   B. *Click the Magnifier icon on the taskbar to see the Magnifier tool.*

   C. *Enlarge (+) or reduce (-) the text in the magnifier.*

   D. *Close the magnifier.*

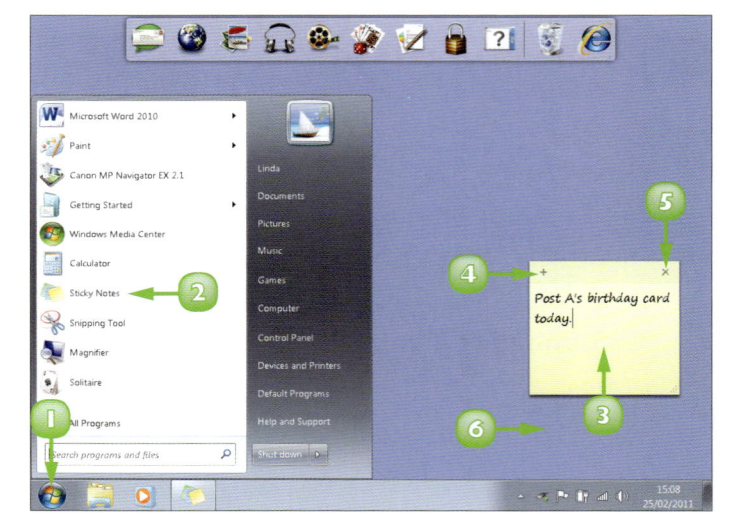

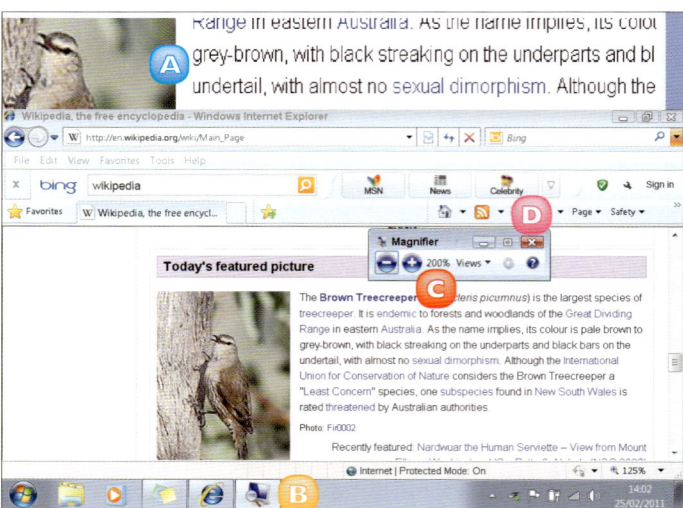

CHAPTER 2 WORKING WITH WINDOWS 7

Calculator

1. Click **Start**.
2. Click **Calculator**.

   The **Calculator** appears.

3. Point to and click the buttons on the calculator.

   The result appears in the calculator window.

4. Click ❌ to close the calculator.

Snipping Tool

1. Open the file from which you want to take the cutting.
2. Click **Start.**
3. Click **Snipping Tool.**
4. Click the **New** ▾ to choose the type of snip from the drop-down menu.
5. Click **New**.

   The screen fades and the cursor turns into a white cross.

6. Hold down the left mouse button and drag across the area to be snipped.
7. Release the mouse button.

   A new menu appears allowing you to save the snip.

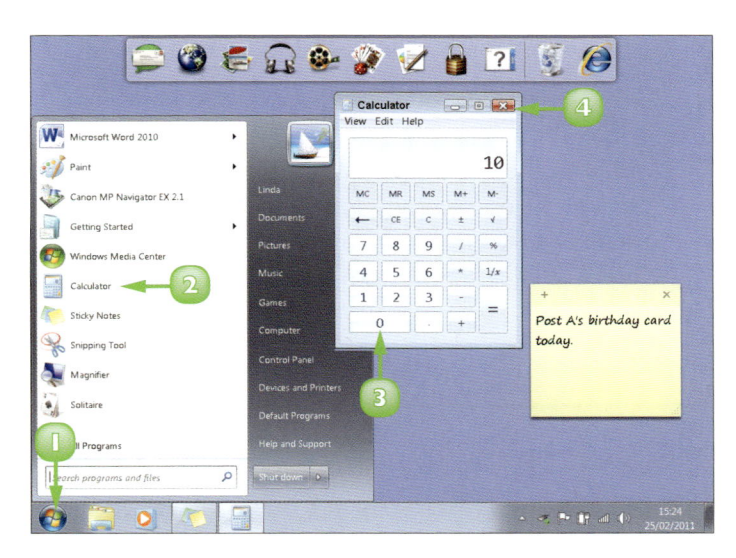

> ✓ *If the Accessories tool you are looking for does not appear in the Start menu, click **Programs**, scroll down the list and click **Accessories**.*

CHAPTER 2 WORKING WITH WINDOWS 7

FAST ACCESS TO FILES

Jump Lists and Aero Peek are two features of Windows 7 that provide quick access to folders and files. A Jump List contains a list of files and software that you visit frequently. Aero Peek allows you to view files that are open on the taskbar. Snap and Aero Shake help you to organise open windows on your desktop.

Jump List on the Start Menu

1. Click **Start**.
2. Click **Getting Started**.

   A. *A list of tasks appears.*

If you click the arrow next to a program, the Jump List shows a list of files that can open in the program.

Jump List on the Taskbar

1. Point to a program on the taskbar and right-click.

   A. *A Jump List of files that you have worked on recently appears.*

2. Click the one you want to open.

   The file opens on the screen.

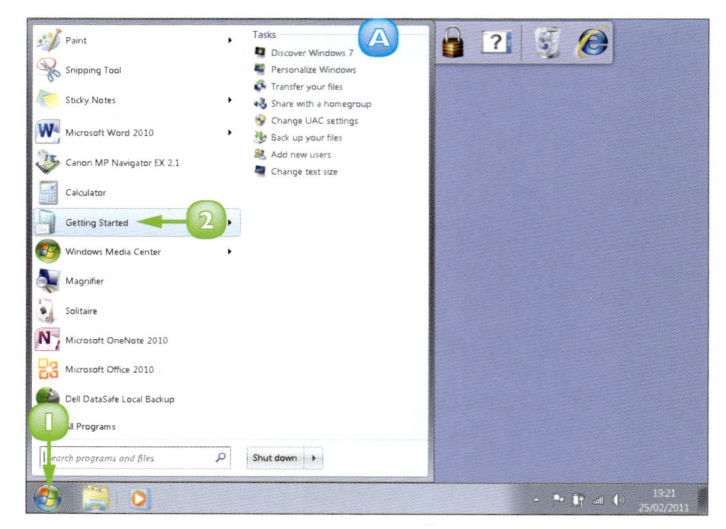

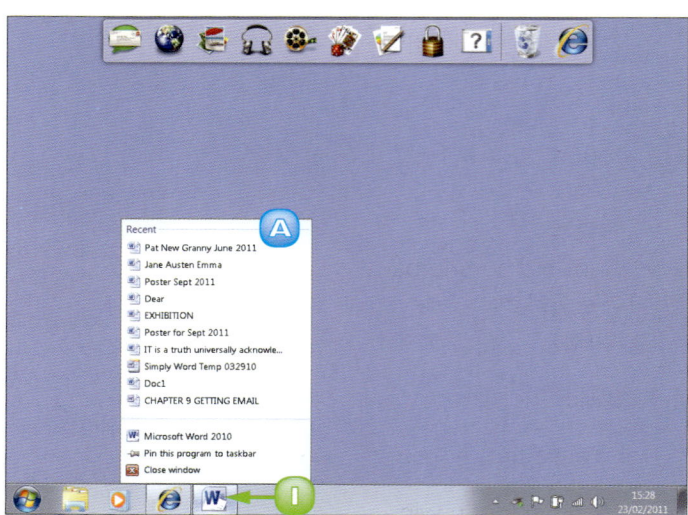

CHAPTER 2 WORKING WITH WINDOWS 7

Aero Peek

1. Move your cursor over a program icon on the taskbar.

   A thumbnail (small picture) of each file open in that program is displayed.

2. Move your cursor over the thumbnails.

   The window that relates to the thumbnail under the cursor is shown on top of the other windows.

3. Click a thumbnail to switch to that window.

Reproduced by permission of thetrainline.com

Snap

1. Point to the title bar of the selected program and hold down the left mouse button.

2. Move the cursor to the top, left or right of the screen until the screen turns blue.

3. Release the mouse button.

   The window fills the whole screen if you moved towards the top of the screen or half the screen if you moved to the left or right.

Aero Shake

1. Point to the title bar of the selected program and hold down the left mouse button.

2. Shake the cursor from side to side.

3. Release the mouse button.

   All other open windows are minimised to the taskbar.

✓ **Repeat these steps to restore all the open windows.**

CHAPTER 2 WORKING WITH WINDOWS 7

CONTENTS

34 Start and Explore Word 2010

36 Start a Document and Move Around

37 Correct Mistakes

38 Check Spelling and Grammar

40 Save and Close a Document

42 Open a Saved Document

44 Create Labels

3

WRITING A LETTER

In this chapter, you find out how to use Microsoft Office's word-processing package, Word 2010. There is an explanation of the menus and how to correct mistakes in your document. We look at parts of the Home, Review and File menus to see how to save a document and how to get it back the next time you want to use it. We also look at creating address labels, useful for Christmas cards, invitations, etc.

START AND EXPLORE WORD 2010

In this section, we create a letter, make corrections and changes and save it so that it is easy to find next time it is needed.

The Quick Access Toolbar contains buttons that give immediate access to the functions you use most often. When Word is installed, it has some standard buttons but you can change them.

Start Word

1. Click **Start**.
2. Click **Microsoft Word 2010**.

   The program opens.

Note: *If your computer has Microsoft Office Starter installed, click **Microsoft Word Starter 2010**. If neither of these two options is in the list, type "word" into the Search Programs and Files box (see Chapter 2).*

Modify the Quick Access Toolbar

1. Click the drop-down (▼) to open the customisation list.
2. Select the items for which you want buttons on the toolbar.

Note: *If you are using Microsoft Office Starter, you may see different options from the ones shown here.*

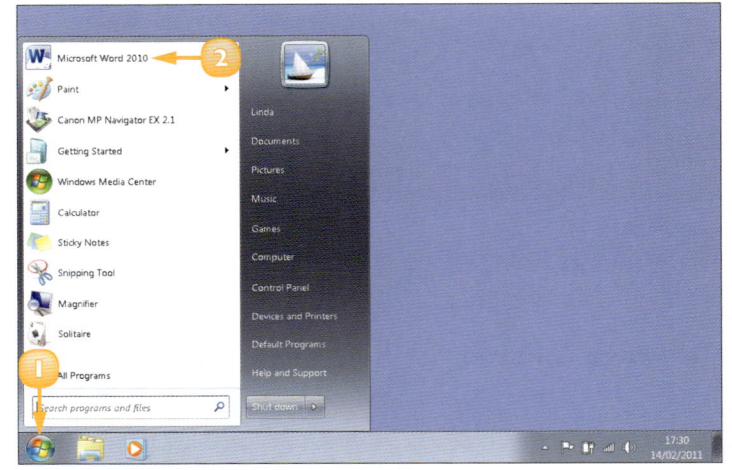

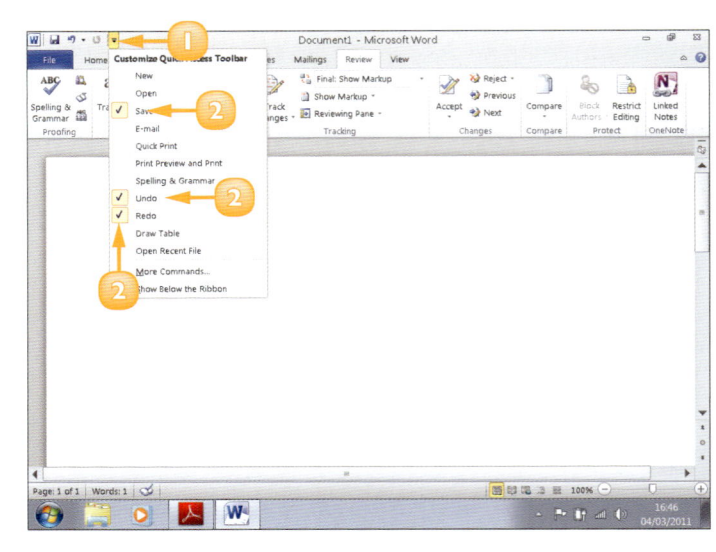

CHAPTER 3 WRITING A LETTER

A **Quick Access Toolbar**

By default, this toolbar holds the Save (📄), Undo (↶) and Redo (↷) buttons.

B **Title of file and program**

C **The Minimize (–), Restore Down/Maximize (▢) and Close (✕) buttons**

D **Ribbon tabs**

Click on a tab to view a ribbon's options.

E **Scroll Bar**

Position the pointer on the Scroll Bar, hold the left mouse button down and move the pointer up and down to look through your document.

F **Page Counter**

G **Word Counter**

H **Zoom Tool**

Drag the slider to zoom in (make the text larger) or zoom out (make the text smaller) on the screen.

Note: *If you are using Microsoft Office Starter, the screen may look a little different.*

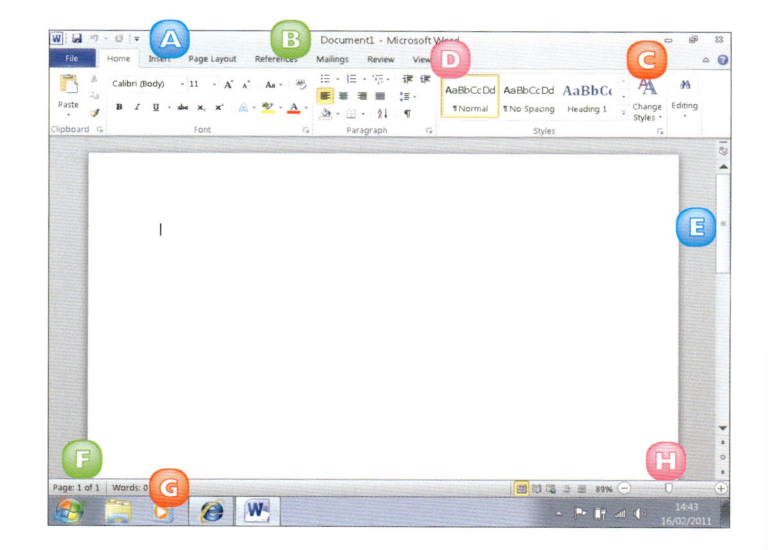

START A DOCUMENT AND MOVE AROUND

Creating a letter will help you find out how to move around the document to make changes to the text and layout.

A The **insertion point** (|) is the point at which text appears when you type.

1 Type text into the document.

When you get to the end of a line, Word automatically wraps the text onto the next line.

2 Press **Enter** to start a new paragraph.

The | moves down to the next line.

3 Move the cursor around the text using the mouse.

The cursor appears as a large capital I (I).

4 Click when the cursor is at the position you want.

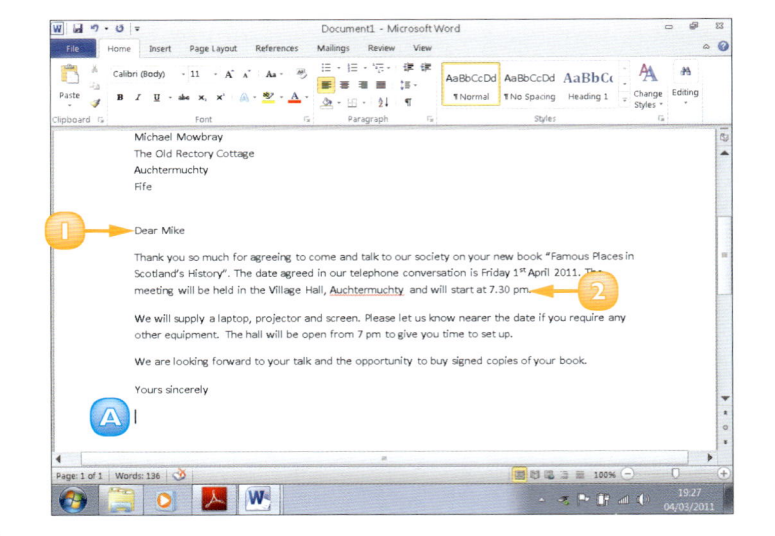

✓ You can use the scroll bar to move through the pages. Hold down the left mouse button and move the slider up and down.

✓ You can also use the arrow keys (◄, ►, ▲ and ▼) to move around the text.

🛑 The cursor moves around only on the text you create.

CHAPTER 3 WRITING A LETTER

CORRECT MISTAKES

There are several ways of deleting, cutting and pasting text to turn your draft into a perfect document.

Delete Text

1. Press Backspace (Backspace) or Delete (Del) to delete characters to the left or right of the cursor.
2. Position the cursor at the start of text you want to delete.
3. Highlight the text (hold down the left button and drag to the end of the text).
4. Release the mouse button and press Del.
5. Click the **Undo** button to remove the last change.
6. Click the **Redo** button to repeat the change.

Move a Block of Text

1. Position the cursor at the start of text you want to move.
2. Highlight the text to be moved.
3. Click **Cut** (✂).
4. Move the cursor to the place where you want to put the text.
5. Click **Paste** (📋).

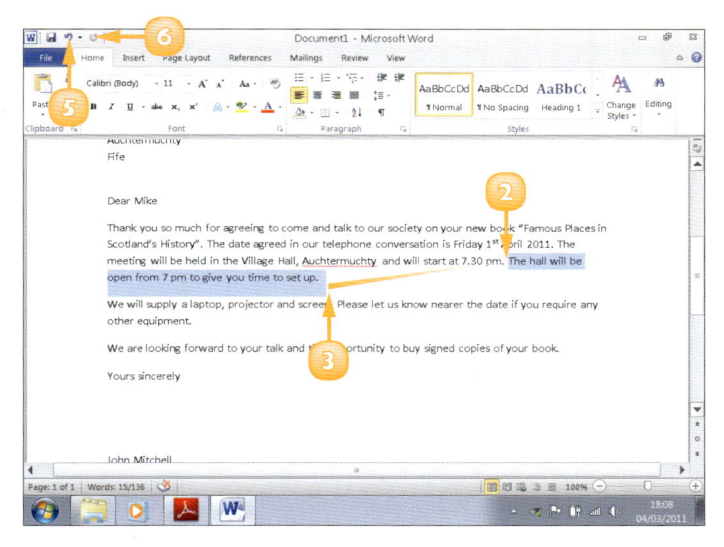

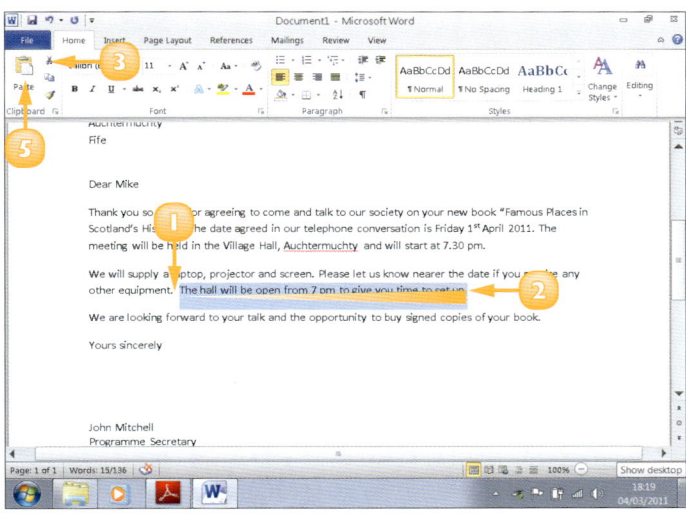

CHAPTER 3 WRITING A LETTER

CHECK SPELLING AND GRAMMAR

Once the document is complete, it is useful to check for grammar and spelling errors. You are alerted to errors in the text before running these checks. Spelling errors are underlined with a red wiggly line and grammar errors with a green wiggly line.

Spelling Check

1. Click the **Review** tab.

   The Review ribbon appears.

2. In the Proofing menu, click the **Spelling and Grammar Check** button ( ).

Note: If you are using Microsoft Office Starter, click the **Spelling** on the Home tab.

   If a word does not exist in the dictionary, a dialog appears.

3. If the correct word is in the list of suggestions, click it.

Note: If the correct word is not suggested, type over the red word in the text pane.

4. Click **Change** to change that occurrence.

   A. You can **Change All** occurrences.

   B. You can add the change to the automatic correction list.

5. When the spelling check is finished, click on **Close**.

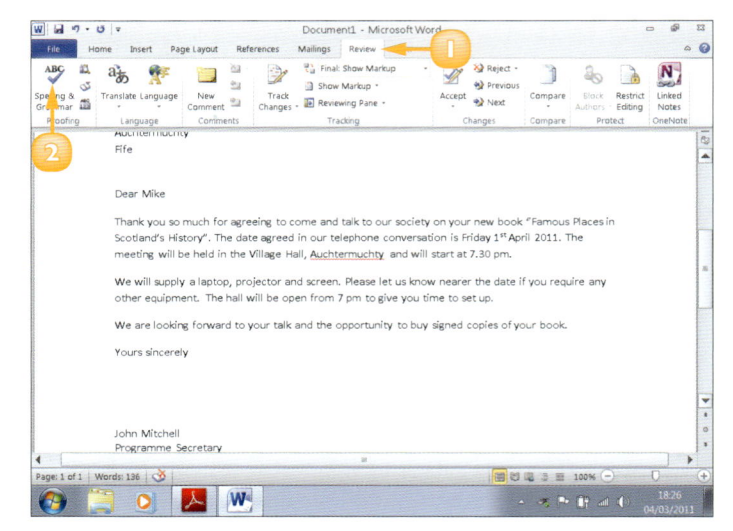

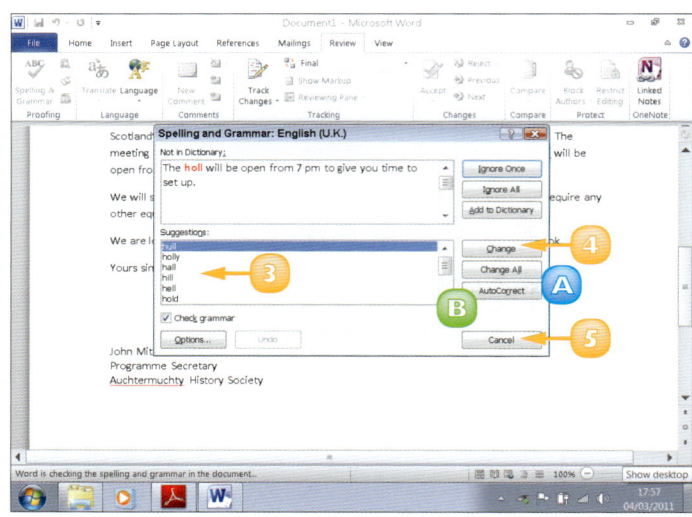

CHAPTER 3 WRITING A LETTER

Grammar Check

1. In the Proofing menu, click the **Spelling and Grammar Check** button ( ).

2. When a grammar error is found, a dialog box appears.

3. If the correct option is in the list of suggestions, click it.

4. Click **Change** to change that occurrence.

    A. Click **Ignore Once** to ignore this error.

Note: *The buttons change depending on the type of error. Use Help to find out what each option does.*

Using the Thesaurus

1. Highlight the word you want to change.

2. Click the **Thesaurus** button ( ) in the Proofing menu.

Note: *If you are using Microsoft Office Starter, click the **Spelling** ▾ and choose **Thesaurus**.*

3. Click the word you want to use.

4. Click the arrow (◢) and choose an option.

    A. **Insert** *replaces the word.*

    B. **Copy** *enables you to paste the word more than once.*

    C. **Look Up** *shows the definition of the word.*

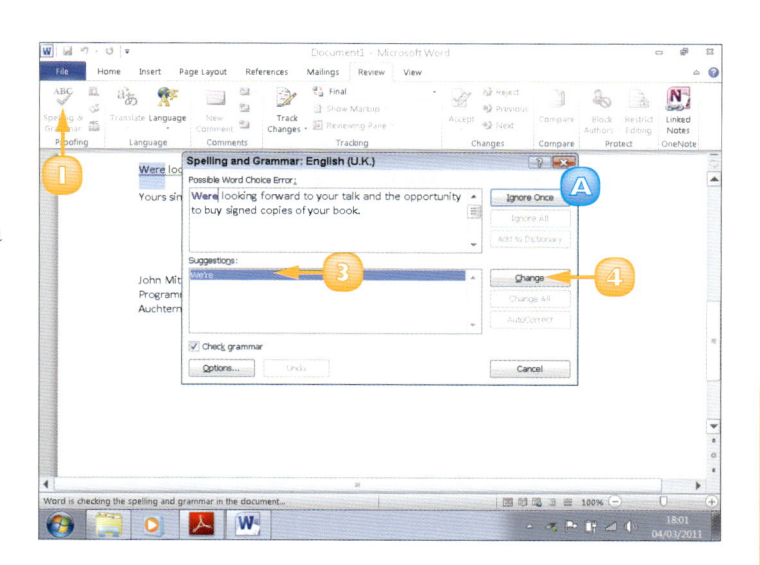

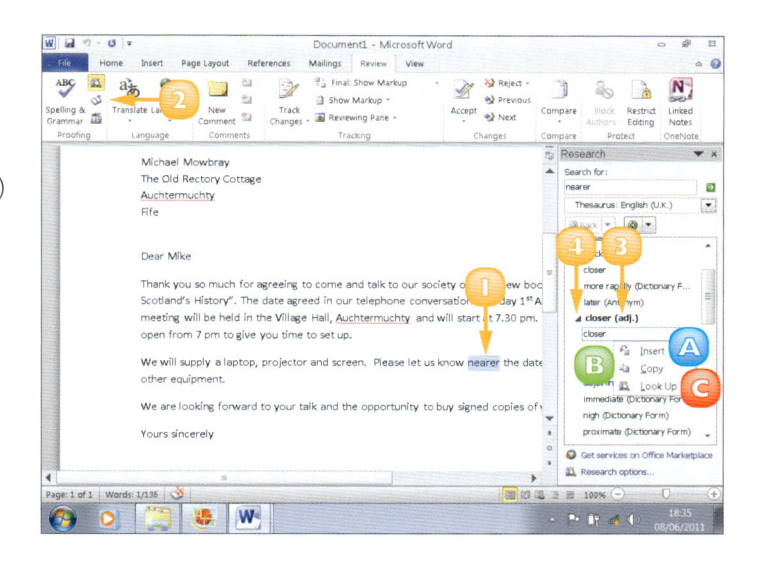

CHAPTER 3 WRITING A LETTER

SAVE AND CLOSE A DOCUMENT

You may wish to continue typing the letter, or to refer to it, later. You need to save it with a relevant name somewhere on your computer where you will easily be able to find it.

Save a Document

1. Click the **File** tab.

   The **File** menu appears.

2. Click on **Save As**.

   The **Save As** dialog appears.

   Note: *The Documents library opens but you can navigate to another folder.*

3. Click in the **File Name** box.

4. Type in a name that will remind you what the letter is about.

   Note: *Two files in the same folder cannot have the same name.*

5. Click **Save**.

   The letter is saved and is displayed with the file name you chose at the top of the screen.

6. As you continue to work on the letter, click **Save** (💾) on the Quick Access toolbar to update the saved file.

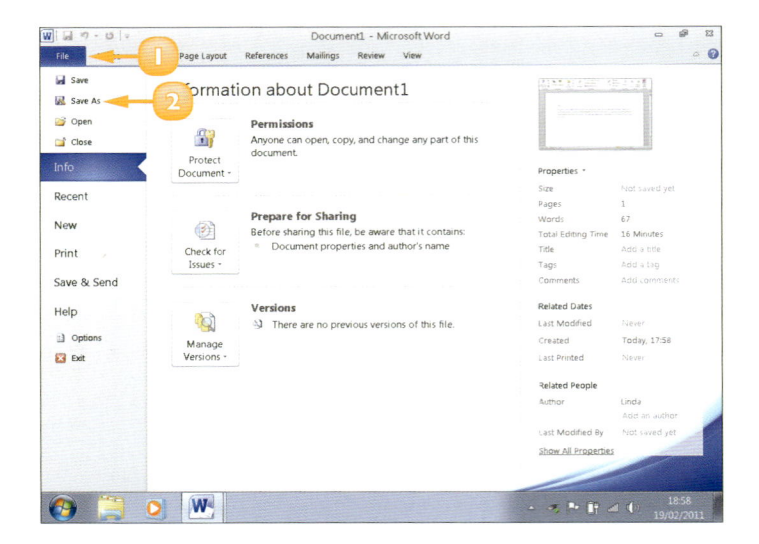

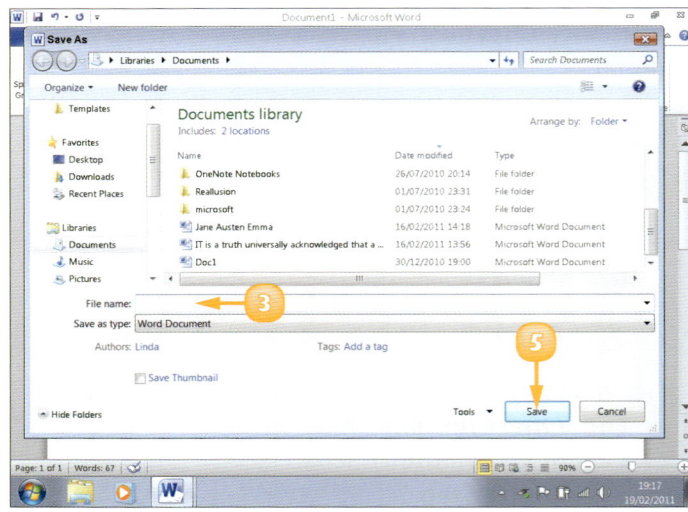

   ✓ *It is good practice to save a file as soon as you have created it.*

CHAPTER 3 WRITING A LETTER

Close a Document

1. Click the **File** tab.

   The **File** menu appears.

2. Click **Close**.

   If the file contains unsaved changes, a dialog appears.

3. Click **Save** to save the changes and close the document.

   A **Don't Save** closes the document without saving the changes.

   B **Cancel** does not save or close the document.

4. To exit Word, click ⊠.

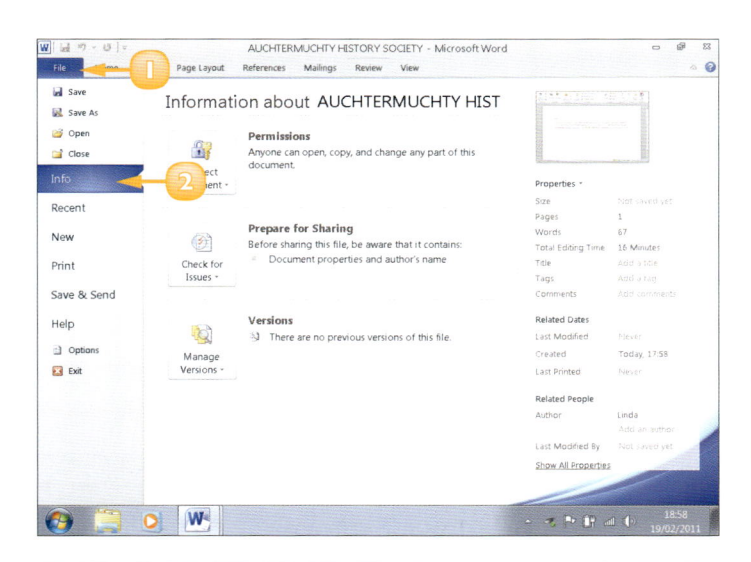

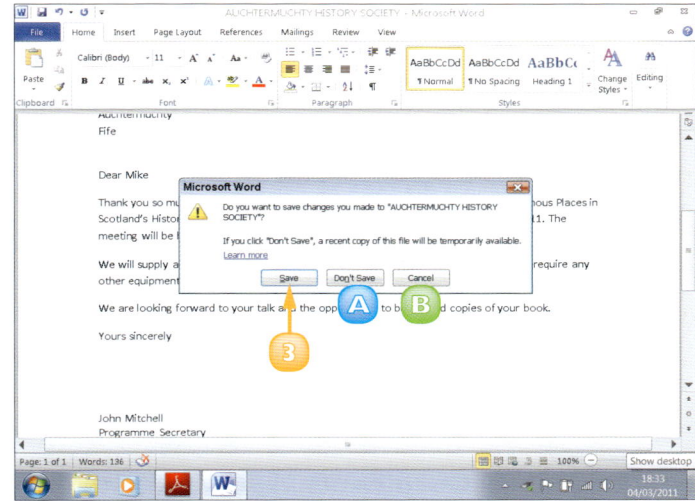

✓ *If you click ⊠ when a document has unsaved changes, you are shown the options in Step 3.*

CHAPTER 3 WRITING A LETTER

OPEN A SAVED DOCUMENT

You would like to access your document again and perhaps make a few changes or additions before printing it out. Chapter 5 covers information on printing documents.

1. Access the **Desktop**.
2. Click the **Windows Explorer** icon ( ).

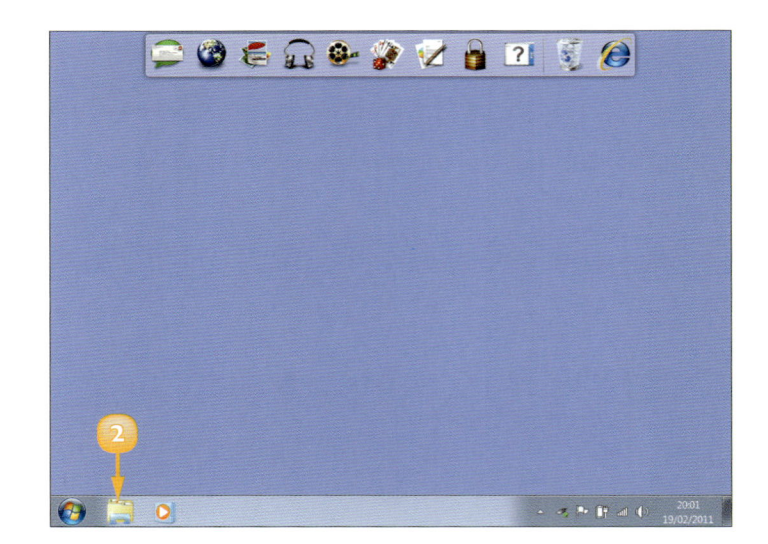

The **Libraries** folder appears.

3. Double-click **Documents.**

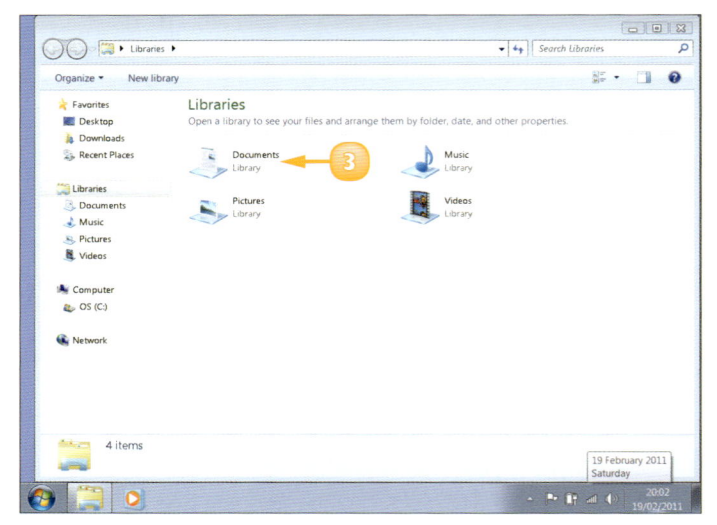

CHAPTER 3 WRITING A LETTER

The Documents folder appears with a list of all the documents that you have saved.

If you have created any folders, they also appear here.

4. Move down the list using the arrow keys (←, →, ↑ and ↓) or the scroll bar until you find the file you want to use.

5. Double-click the file that you want to work with.

Word opens with your selected document on the screen.

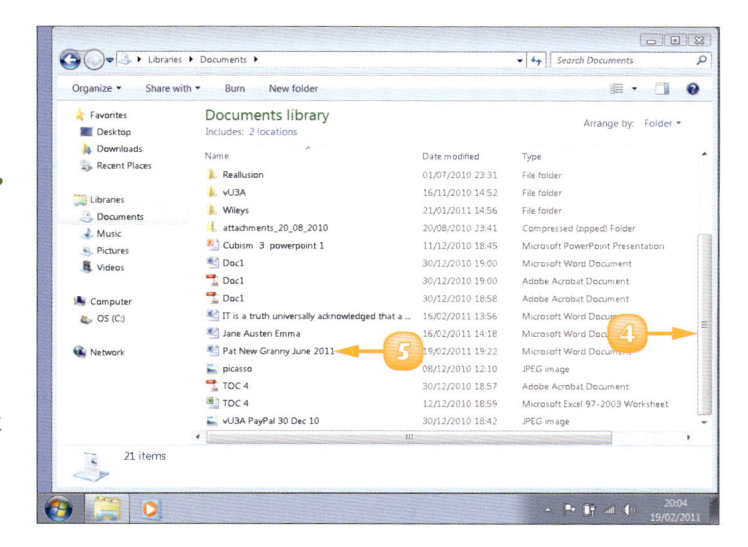

CHAPTER 3 WRITING A LETTER

CREATE LABELS

Once it is set up, making up labels in Word removes the task of writing names and addresses on envelopes for Christmas cards or invitations and they are easily updated to include new friends and relations or when somebody moves house. You need to buy a pack of 21 labels to an A4 sheet, usually sold in packs of 50 or 100 sheets, available at most large supermarkets and computer shops.

Create a Blank Label Document

1. Open a new Word document.
2. Click **Mailings**.

   The Mailings ribbon menu opens.

3. Click **Labels**.

   The Envelopes and Labels menu appears.

4. Click **Options**.

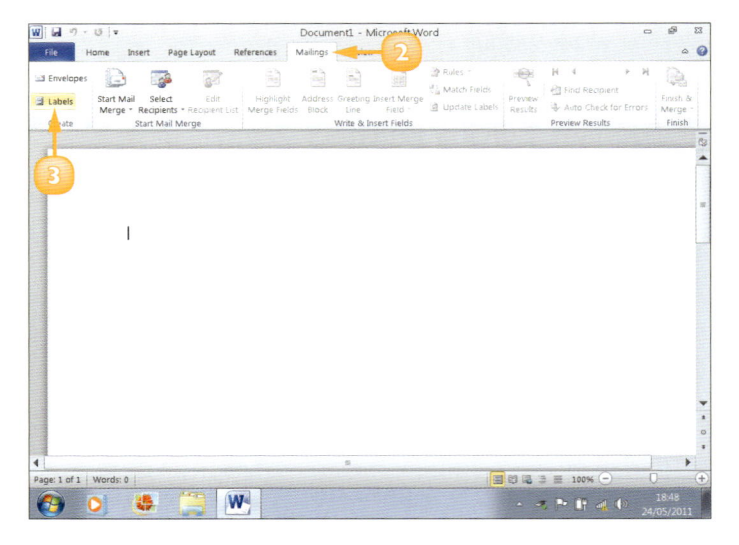

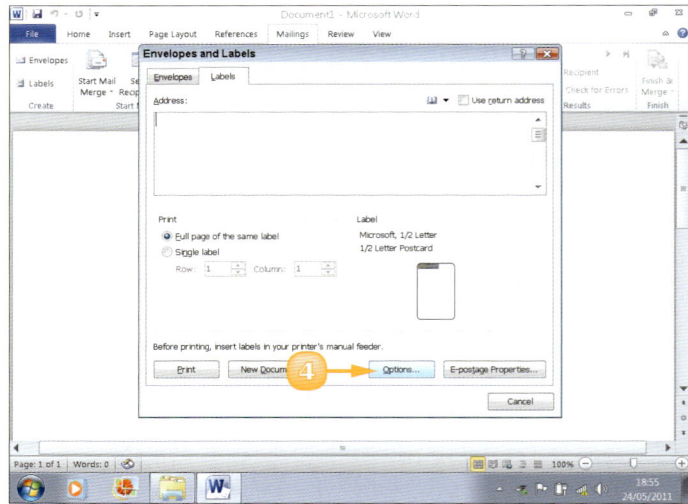

CHAPTER 3 WRITING A LETTER

5 Click the **Label vendors**.

6 Click **Avery A4/A5**.

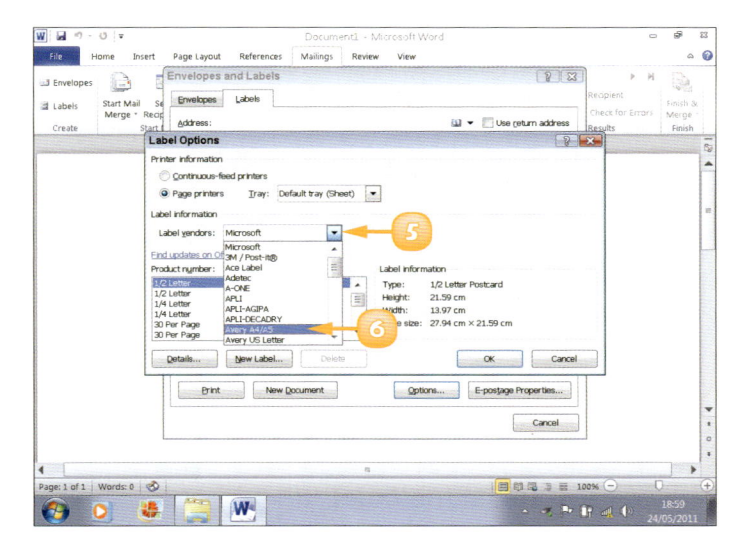

7 Scroll down the Product number list and click **L7160**.

8 Click **OK**.

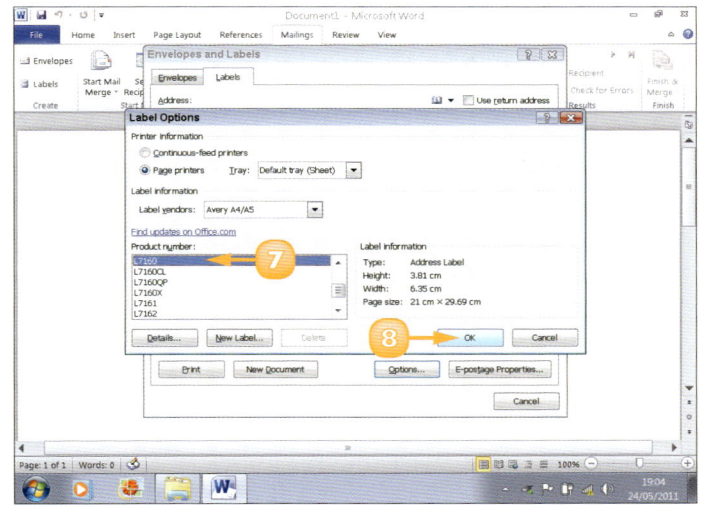

> *If you have bought a different type of label, find the code on the packaging and select it from the list.*

continued ➜

CHAPTER 3 WRITING A LETTER

CREATE LABELS (continued)

Once you have selected the type of label, you can save them into a new document. Word sets up a table in the document and you create the labels themselves by typing into the table cells.

9. Click the check box next to **Full page of the same label**.

10. Click **New Document**.

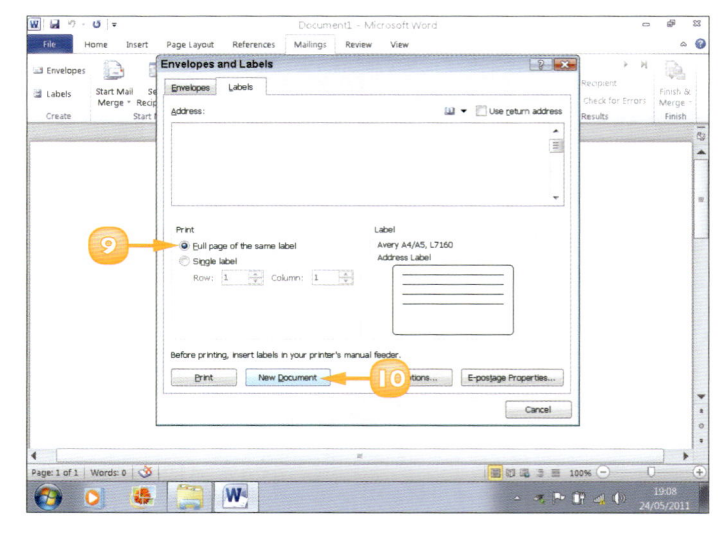

The label format appears in the document.

11. Click **Save**.

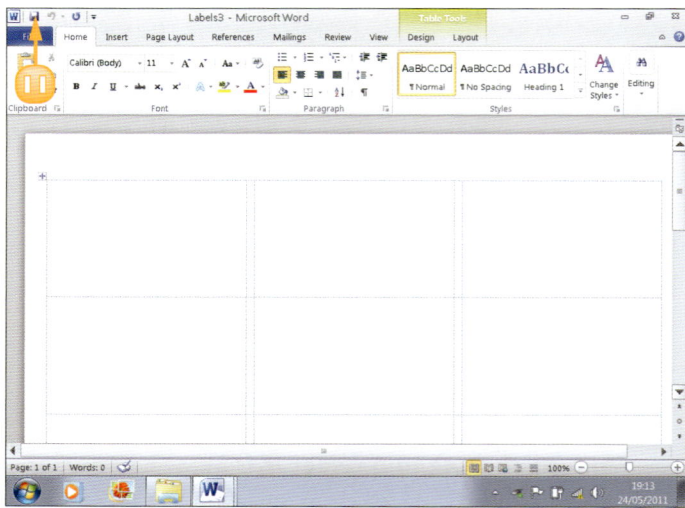

CHAPTER 3 WRITING A LETTER

Create the Labels

1. Type in the name and address.
2. Click **Layout**.
3. Click the start of the text.
4. Hold down the left mouse button and drag to highlight the whole page.
5. Click an alignment style from the Layout menu.

    All labels are converted to the new layout.

6. Click a blank box.
7. Type in a name and address.
8. Repeat Steps 6–7 to complete your list.
9. Press Tab when you get to the end of the page to create a new page.

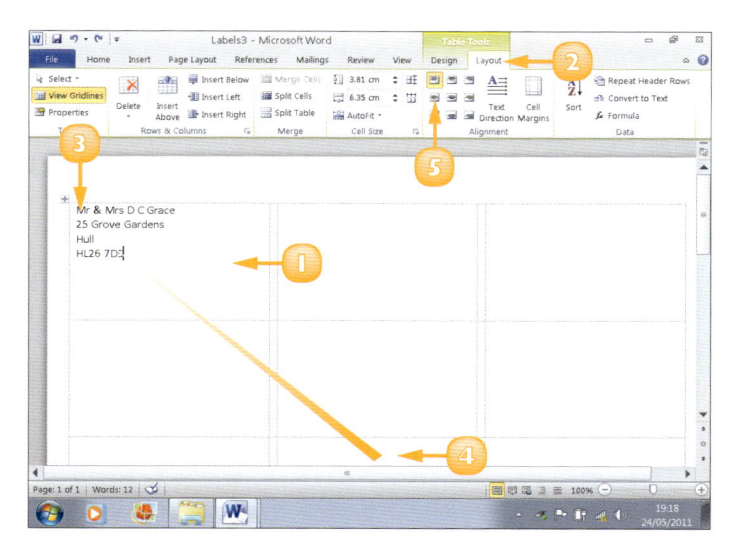

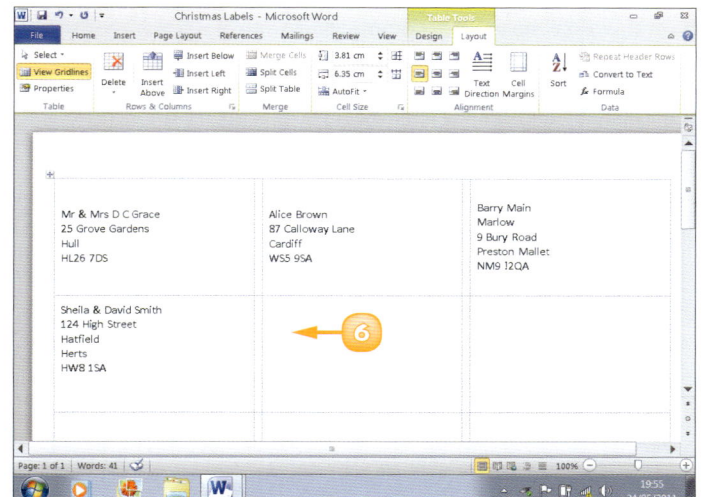

CONTENTS

- **50** Create a Document and Add Text
- **52** Choose the Text Style, Size and Colour
- **54** Align and Number Paragraphs
- **56** Change the Margins and Page Size
- **57** Add a Picture
- **58** Modify a Picture

4

MAKING A POSTER

This chapter continues exploring Word 2010 while creating a more complex document, a poster, using the Home menu to change the layout of the document and enhance the text. The Insert, Page Layout and Picture menus are also used to produce an eye-catching poster. Using the information in Chapters 3 and 4, you can create a variety of documents. For example, a newsletter, a programme or an invitation to a party.

CREATE A DOCUMENT AND ADD TEXT

Using Word 2010, you can easily produce a poster advertising an event, an invitation or a short newsletter and make it look attractive.

Create a File

1 Open Microsoft Word 2010.

Note: *If your computer has Microsoft Office Starter installed, open* **Microsoft Word Starter 2010**.

2 Click the **File** tab.

The **File** panel appears.

3 Click **Save As**.

The **Save As** dialog appears.

4 Type a file name that identifies the file e.g. Ferry Exhibition Poster 1.

5 Click **Save.**

The file name appears at the top of the empty document.

✓ *Before getting started, assemble all the information you need, for example, the date, time and place of the event.*

✓ *For an eye-catching poster, try to include a picture but not too much text.*

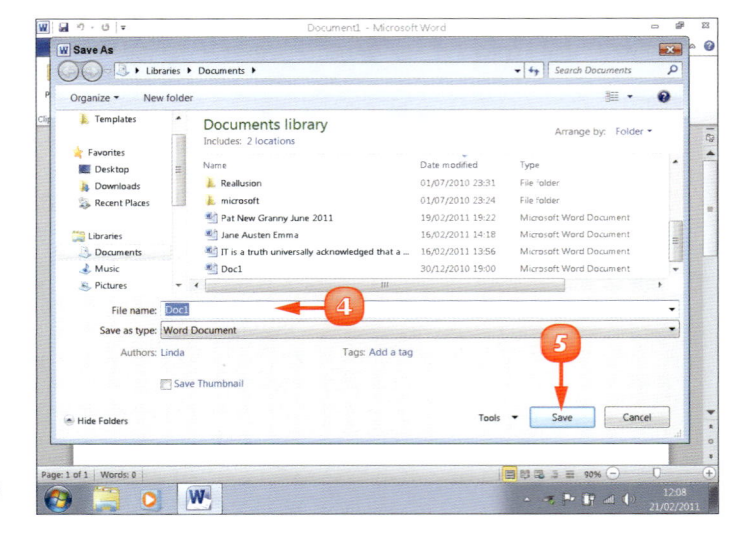

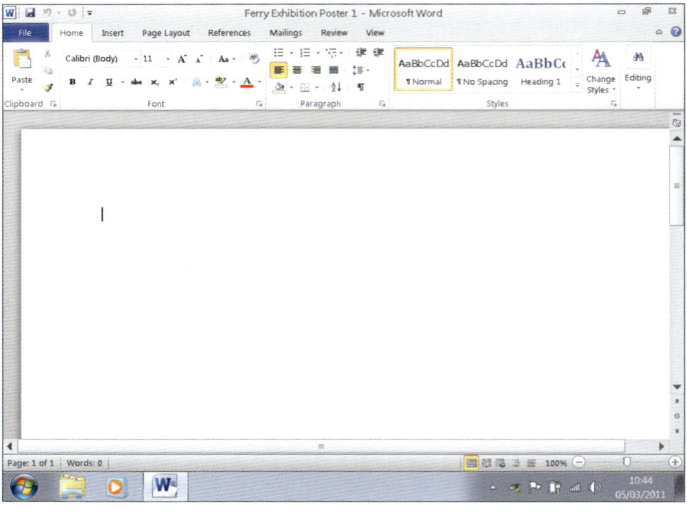

CHAPTER 4 MAKING A POSTER

Add Text

1. Type in the text.
2. Press **Caps Lock** (**Caps lock**) to type in capital letters.

Note: Press **Caps lock** again to turn off capital letters.

3. Press **Enter** at the end of each line of text.
4. Click the **Review** tab.

Note: If you are using Microsoft Office Starter, click the **Proofing** tab.

5. To check for errors, click ABC.
6. Click the **Save** button (💾).

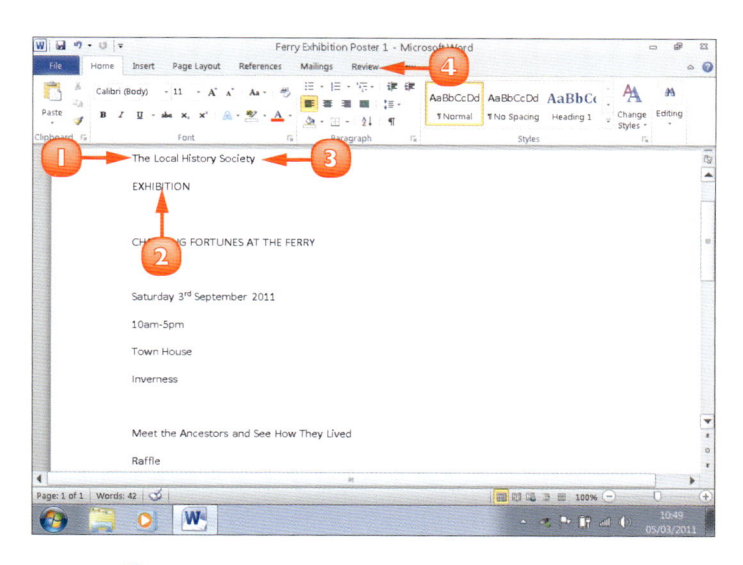

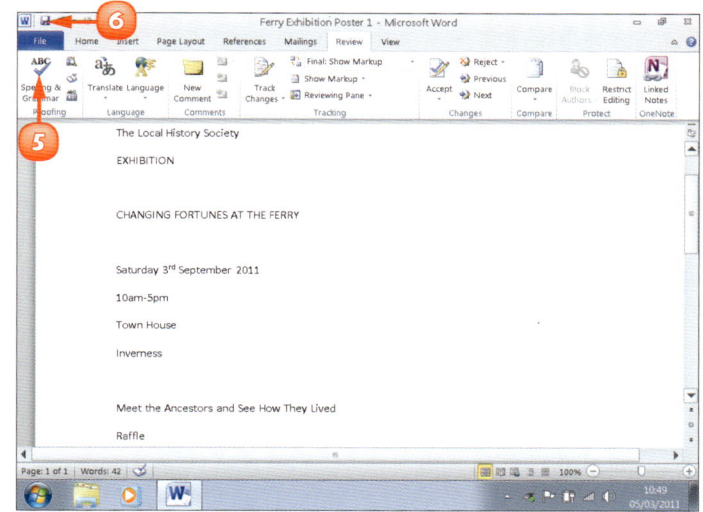

CHAPTER 4 MAKING A POSTER

CHOOSE THE TEXT STYLE, SIZE AND COLOUR

You use the Font menu in the Home tab to select and change text styles and size. You can also add colour and other visual effects to enhance the text in your poster.

Change the Font

1. Move the insertion point (I) to the left of text to be changed.

2. Hold the left mouse button down and drag the cursor to the end of the text to highlight it.

3. Release the mouse button.

4. Click the font ▾.

    A drop-down list of fonts appears.

    A *To view the complete list point at the scroll bar, hold down the left mouse button and scroll down the list.*

5. Click a font.

    The text appears in the new font.

6. Click on a blank area of the document to remove the highlighting.

✓ ***To choose a different font, repeat these steps.***

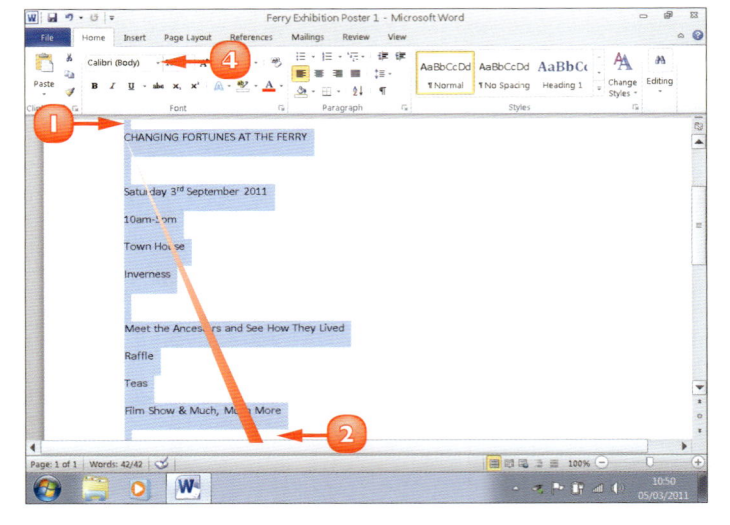

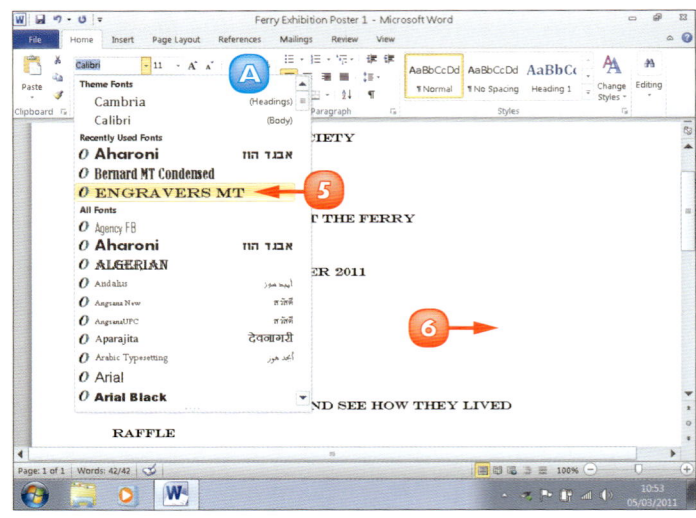

CHAPTER 4 MAKING A POSTER

Change the Text Size

1. Highlight text to change.
2. Click the font size ▼.
3. Point to the size you want to use.

   The text appears in the new size behind the drop-down menu.
4. Click to choose the size.

Change the Font Colour and Text Effects

1. Highlight a piece of text.
2. Click the font colour button (**A**) to choose a colour from the drop-down menu.
3. Click **A** to choose an effect from the drop-down menu.
4. Click **Bold** (**B**) to embolden the text.

   A *You can set the text to **Italics** (I).*

   B *You can underline the text using the **Underscore** button (U).*

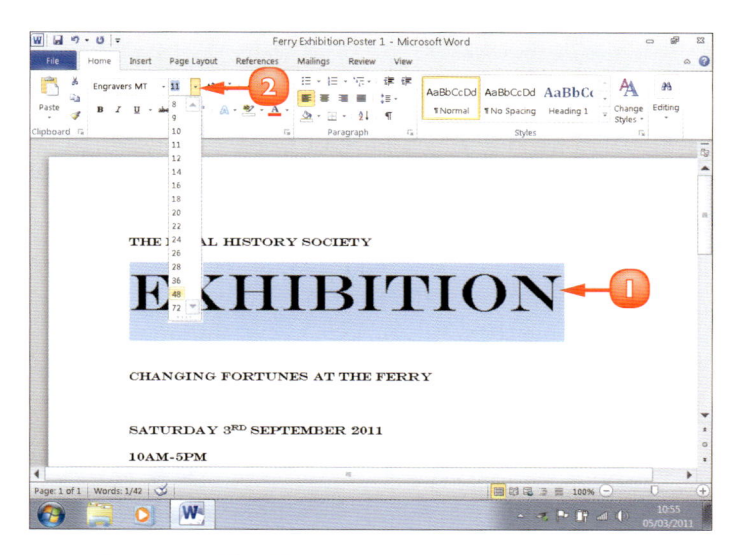

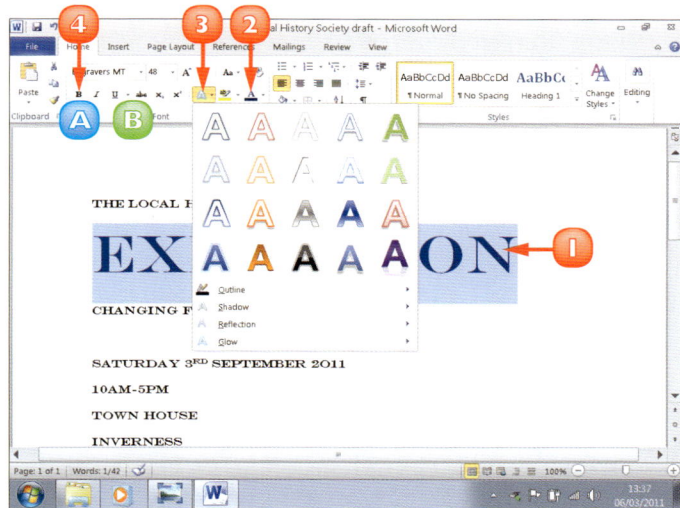

✓ ***Click the Underscore ▼ to choose a line style and colour for the underscore.***

✓ ***You can use A˄ to enlarge the highlighted text and A˅ to reduce it.***

CHAPTER 4 MAKING A POSTER

ALIGN AND NUMBER PARAGRAPHS

You can use the alignment buttons on the Home tab to align the text to the left, right or centre of the document. You can also 'justify' text to make it touch the margins on the left and right of the document.

Paragraphs of text can be made to stand out by putting a bullet point or number before them.

Change the Alignment

1. Highlight the text to be realigned.

    A *Text is usually left aligned and the Left button (≡) is highlighted in the **Paragraph** menu.*

2. Click **Center** (≡).

    The text is centred in the document.

    B *You can click **Right Align** (≡) to align the text to the right margin.*

    C *You can click **Justify** (≡) to align the text to both margins.*

3. Click Line & Paragraph Spacing (≡).

    You can change the spacing between lines and paragraphs by selecting options from the drop-down menu.

✓ **Made a mistake? Remember you can click ↶ and ↷ to correct errors.**

🛑 **You must highlight text before attempting to enhance it.**

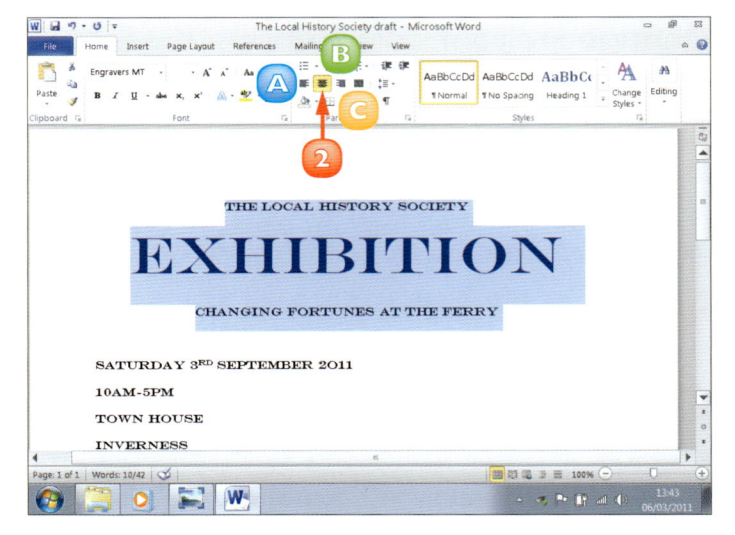

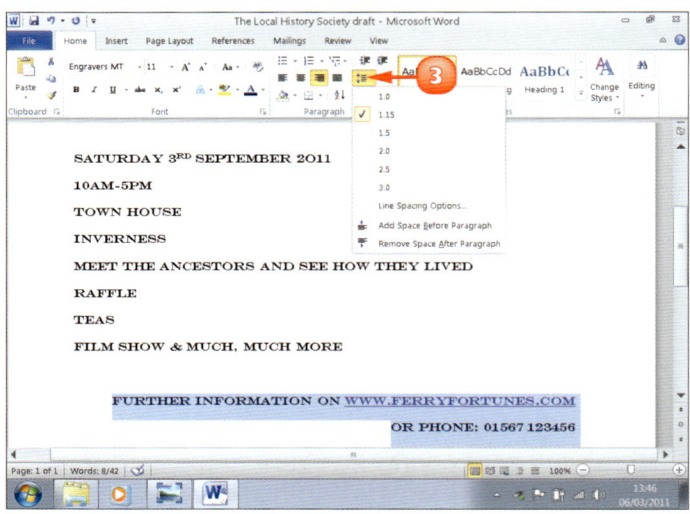

CHAPTER 4 MAKING A POSTER

Add Bullet Points and Numbering

1. Highlight the text which is to have bullet points.

2. Click on the **Bullets** icon ( ).

   Bullet points appear.

3. Click on the Bullets ▼ to see a list of alternative designs.

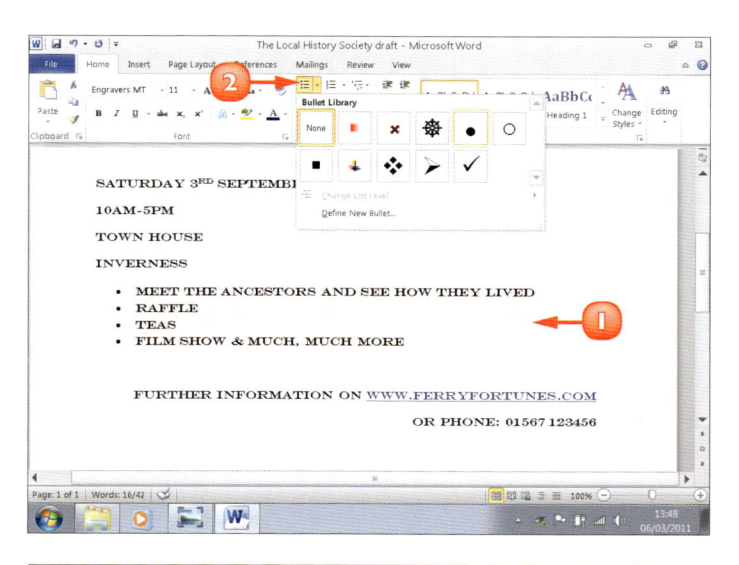

4. Click on the **Numbers** icon ( ).

   Numbering appears.

5. Click on the Numbers ▼ to display a list of alternative numbering styles.

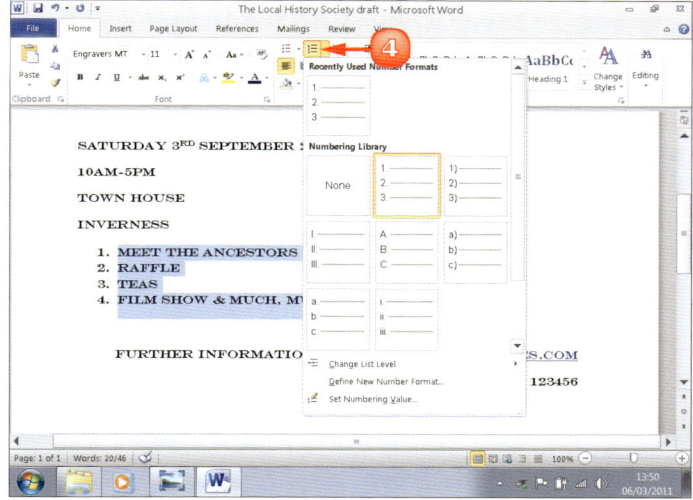

Highlight a block of text and move it to the left or right by clicking or .

CHAPTER 4 MAKING A POSTER

CHANGE THE MARGINS AND PAGE SIZE

The Page Layout menu contains options to control the margins, orientation and page size.

1. Click the **Page Layout** tab.
2. Click **Margins** ( ).

   The Margins drop-down menu appears.

3. Click **Narrow** for a poster or newsletter to allow maximum space on the page.

4. Click **Orientation** ( ) to change from portrait (the standard format) to landscape.

5. Click the arrow at the bottom right of the Page Layout tab.

   The Page Setup dialog appears.

   - **A** You can adjust the margins and orientation in the Margins tab.
   - **B** You can change the size of the paper in the Paper tab.
   - **C** The effect of the changes are shown in the Preview pane.

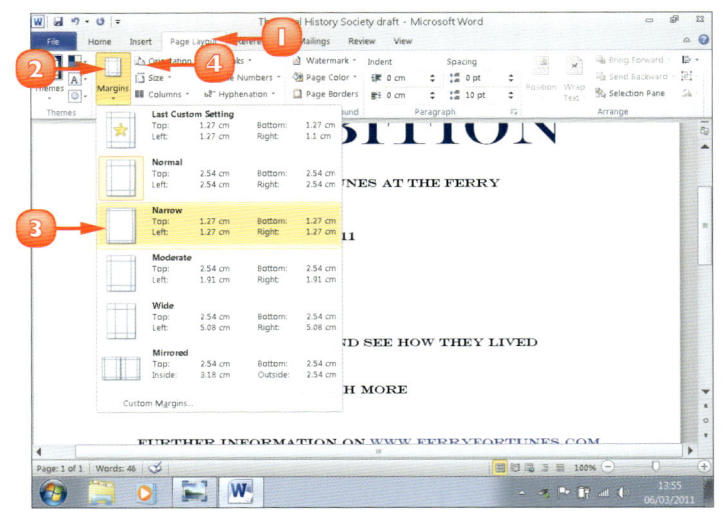

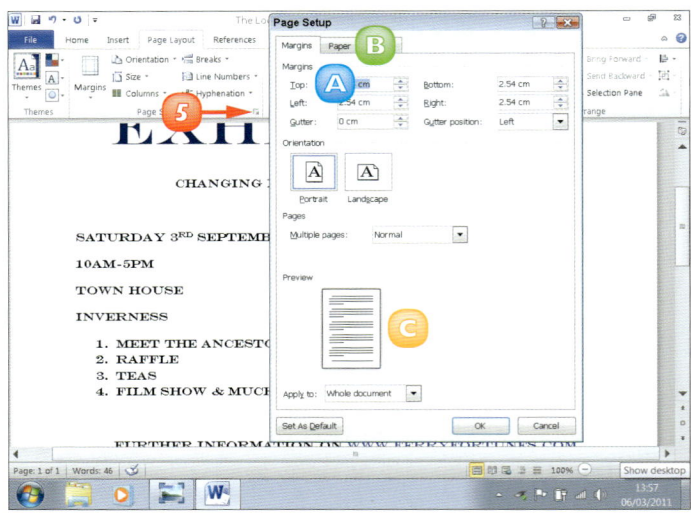

CHAPTER 4 MAKING A POSTER

ADD A PICTURE

To make the poster more effective, we use the Insert menu to add a picture.

Chapter 11 provides information on how to download digital pictures from your camera. With access to the Internet (see Chapter 6), a vast range of Microsoft clipart becomes available to you. Clipart is inserted into a document in much the same way as a picture.

① Click the **Insert** tab.

The **Insert** ribbon appears.

② Click **Picture**.

The **Pictures Library** appears.

③ Double-click a folder to see the pictures in it.

④ Double-click a picture.

The picture appears in the document and the **Picture Tools** menu from the **Format** tab appears at the top of the screen.

✓ *You can click a picture to access the Picture Tools. Click outside the picture to return to the text.*

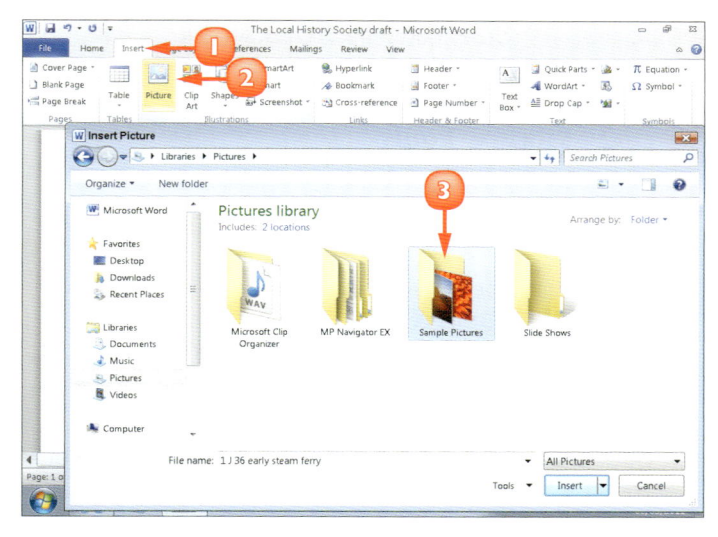

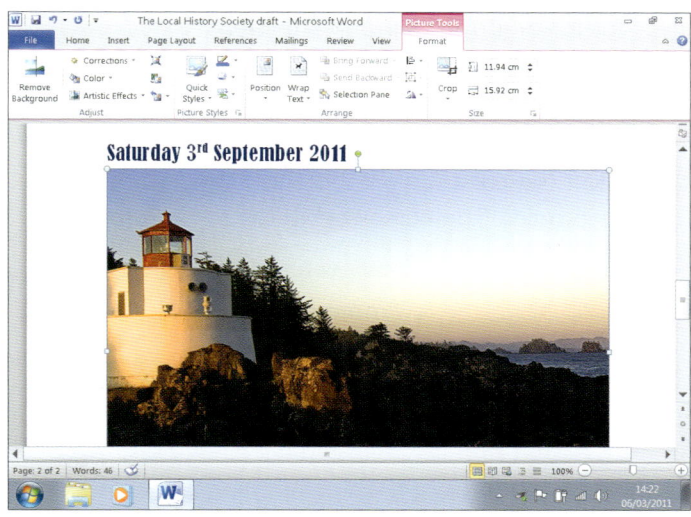

CHAPTER 4 MAKING A POSTER

MODIFY A PICTURE

Once you have inserted an image into a document, you can change its size or crop it to remove unwanted details. You can also wrap text around a picture and move the picture to a different position in the document.

Reduce the Size of a Picture

1. Click on the picture.
2. Click **Picture Tools.**
3. Point the cursor to a corner of the picture.

    The cursor becomes a double-headed arrow (⤡).

4. Hold the left mouse button down and drag towards the middle of the picture. Release the button.

Crop a Picture

1. Click the picture and the **Picture Tools** menu.
2. Click **Crop** (▦).
3. Point the cursor at the bottom crop mark. The cursor becomes a black T shape.
4. Hold down the left mouse button and drag up towards the centre of the picture. Release the button.
5. Click **Crop**.

Note: You can also just click outside the picture.

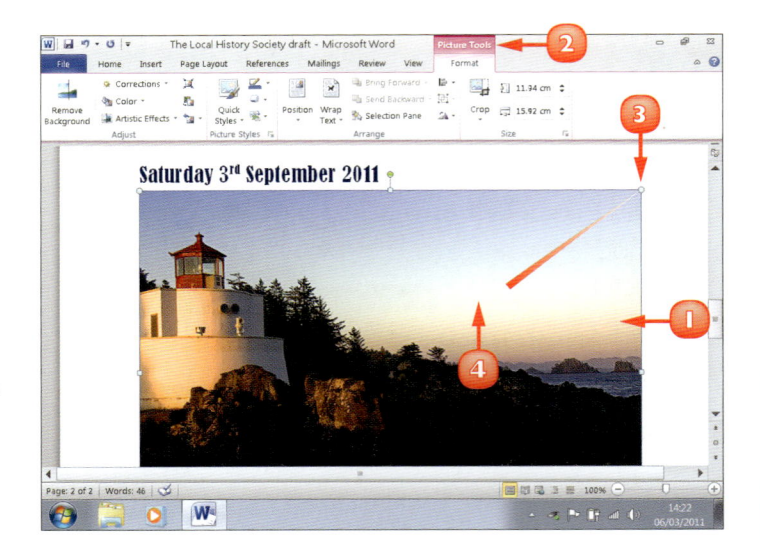

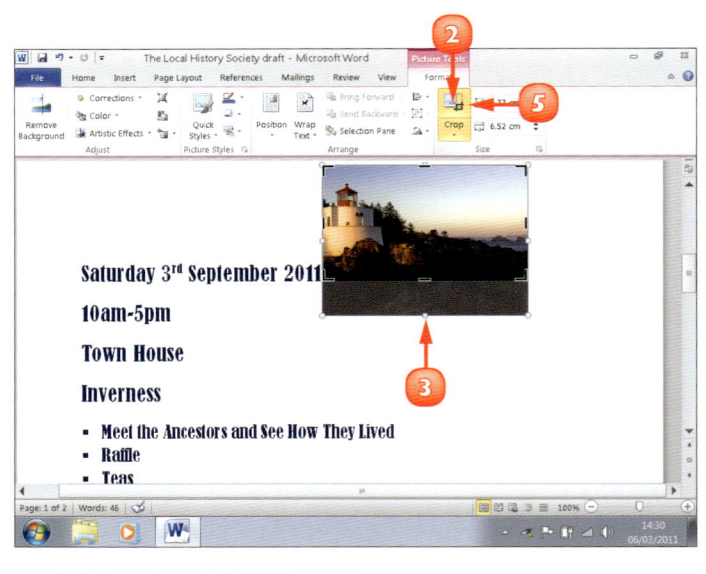

CHAPTER 4 MAKING A POSTER

Moving a Picture

1. Click the picture and the **Picture Tools** menu.

2. Click **Wrap Text** ( ).

   A drop-down menu of wrapping options appears.

3. Click **In Front of Text**.

   The picture sits on top of the text.

4. Point the cursor somewhere in the picture and hold down the left mouse button.

   The cursor becomes a cross ( ).

5. Move the cursor around to choose a new position for the picture.

   The picture moves with the mouse.

6. Release the mouse button.

   The picture remains in its new position.

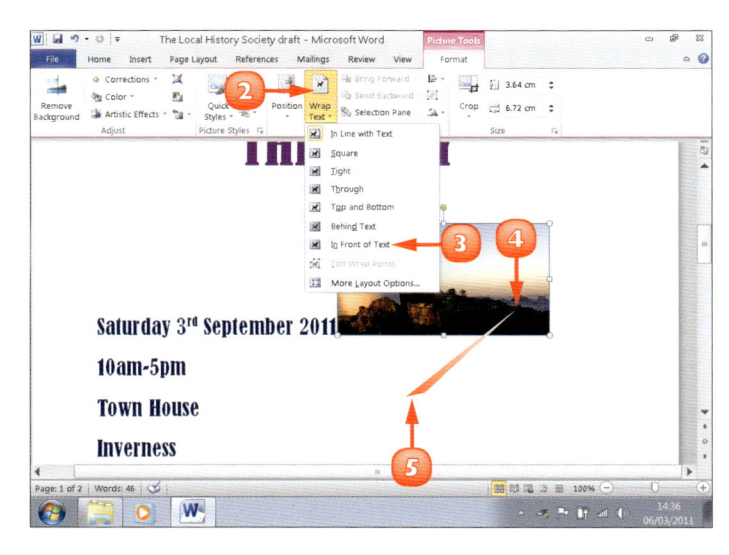

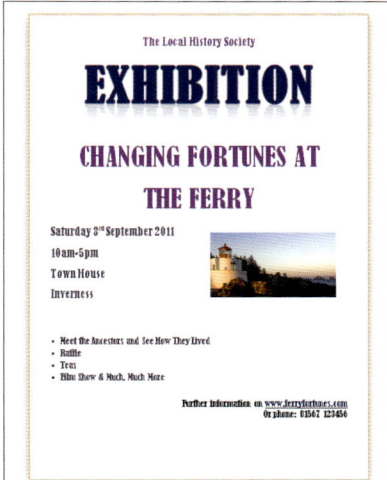

CHAPTER 4 MAKING A POSTER

CONTENTS

62 Use Print Preview
64 Print a Document
66 Print a Picture
68 Copy Documents and Pictures
70 Scan Documents and Pictures

5
USING A PRINTER AND SCANNER

This chapter shows you how to copy, scan and print documents and pictures using an all-in-one printer. All-in-one printers can copy and scan documents as well as printing them.

A printer that can only print is usually cheaper than an all-in-one printer. A laser printer is more expensive than an inkjet printer. Inkjet printers produce good-quality, black-and-white and colour printouts. When considering which printer to buy, bear in mind the cost of replacement ink cartridges and how many copies a cartridge can produce.

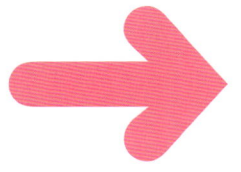

USE PRINT PREVIEW

Print Preview allows you to see what the finished document will look like when it is printed. If you have made a mistake, it can be corrected before printing, saving time, paper and ink. It is assumed that you have a printer connected to your computer.

In this section, we work with the Backstage menu (accessed from the File tab in Office 2010) to preview documents. We use Windows Photo Viewer to preview pictures.

Preview a Document

1. Click **Start**.

2. Point to Microsoft Word 2010.

   A Jump List appears.

3. Click the document to be opened.

   Word 2010 opens and the document appears.

4. Click the **File** tab.

   The Backstage menu appears.

5. Click **Print**.

   The Print menu appears.

   A. *You can change the size of the document preview.*

   B. *You can scroll through the pages of the document.*

   C. *You can click the **Home** tab to go back to the document.*

✓ Remember to click the **SAVE** button (💾) if you change the document.

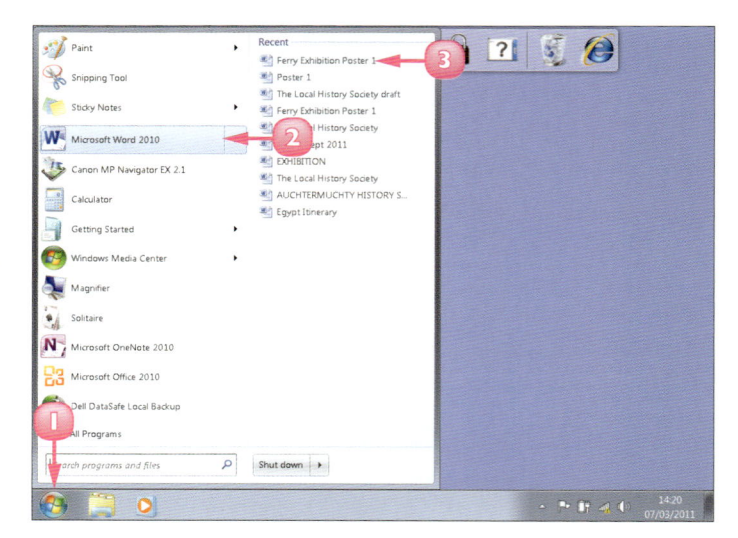

CHAPTER 5 USING A PRINTER AND SCANNER

Preview a Picture

1. Click the **Folder** icon (📁) on the Taskbar.

   The **Libraries** folder opens.

2. Double-click the **Picture Libraries** icon.

   The Pictures Library folder appears.

3. Double-click the folder that contains the image and double-click the picture.

   Windows Photo Viewer opens.

4. Click **Print**.

5. Click **Print** in the drop-down menu.

   The Print Pictures screen appears.

6. Choose a layout.

   The picture changes size depending on your choice.

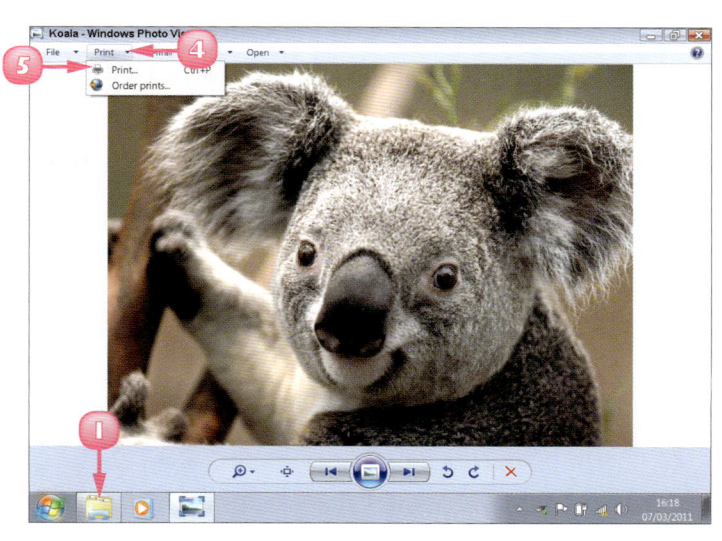

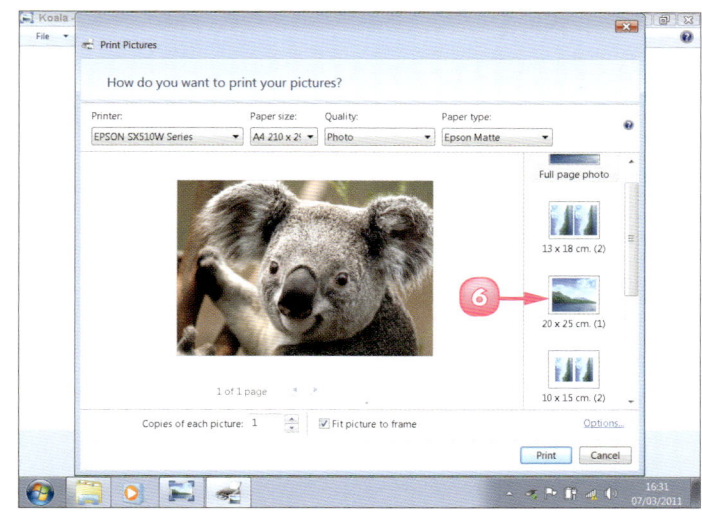

> ✓ *Click **Cancel** to return to Windows Photo Viewer or ❌ to return to the Pictures Library.*

CHAPTER 5 USING A PRINTER AND SCANNER

PRINT A DOCUMENT

An Epson All-in-One printer has been used to illustrate this chapter. There will be some differences in the way your printer works and how its software operates but you will find that all modern printers have similar features.

1. Open the document to be printed.
2. Click the **File** tab.
3. Click **Print**.
4. Click the **Print** button.

Change Printer Properties

1. In the Print screen, click **Printer Properties**.

Note: *The Properties dialog differs depending on the printer.*

2. Click a **Quality Option** button to choose the quality of printout required.
3. Click the **Type** and select the type of paper.
4. Click the **Size** and select the paper size.
5. Click **OK**.
6. In the Print screen, click **Print**.

✓ *If the document does not print, check that the printer is connected to the computer, switched on and loaded with paper.*

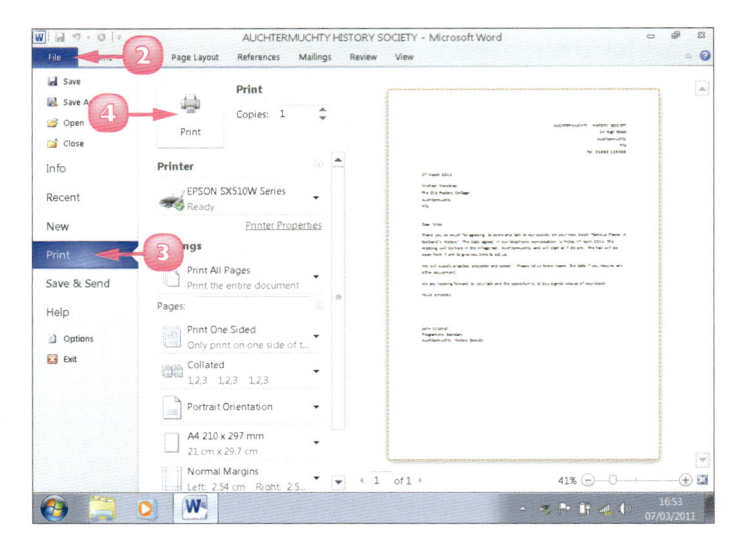

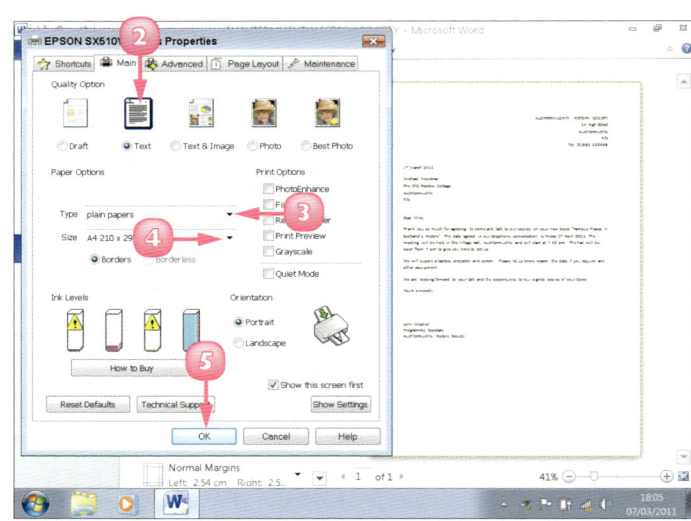

CHAPTER 5 USING A PRINTER AND SCANNER

Change the Print Settings

1. In the Print screen, use the **Copies** ⇕ to choose the number of copies required.

Note: You can also type a number into the box.

2. Click **Print All Pages** to view the options.

3. Click **2 Pages per Sheet**.

4. Click **Print**.

Both pages are printed on the same sheet of paper.

> You can click on any **Settings** ▾ to see a list of changes that you can make.

Move and Zoom

1. Click **Next Page** (◀) to move to the next page in the document.

   Ⓐ You can click **Previous Page** (▶) to move to earlier pages in the document.

   Ⓑ You can enter a number to move to a specific page.

2. Click **Zoom In** (⊕) to enlarge the type on the preview.

   Ⓒ You can click **Zoom Out** (⊖) to reduce the type on the preview.

   Ⓓ You can drag the slider (▯) to zoom in and out.

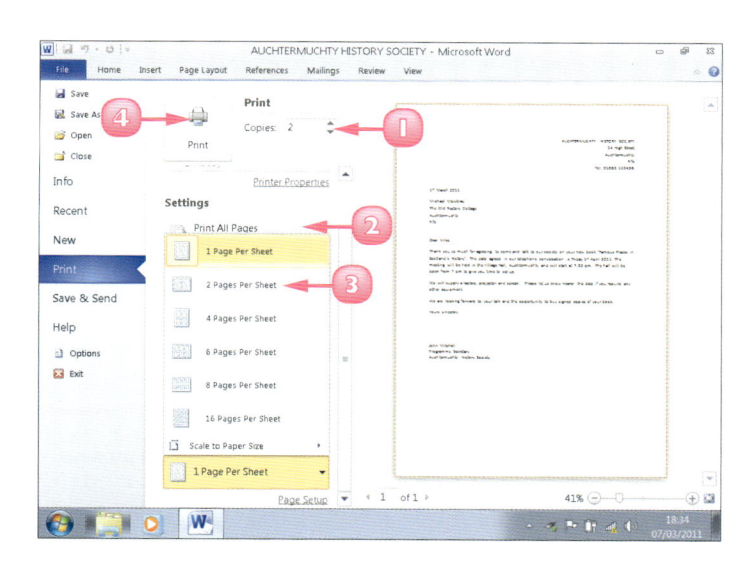

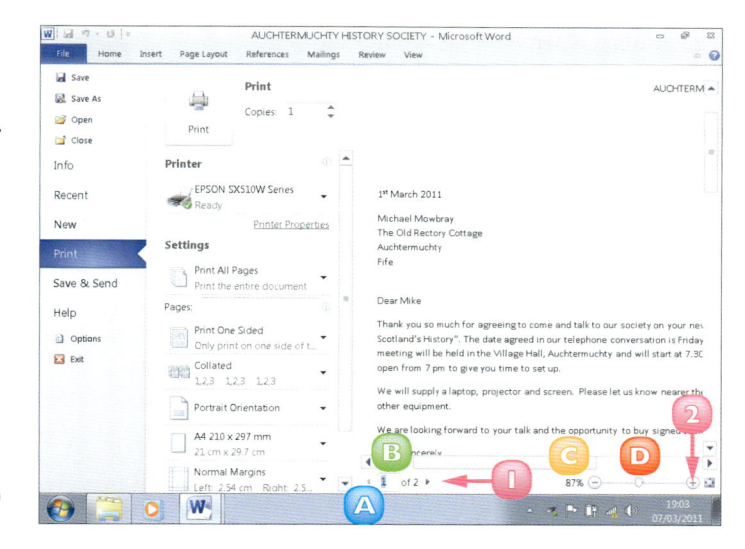

CHAPTER 5 USING A PRINTER AND SCANNER

PRINT A PICTURE

We use Windows Photo Viewer, part of Windows 7, and Office 2010 Picture Editor to print pictures. To get high-quality printouts, you need to use special photo paper. You can then produce glossy or matte finish pictures.

① Open the picture to be printed (see Steps 1–3 of "Preview a Picture").

② Click **Print**.

③ Click **Print** in the drop-down menu.

The Print Pictures screen appears.

④ Click a print layout.

⑤ Click the **Printer** to choose a printer (if you have more than one).

⑥ Click the **Paper Size** to select the size of paper to be used.

⑦ Click the **Quality** to choose **Photo** or **Best Photo**.

⑧ Click the **Paper type** to select the type of paper.

⑨ Click the **Copies of each picture** to change the number of copies.

⑩ Click **Options** and **Printer Properties**.

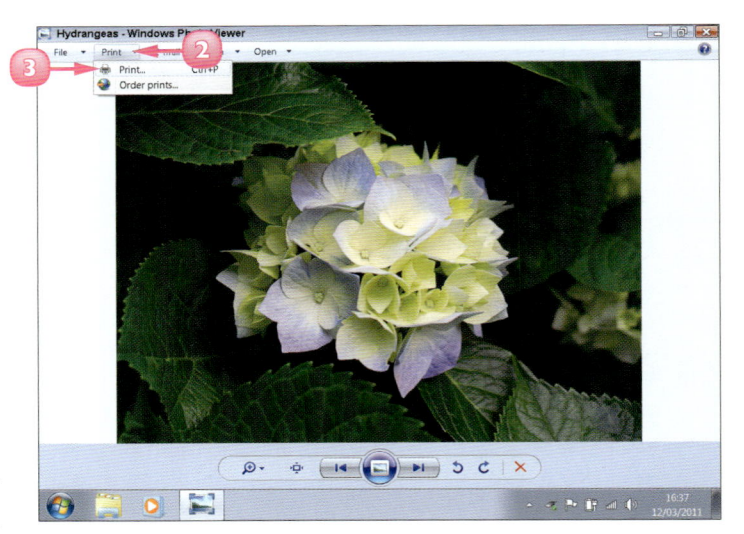

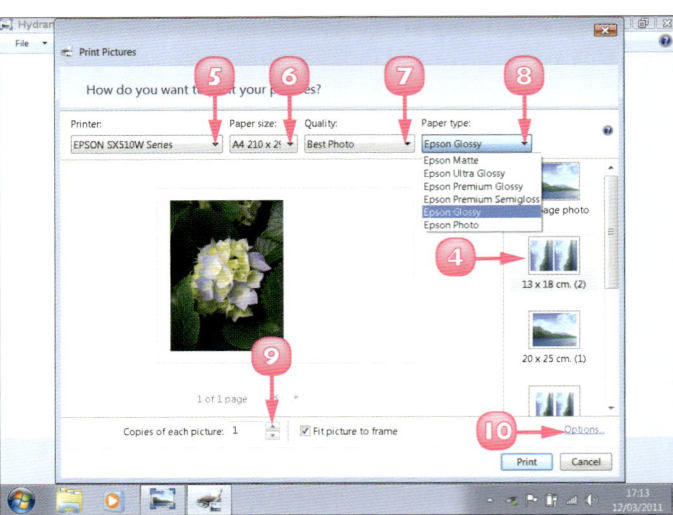

CHAPTER 5 USING A PRINTER AND SCANNER

The Printer Properties menu appears.

Ⓐ *The options set in the Print Pictures screen are shown.*

⓫ Click **Print Preview.**

⓬ Click **OK.**

⓭ Click **Print**.

The Print Preview window appears.

⓮ Click **Print** in the Preview window to print the pictures.

Ⓑ *You can click **Cancel** to cancel the print process and make changes.*

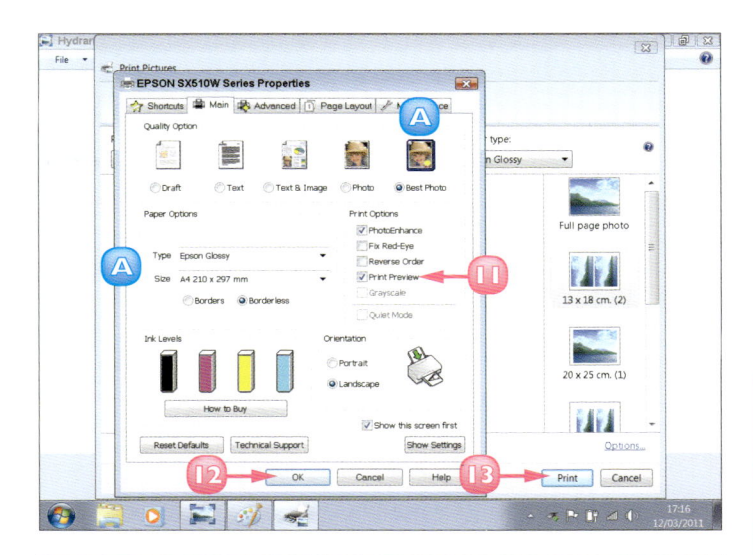

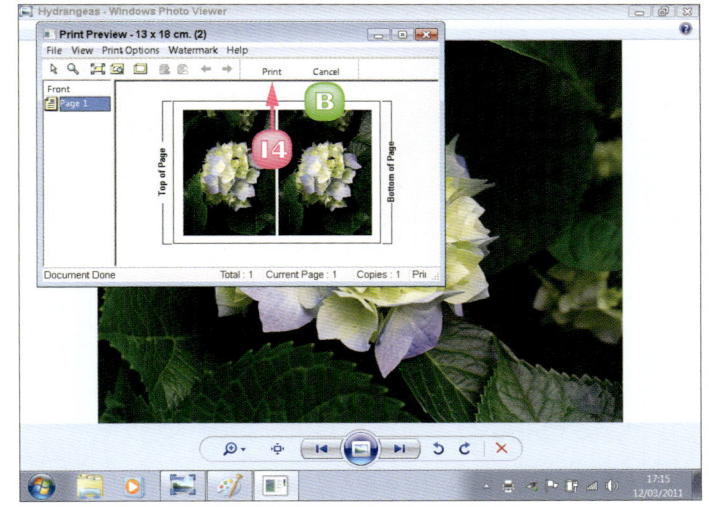

Check the printer is loaded with photo paper and is connected to the computer before pressing the Print button.

CHAPTER 5 USING A PRINTER AND SCANNER

COPY DOCUMENTS AND PICTURES

An all-in-one scanner and printer makes it easy to produce copies of documents and pictures. All models of all-in-one printers have a lid that lifts up to reveal a glass plate on which the document is placed and a keypad for quick copies. Software is provided to improve and enhance the quality of your documents and pictures.

Use the Keypad to Copy

1. Lift the lid of the scanner.

2. Find the arrow at the corner of the glass telling you where to place the document or picture and put it face down on the glass.

Source: Epson UK

3. Press **Copy** on the keypad.

4. Use the arrow keys to choose **colour** or **black & white** copy.

5. Use the – and + keys to choose the number of copies.

6. Press Settings to choose Paper Size, Type and Quality.

7. Press **Start**.

    The document or picture is scanned and printed.

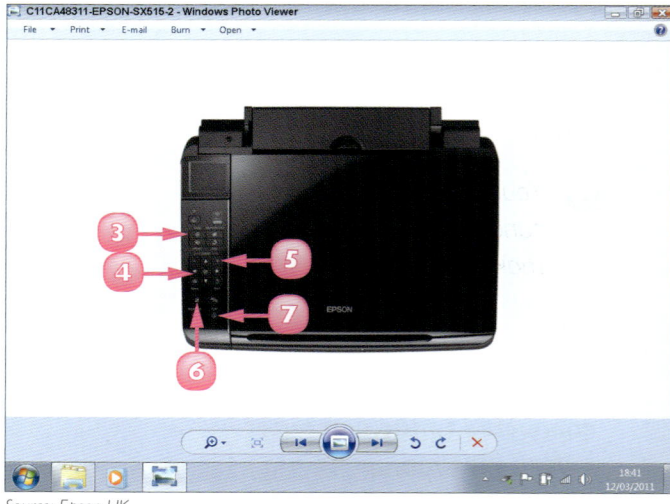

Source: Epson UK

CHAPTER 5 USING A PRINTER AND SCANNER

Use the Software to Copy

1. Double-click the **Scanner** icon on the Desktop.

   The scan dialog opens in **Full Auto Mode**.

2. Lift the lid of the scanner and place the document face down on the glass.

3. Click **Scan**.

   The document is scanned and saved in the Pictures Library.

4. Go to the **Pictures Library** and double-click the picture.

   Windows Photo Viewer opens.

5. Click **Print** and then click **Print** on the drop-down menu.

   The **Print Pictures** menu appears.

6. Click **Fit picture to frame** (☑ changes to ☐).

7. Click **Print**.

   The Print Preview window appears.

8. Click **Print** to print the pictures.

   Ⓐ You can click **Cancel** to cancel the print process and make changes.

   ✓ **No scanner icon on your desktop? Click Start. Type the name of the scanner into Search programs and files. Select the scanner from the list.**

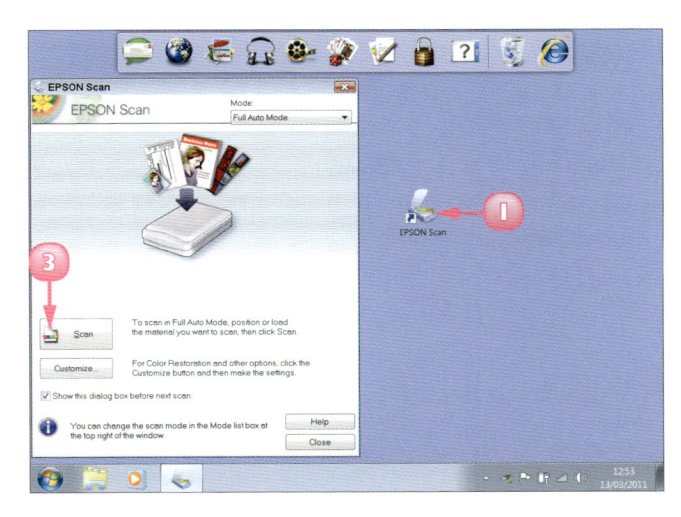

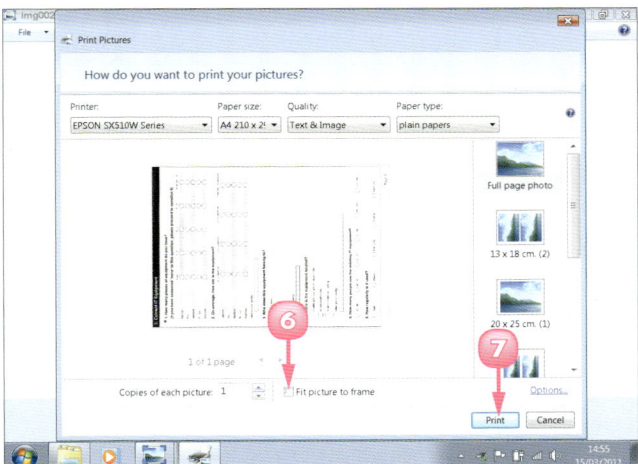

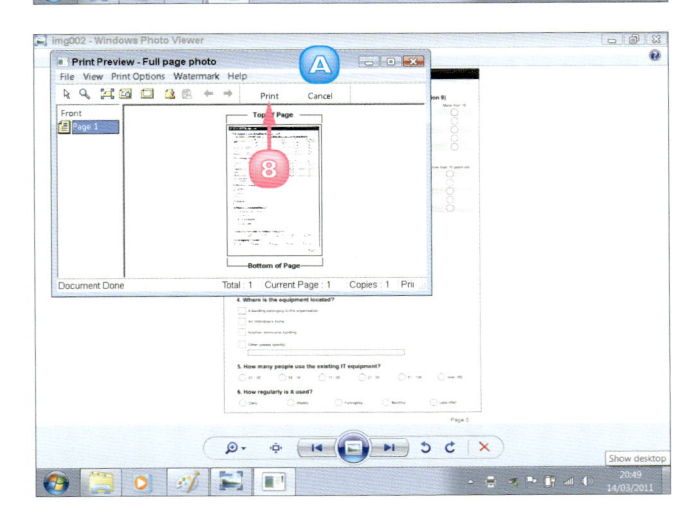

CHAPTER 5 USING A PRINTER AND SCANNER

SCAN DOCUMENTS AND PICTURES

You may have some birth certificates or other important documents of which you would like to make digital copies for safe-keeping. Perhaps you have some old pictures that you have borrowed and need to give back. If you scan them into your computer, you can improve the quality before printing them out.

Scan a Document

1. Double-click the **scanner** icon on the Desktop.

   The Scan Menu opens in **Full Auto Mode**.

2. Click the **Mode** and choose **Home Mode**.

   The Home Mode menu appears.

3. Place the picture face down on the glass.

4. Click **Preview**.

   The Preview window opens.

   A *You can select the Document Type.*

   B *You can select the Image Type.*

5. Click **Other** Destination.

6. Click **Scan**.

7. Click **OK** in the File Save Settings menu.

   The document is scanned and saved in the Pictures Library.

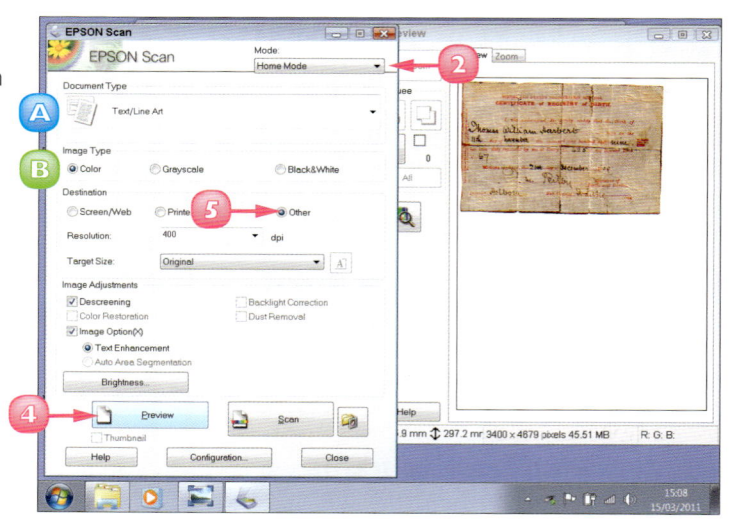

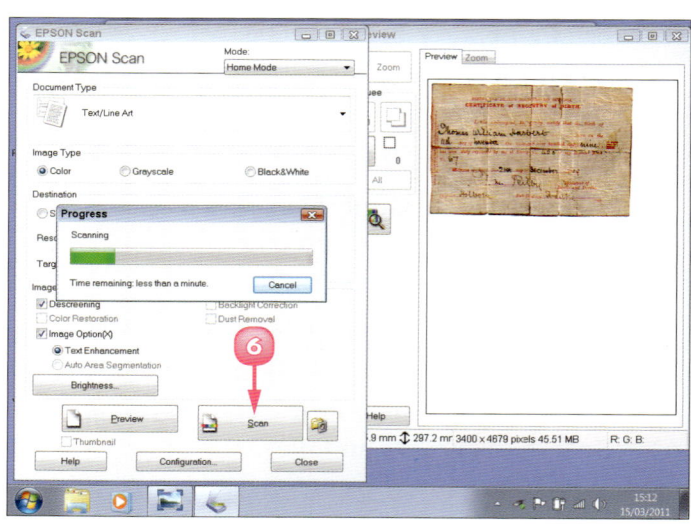

CHAPTER 5 USING A PRINTER AND SCANNER

Scan a Picture

1. Repeat Steps 1–3 on the previous page.

2. Click **Preview**.

   The Preview window opens.

3. Click to select the appropriate document type.

4. Click to select the appropriate image type.

5. Click **Other** destination.

6. Click the **Resolution** and change to **600** dpi (dots per inch) for a better quality picture.

7. Click the **Brightness** button.

8. Drag the **Brightness** to adjust the brightness of the picture.

9. Drag the **Contrast** to improve the clarity of the picture.

10. Click **Close**.

11. Click **Scan**.

    The **File Save Settings** menu appears.

12. Click **My Pictures** in Location to choose where to save the picture.

13. Click **OK**.

    The picture is scanned and saved to the location you have chosen.

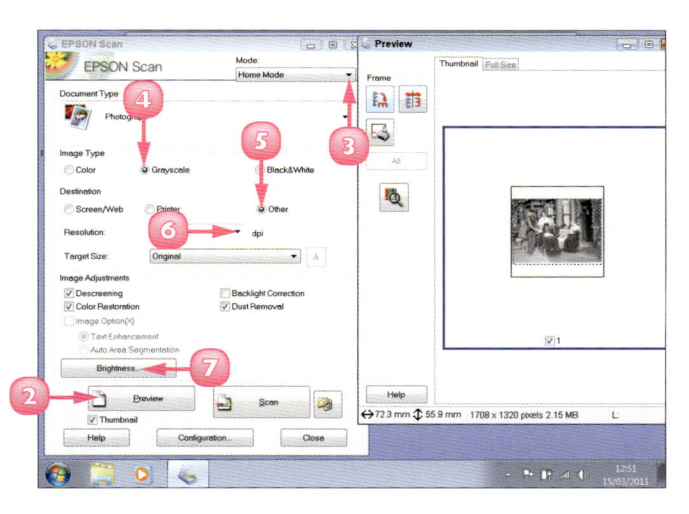

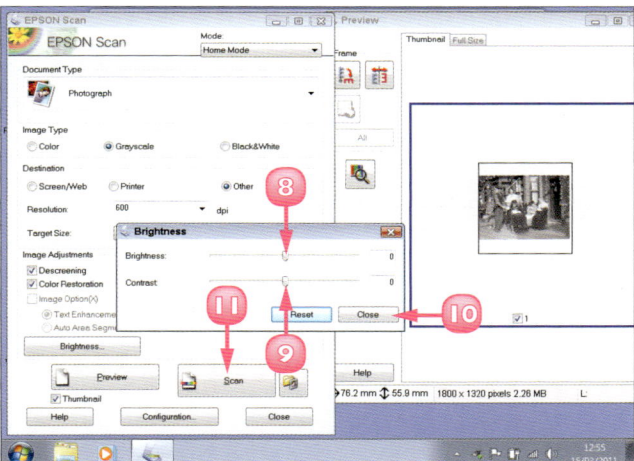

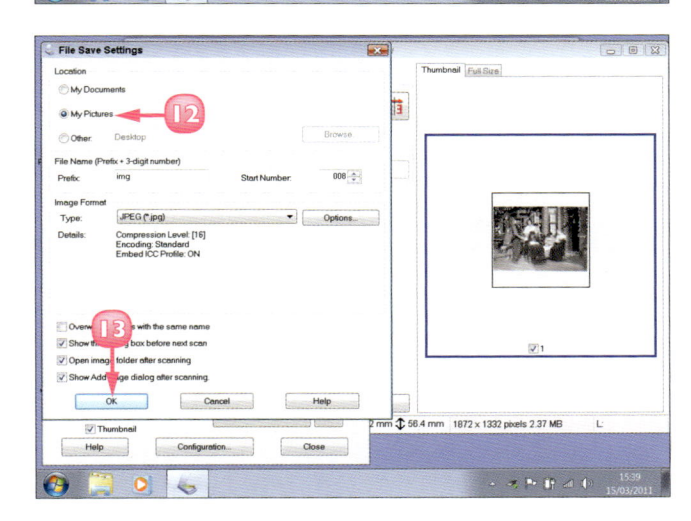

CHAPTER 5 USING A PRINTER AND SCANNER

CONTENTS

74 Choose an ISP
75 Connection Types
76 Get Started on the Internet
78 Keep Safe
80 Windows Live Essentials
82 Social Networking

6

GETTING CONNECTED

This chapter helps you to choose a provider and set up the Internet. It explains how to keep your computer safe and secure when you go online. It also looks at what Windows Live Essentials has to offer and dips into social networking.

CHOOSE AN ISP

If you have already been set up with an Internet connection, skip to the "Keep Safe" section; if not, read on.

To connect to the Internet, you need to pay a subscription to an Internet service provider (ISP). The ISP provides a connection (through a telephone line or cable) and will probably supply a modem or router to connect your computer to the network. ISPs offer packages that include access to the Internet, a web browser, email addresses and web space.

1. Using a computer belonging to a friend, a library or an Internet café, open Internet Explorer.

2. Enter **www.ispreview.co.uk** into the address bar.

3. Make a list of questions to help you decide what you need to know.

4. Visit neighbours and friends who live close by and ask them about their broadband experience.

5. Use a comparison website (such as **www.top10.com**) to find out which ISP is offering the best deals.

6. Check how much it will cost and how long it will take for your telephone company to set up a broadband connection to your line.

✓ *Many ISPs offer packages including broadband, telephone and television or broadband and telephone. You need to work out which one is best suited to your needs.*

Reproduced by permission ISPreview.co.uk Copyright © 1999–2011

All website information, including prices and privacy settings, correct at time of going to press. Please check appropriate website for current details.

CHAPTER 6 GETTING CONNECTED

CONNECTION TYPES

Wireless broadband allows you to sit with your laptop anywhere in the house (or garden) and access the Internet or print a document. Other people can access the Internet remotely via the wireless router at the same time.

Dial-up Internet access is slow but can cost less if you use the Internet infrequently. Phone calls cannot be made while the line is connected to the Internet. If you want to download software or music, find your ancestors online or put photographs on a website, a dial-up connection is not for you.

Wireless Broadband Access

1. Look at the diagram of a typical system.
2. Make a list of things to consider.
3. Talk to family and friends who have a wireless system.
4. Go to the library or Internet café and access a website for information.
5. Check out whether you need to buy additional equipment.

Dial-up Access

1. Look at the diagram of a typical system.

    The dotted line shows that the telephone cannot be used because the computer is using the line to access the internet.

    ✓ *If this all sounds a bit too much you could ask a friend or relative to help or perhaps they could recommend a good and reliable IT technician to help you.*

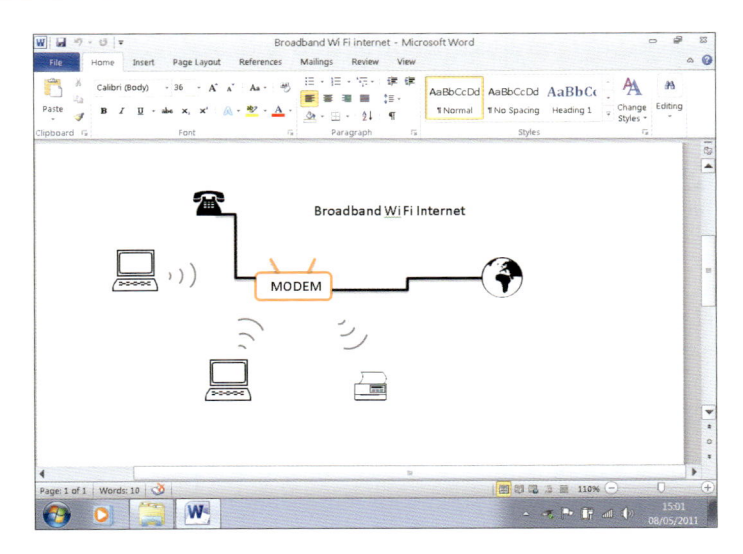

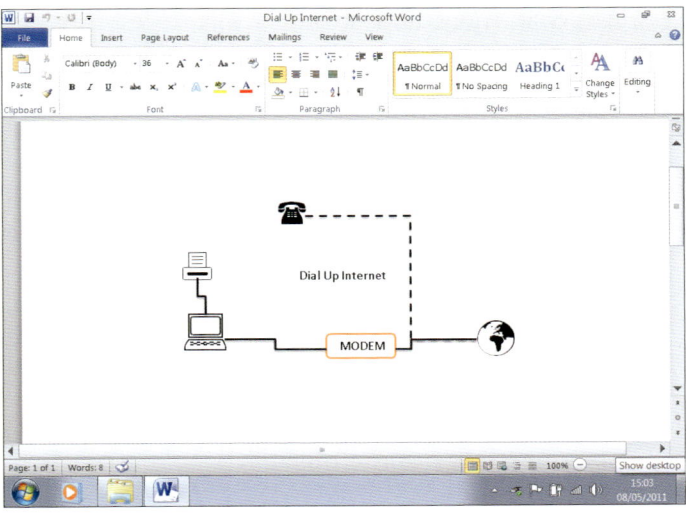

CHAPTER 6 GETTING CONNECTED

GET STARTED ON THE INTERNET

So you have a computer, a telephone (or cable) connection, a modem or router and an Internet Service Provider (ISP). Now you need a web browser, an application that allows you to view web pages. Most ISPs provide a web browser but you have a choice as to which one you prefer to use.

The most common browsers are Internet Explorer (developed by Microsoft), Firefox (developed by Mozilla) and Chrome (developed by Google), but there are many others. All browsers have similar features to make it easier to move around, search and access websites (see Chapters 7 and 8 for more detail).

We assume here that whoever has set up your Internet connection has provided you with a web browser.

Connect to the Internet

1. If you have a dial-up connection to the Internet, start it.

Note: *Broadband connections are permanently switched on.*

2. Click **Start**.

The Start menu appears.

3. In the Search programs and files box, type **internet**.

4. Click **Internet Explorer**.

The Internet Explorer web browser appears with the default home page.

> *If you are not using Internet Explorer, the web browser will look different to the one shown here.*

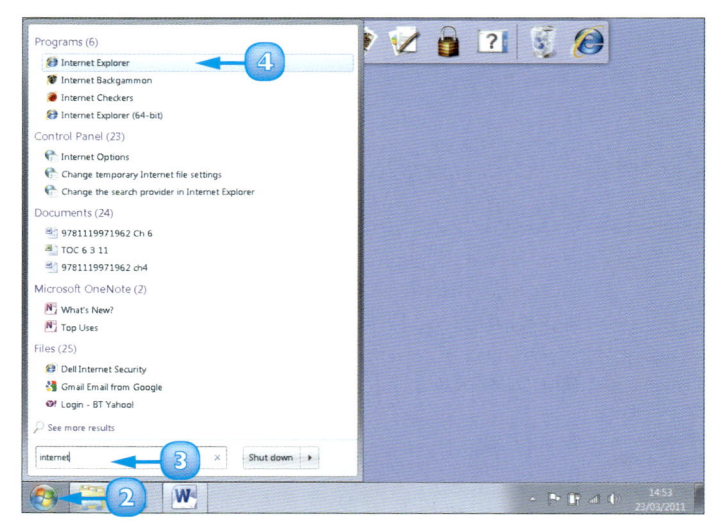

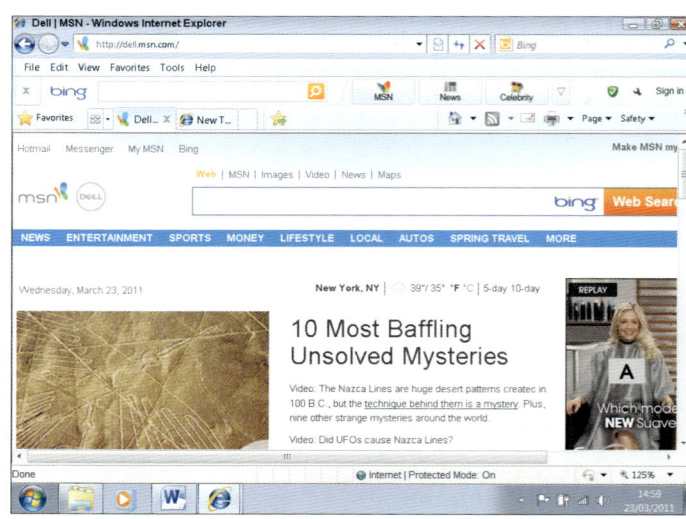

CHAPTER 6 GETTING CONNECTED

Use a Web Browser

1. Click the address bar at the top of screen.

   The web address (URL) is highlighted.

2. Type in **www.microsoft.com**.

3. Press **Enter**.

   The Microsoft website appears.

4. Click ⬅ to move back to the previously open website.

   - **A** You can click ➡ to move to the next website at which you looked.

   - **B** You can click 🔄 to update a page.

   - **C** You can click ✖ to stop loading a website.

5. Click ✖ to close the browser.

   - **D** You can click ➖ to send the browser to the Taskbar.

   - **E** You can click 🗗 to resize the window.

> ✔ The most widely used web browsers are Internet Explorer (Microsoft) and Firefox (Mozilla), but there are others. You can download your preferred browser from the Internet.

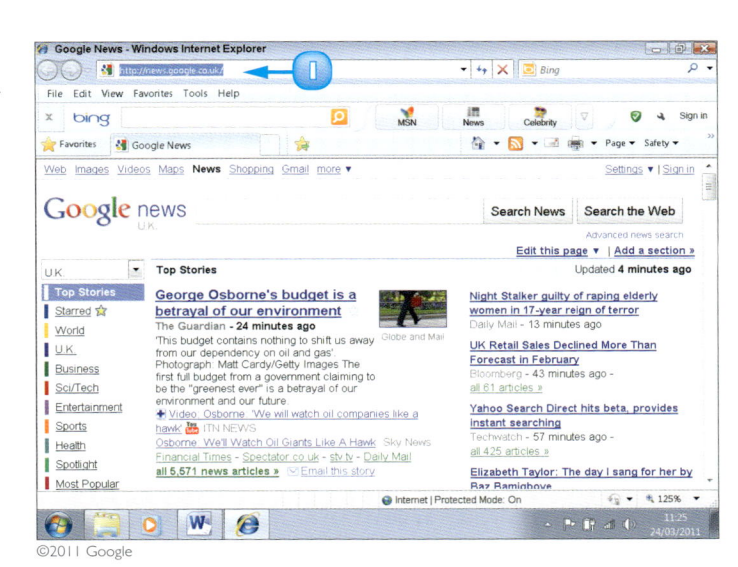

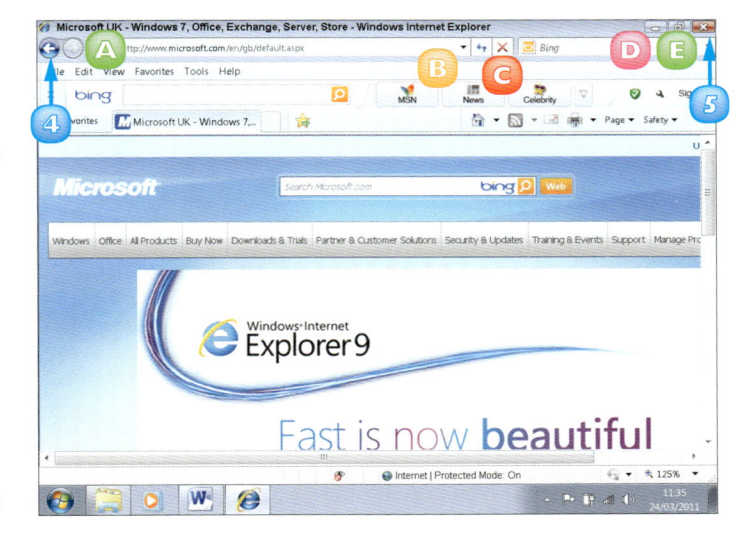

CHAPTER 6 GETTING CONNECTED

KEEP SAFE

To protect your computer from malicious software on the Internet, you need to keep the firewall, antivirus software, antispyware software and Windows Defender (Windows 7 operating system software) switched on and up to date. You control these items in the Action Center, which is new to Windows 7.

You probably have antivirus software installed on your computer. Windows Action Center monitors it and informs you of any changes that become necessary. If there is no antivirus software, you need to download and install some immediately to protect your computer from harm.

Use the Action Center

1. Click **Start**. Click **Control Panel**.

2. Click **Review your computer's status**.

   The Action Center appears.

3. Click **Security**.

4. Scroll through the list to check that Network Firewall, Windows Update, Virus Protection, and Spyware and unwanted software protection are all switched on and OK.

5. Click any message buttons and deal with any problems.

6. Click on **How do I know what security settings are right for my computer?** for a checklist of how Windows 7 can help keep your computer safe and secure.

Security is vitally important if you intend using the Internet in a public place, such as a coffee shop.

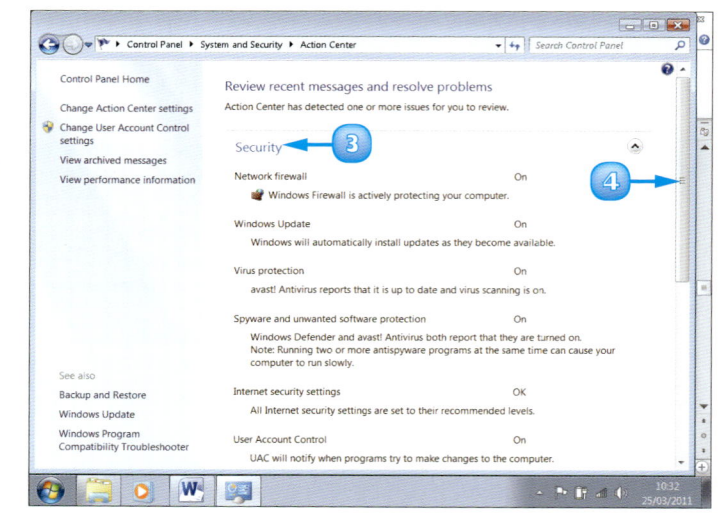

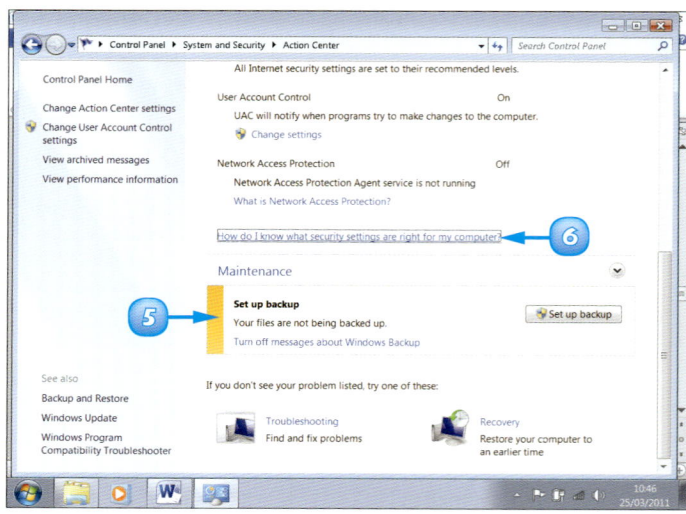

CHAPTER 6 GETTING CONNECTED

Antivirus Software

1. Click **Internet Explorer**.

   The default home page opens.

2. Type **www.avast.com** in the address bar.

3. Press **Enter**.

   The Avast! home page appears.

4. Click **Go to downloads**.

   The download page appears.

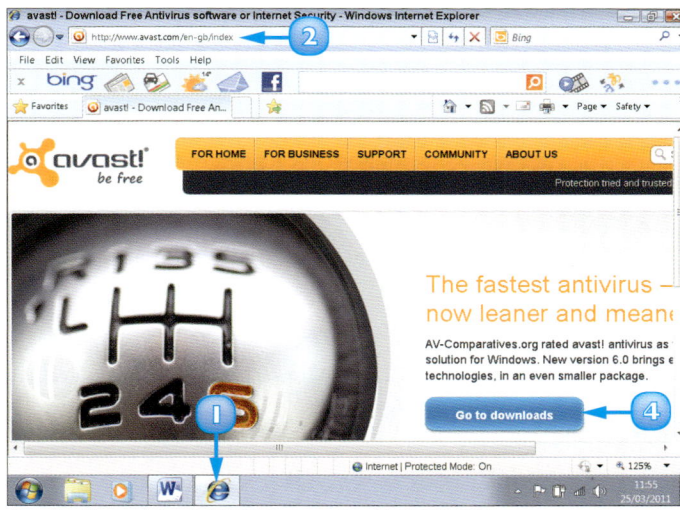

5. Scroll down the page and click **Download** in the Free Antivirus column.

6. Close any additional information windows that appear.

7. Click the **Download Now** link and follow the on-screen instructions to download and register the product.

Reproduced by permission of AVAST Software a.s. Copyright © 1988–2011

Reproduced by permission of AVAST Software a.s. Copyright © 1988–2011

✓ *There are many free versions of antivirus software available on the Internet. Ask around before deciding which one to install.*

✓ *Ask a friend or relative if you are unsure about how to do this as it is important that you protect your computer.*

CHAPTER 6 GETTING CONNECTED

WINDOWS LIVE ESSENTIALS

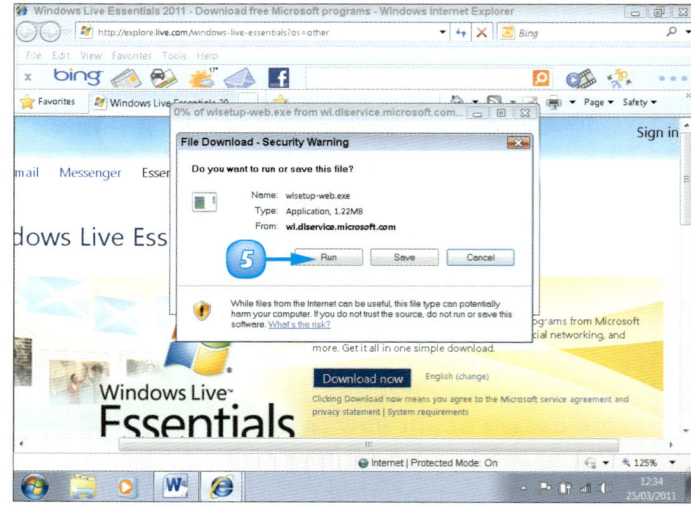

Windows Live Essentials does not come pre-installed on your computer. Now that you have connected to the Internet, you can download several useful free programs from Microsoft for email, photos, videos, social networking and much more.

Get Started

1. Click **Start**.

   The Start menu appears.

2. In the Search programs and files box, type **Get Windows Live**.

3. Click **Get Windows Live Essentials**.

   The Windows Live Essentials home page appears.

4. Click **Download now**.

5. Click **Run**.

   A dialog appears asking, "Do you want to allow the following program to make changes to this computer?"

6. Click **Yes**.

The Windows Live Essentials dialog appears.

7 Click **Install all of Windows Live Essentials**.

The software may take a few minutes to download.

8 Click **Restart Now**.

Your computer closes down and restarts.

Note: *You can choose to restart later.*

Find Out More

1 Open Internet Explorer.

2 In the address bar, type **explore.live.com/home**.

The Windows Live Essentials website opens.

3 Click **Home**.

The Windows Live Home page appears.

You can now discover the many features that are available in Windows Live Essentials, such as Hotmail and Messenger.

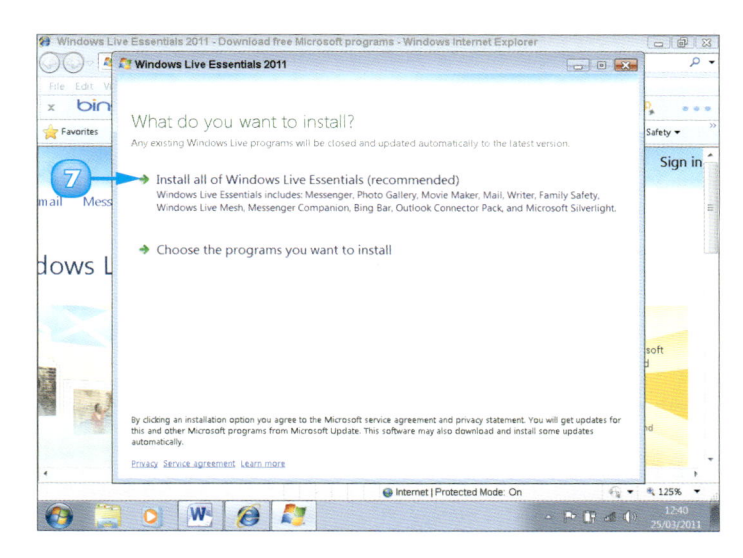

CHAPTER 6 GETTING CONNECTED

SOCIAL NETWORKING

A social networking website focuses on relationships among people who share common interests or activities. For example, mums (www.mumsnet.com) and seniors (www.vu3a.org) have websites where the interests and concerns of the social group can be shared. Facebook, Twitter and YouTube provide similar services allowing people to stay in touch with each other electronically. All social networking sites require you to register, give a few details about yourself and choose a password for security reasons. Microsoft Messenger is part of Windows Live Essentials.

1. Click Start.

2. In the Search programs and files box, type **Messenger**.

3. Click **Windows Live Messenger**.

   The Sign in screen appears.

4. Click **Sign Up**.

   The Create Windows Live ID screen appears.

5. Click **Or get a Windows Live email address**.

6. Think of an email name and type it into the field.

7. Click **Check availability**.

8. Type in a password.

   A. *Windows Live helps you to choose a strong and secure password.*

Note: *You must type your password a second time to ensure that you can enter it correctly.*

9. Click **Or choose a security question for password reset**.

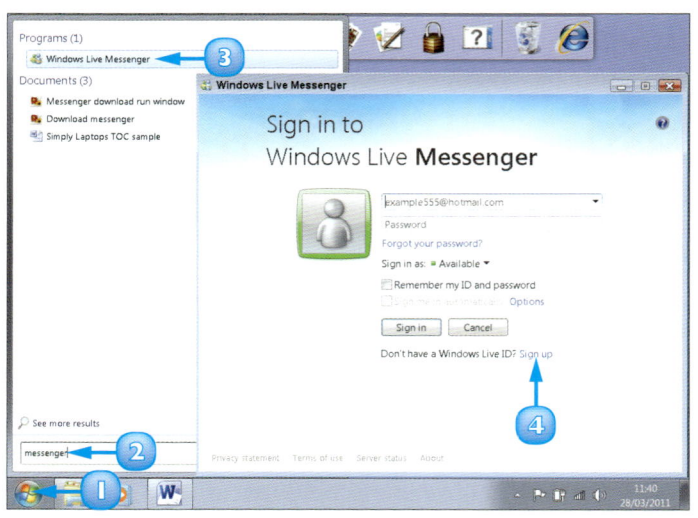

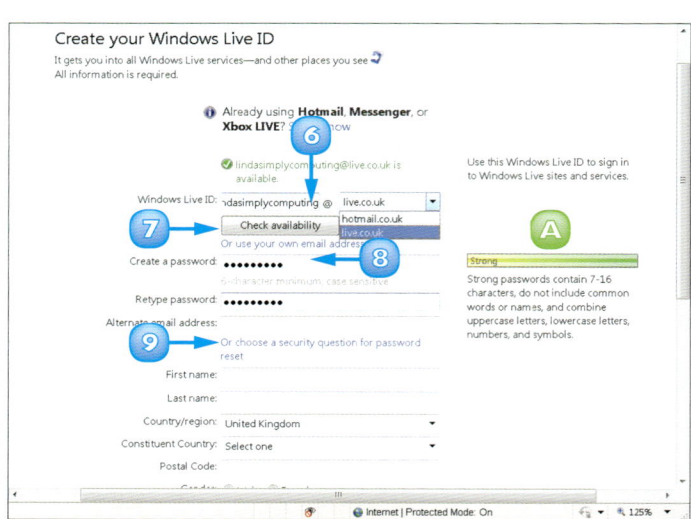

CHAPTER 6 GETTING CONNECTED

10 Select a question.

11 Type the answer to the question.

✓ *If you forget your password, Windows Live will ask this question to verify your identity.*

12 Complete the form.

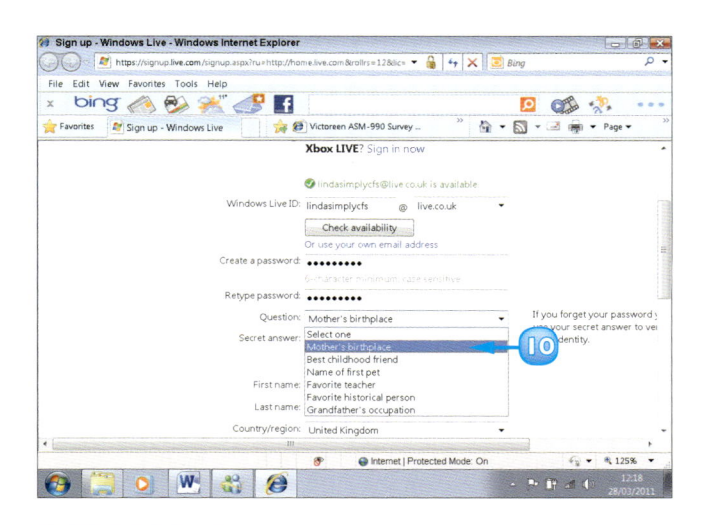

13 Type the security characters you see into the field.

14 Click **I accept**.

The Windows Live home screen appears.

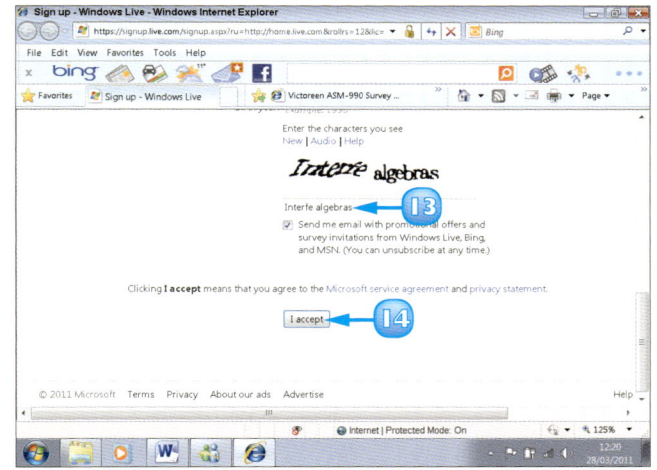

15 Click **Messenger**.

16 Click **Add friends**.

17 Click **Limited** on **Set up your privacy settings** and then **Save**.

The Add people window is displayed.

18 Type an email address into the field and click **Next**.

The invitation screen appears.

19 Click **Invite**.

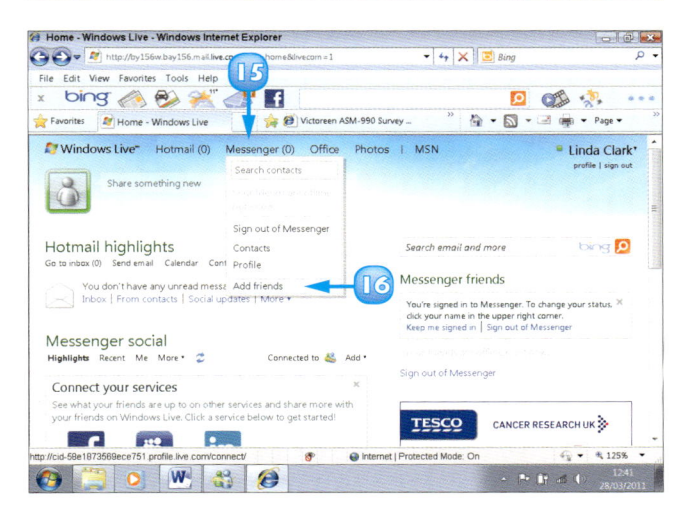

CHAPTER 6 GETTING CONNECTED

CONTENTS

- **86** Explore Internet Explorer
- **88** Change Your Home Page
- **90** Search the Internet
- **92** Save Your Favourite Pages
- **94** Print a Web Page
- **96** Save Text and Pictures

DISCOVERING THE INTERNET

In this chapter, we continue to use the Internet and show how to make changes to the setup to allow easier access to the websites that you want to return to again and again. We cover how to research and save text and pictures that you wish to keep and how to print web pages.

EXPLORE INTERNET EXPLORER

Following on from the brief introduction in Chapter 6, we now look at what else is in the web browser window. We use Internet Explorer 9; if you are using another web browser, the window may well be laid out differently. All of the items mentioned here are common to web browsers so you should be able to find them on the screen somewhere. See Chapter 6 for information about opening Internet Explorer.

A Navigation tools
Use ◄ and ► to move between pages and websites you have visited.

B Address bar
Type a website address.

C Compatibility mode button
Use compatibility mode.

D Refresh button
Reload the current page.

E Stop button
Stop loading the current page.

F Title Bar
Shows open websites.

G Toolbar
These buttons are found in all web browsers (but may be in different places with different icons): Home, Favorites, Tools.

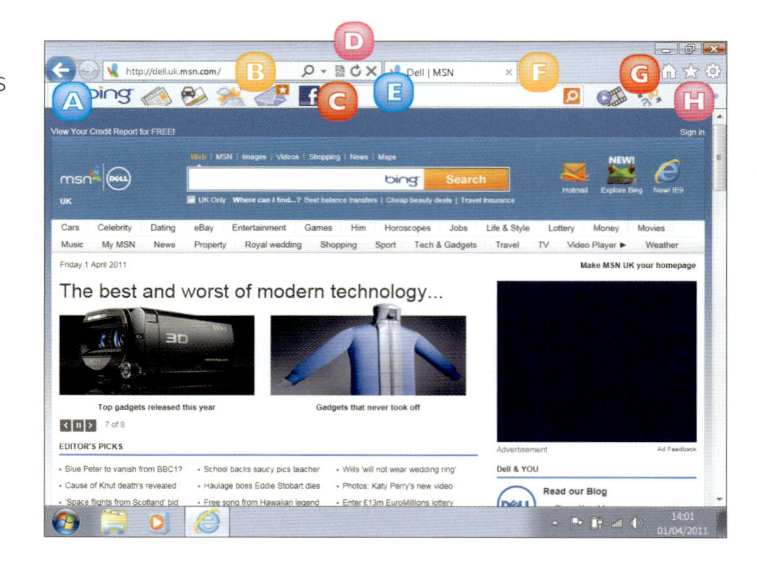

H History
See a list of the websites you have visited.

CHAPTER 7 DISCOVERING THE INTERNET

I **Search Box**
Type a word or phrase here for a list of potential answers.

J **Bing Tools**
Video, Translator, Bing bar settings.

K **Quick Link Tabs**
These tabs are specific to the web page.

L **Main Window**
Information is displayed with links to other pages and sites.

M **Scroll Bar**
Click on this bar and slide it up and down to move up and down the web page.

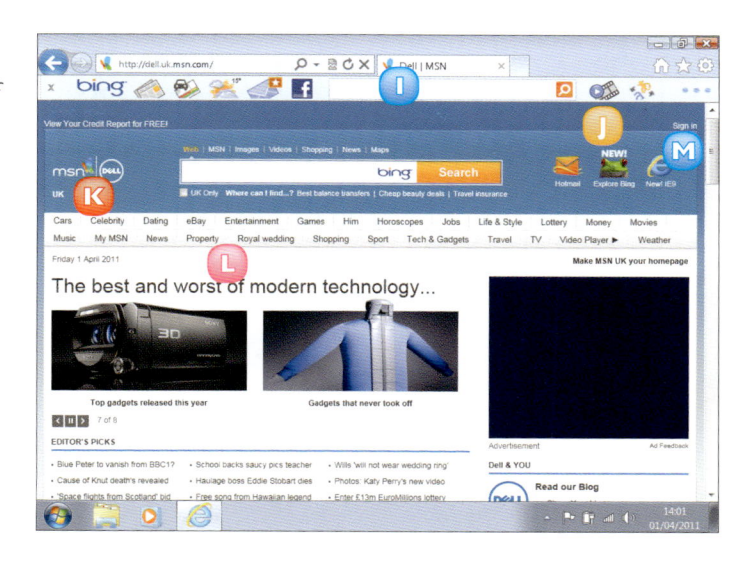

STOP *If you are using a telephone line to receive broadband Internet, the distance from the telephone exchange and the quality of the lines will affect the operating speed.*

CHAPTER 7 DISCOVERING THE INTERNET

CHANGE YOUR HOME PAGE

The home page is displayed when you open your web browser. You can make any website your home page. This means that you can set up your web browser to go to the website of your choice. Perhaps you are interested in keeping up to date with the latest news, want to know what the weather is like at your next holiday destination, want to know what programmes are on TV or want to keep an eye out for Internet bargains.

Choose a Website

1. Click **Start**.

2. Click **Internet Explorer**.

   The browser opens and displays the home page.

3. Click in the address bar.

4. Type in an address and then press `Enter`.

   A You can see all sorts of information and the latest news at **bbc.co.uk** and **sky.com**.

   B You can buy and sell on the Internet at **ebay.co.uk**.

Note: To go to another website, repeat Steps 3 and 4.

Copyright © 1995–2011 eBay Inc. All Rights Reserved

CHAPTER 7 DISCOVERING THE INTERNET

Set Up a New Home Page

1. Display your chosen website in Internet Explorer.

2. Click **Tools** ( ).

   The drop-down menu appears.

3. Click **Internet Options**.

   The Internet Options dialog appears.

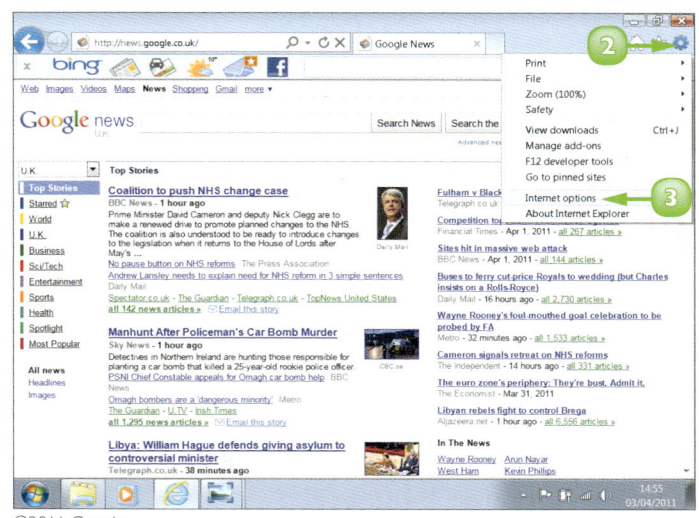

4. Click **Use Current**.

5. Click **Apply** and then **OK**.

6. Click to close Internet Explorer.

7. Click **Start**.

8. Click **Internet Explorer**.

   The browser opens and displays your new home page.

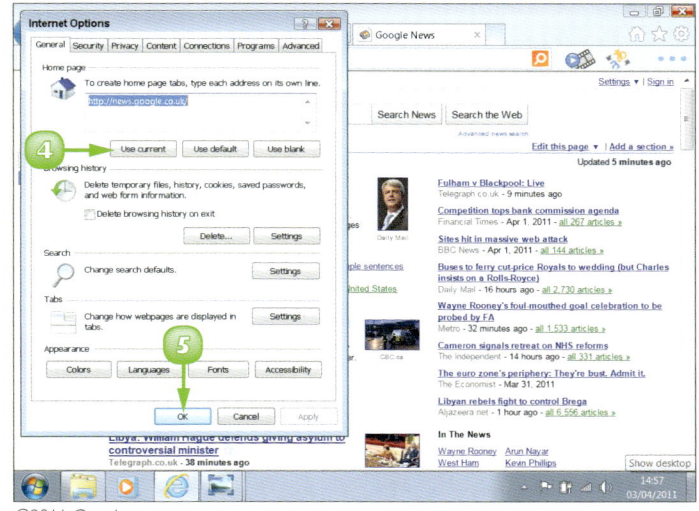

©2011 Google

©2011 Google

You can change your home page as often as you like by following the steps in this section.

CHAPTER 7 DISCOVERING THE INTERNET

SEARCH THE INTERNET

Google is a very good search engine but there are others, for example, Bing and Ask. One advantage of using Google News as your home page is that it also provides the starting point for undertaking searches on the Internet. If you need train times, want to find out where to get the best deals on car insurance or want to find out what's on in Edinburgh, this section explains how to go about it.

1. Click **Start**.

2. Click **Internet Explorer**.

   A. The **Bing** search box is provided by the browser.

   B. The **Google** search box is on the home page.

Note: You can also type **google.co.uk** in the address bar to go to the Google search page.

3. Type some key words into the Google search box.

4. Click **Search the Web**.

   The search list appears.

   C. There could be millions of results (known as "hits").

5. Scroll down the list.

6. Hover over a link (cursor changes to) and then click the link.

   The web page opens.

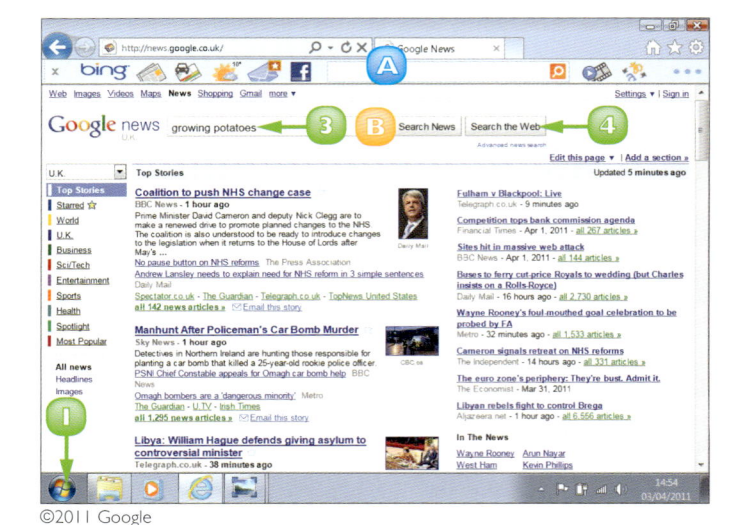

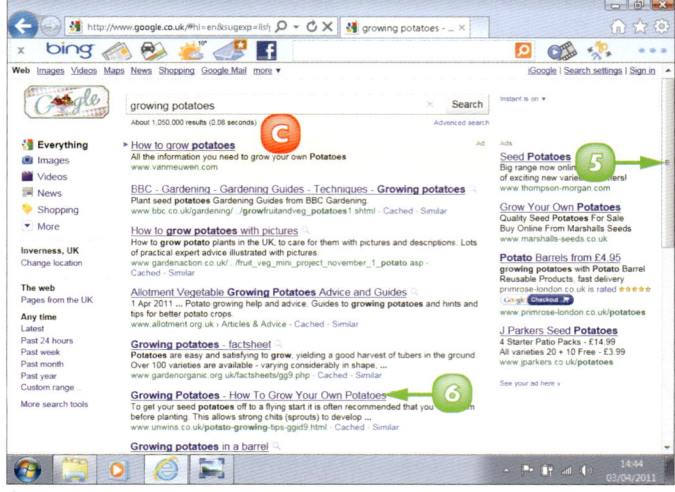

©2011 Google

©2011 Google

CHAPTER 7 DISCOVERING THE INTERNET

Narrow Down a Search

1. Load **google.co.uk** in your web browser.

2. Type some key words into the search box.

   The "I'm Feeling Lucky" menu shows some options to choose from.

3. Click the one which is closest to what you are looking for.

4. Click **Search**.

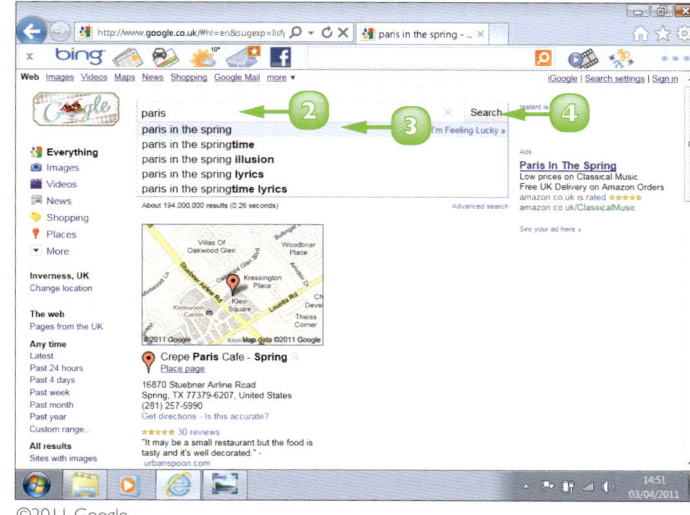

5. If you do not see what you are looking for, type an additional word in the search box.

   A general search will give you millions of web pages. A more specific search will narrow the list down.

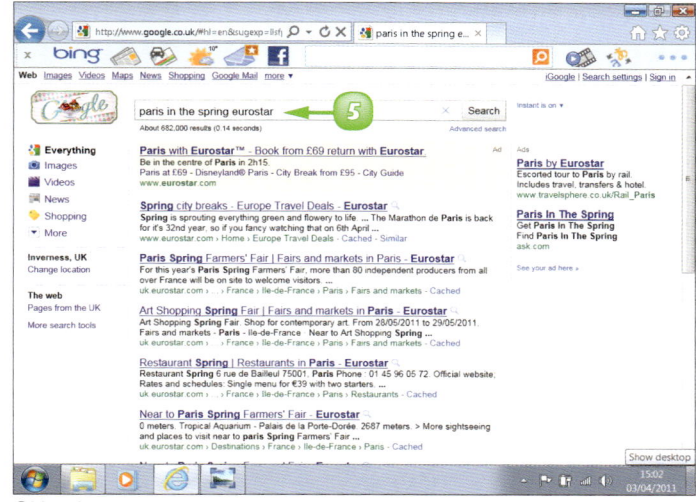

©2011 Google

©2011 Google

> ✓ *The most relevant results appear on the first page. Move to the next page of the search by scrolling to the bottom of the page and clicking the* **Next** *button.*

> ✓ *Go back to your home page at any time by clicking the Home icon ( ).*

CHAPTER 7 DISCOVERING THE INTERNET

SAVE YOUR FAVOURITE PAGES

The equivalent of filing paperwork, keeping a list of websites that you visit frequently saves you time and effort. You do not have to search for the websites all over again. Whether you are planning a holiday, like to buy books online or are helping with a child's school project, the Favorites list saves you the frustration of having to search for that illusive piece of information that you know you saw somewhere.

Add Favourites to a List

1. Open Internet Explorer.

2. Type **northkessockhistory.com** into the address bar.

    The home page appears.

3. Click **View favorites, feeds & history** (☆).

    The Favorites Center appears.

4. Click to pin the Favorites Center to the left of the screen.

5. Click the **Add to favorites** ▾.

6. Click **Add to favorites**.

    The Add a Favorite dialog opens.

Note: You can also click `Ctrl` + `D` to add a favourite to the list without opening this menu.

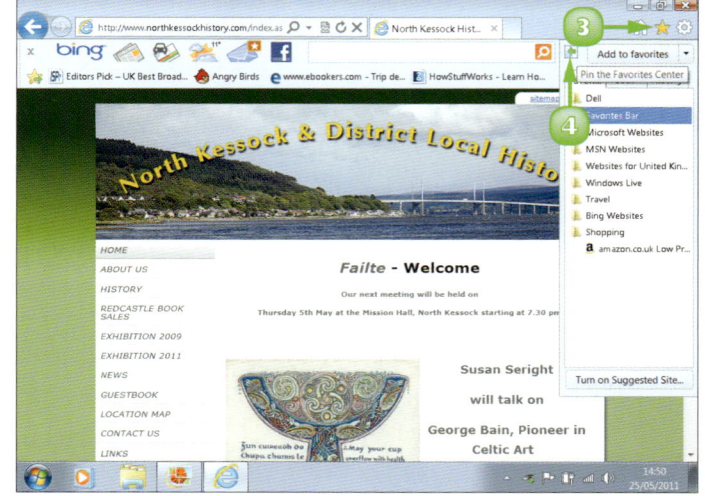

Reproduced by permission of North Kessock & District Local History Society

Reproduced by permission of North Kessock & District Local History Society

CHAPTER 7 DISCOVERING THE INTERNET

7 Click **New folder**.

The Create a Folder window opens.

8 Type **History**.

9 Click **Create**.

Ⓐ *The folder is created in the Favorites list.*

10 Click **Add**.

Ⓑ *The website address is put into the folder.*

Add a Favourite to the Favorites Bar

1 Type **easyjet.com** into the address bar.

The Easyjet home page appears.

2 Click **Add to Favorites bar** ( ).

Ⓐ *The website address is stored on the Favorites bar.*

3 Click to go back to your home page.

4 Click **History** on the Favorites menu.

5 Click **North Kessock History** to reopen that website.

6 Click **Easyjet** on the Favorites menu bar to reopen that website.

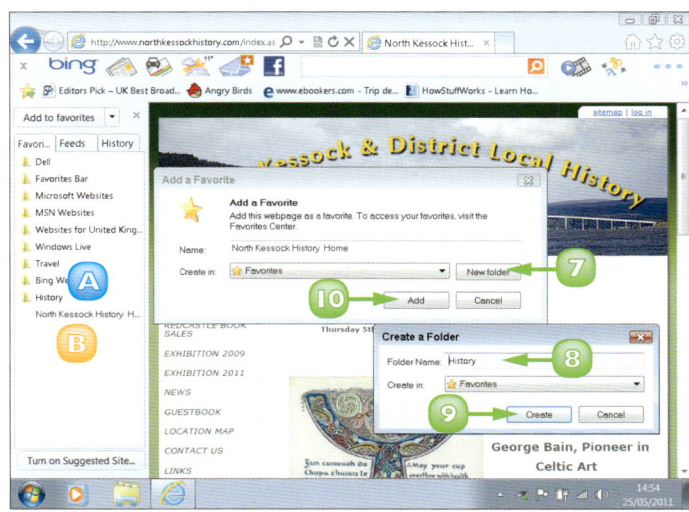

✓ *To delete a website from Favorites, hover over it (changes to) and press Del.*

Reproduced by permission of North Kessock & District Local History Society

Reproduced by permission of easyJet airline company Ltd

✓ *To maximise space on the screen close the Favorites Center by clicking ✗ at the top of the Favorites menu.*

CHAPTER 7 DISCOVERING THE INTERNET

PRINT A WEB PAGE

It is very easy to collect information from the Internet before you go out to buy a new camera or printer, to find out a little bit more about your holiday destination or to investigate a topic that is currently in the news. Sometimes it is useful to print that information and take it with you.

Print a Map

1. Open Internet Explorer.
2. Type **streetmap.com** into the address bar and press Enter.

   The streetmap home page appears.

3. Type **Edinburgh** into the search box.
4. Click **Place**.
5. Click **Go**.

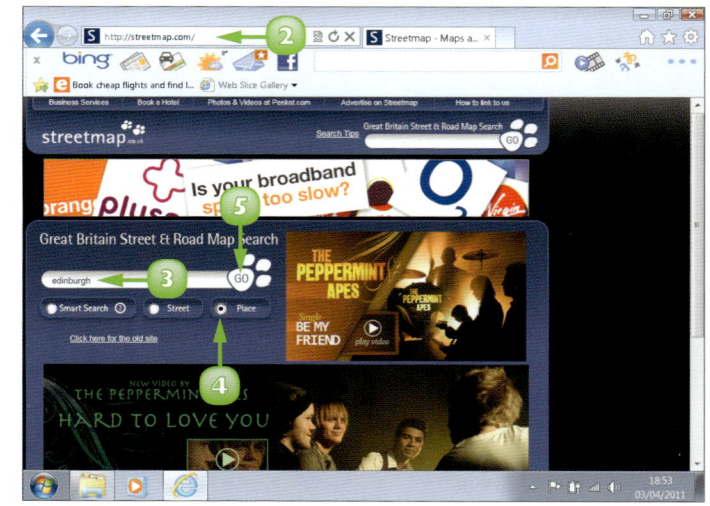

   A list of places is displayed.

6. Hover over Edinburgh Station (☝ changes to ☝) and click.

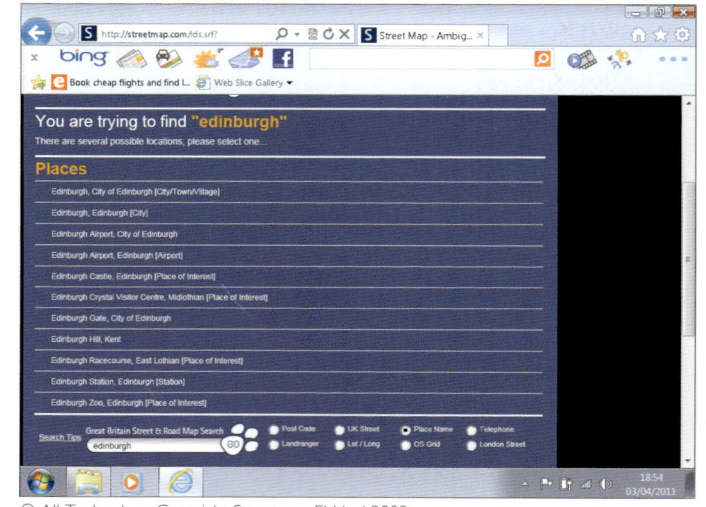

© All Technology Copyright Streetmap EU Ltd 2009

© All Technology Copyright Streetmap EU Ltd 2009

CHAPTER 7 DISCOVERING THE INTERNET

A map of Edinburgh showing the railway station appears.

7 Click **Print**.

A printer-friendly page appears.

8 Click **Tools** (⚙).

The Tools menu appears.

9 Click **Print**.

The Print menu appears.

10 Click **Print Preview** to check that the page looks OK.

11 Click **Print**.

© All Technology Copyright Streetmap EU Ltd 2009

© All Technology Copyright Streetmap EU Ltd 2009

Print Useful Information

1 Type **howstuffworks.com** into the address bar.

2 Type **how do earthquakes work**.

3 Click **Search**.

4 Scroll down and click **How Earthquakes Work**.

5 Hover over the topic you are interested in (▸ changes to ✋) and click.

> *In the Print dialog, you can choose whether to print the whole web page or what will fit onto one printed page.*

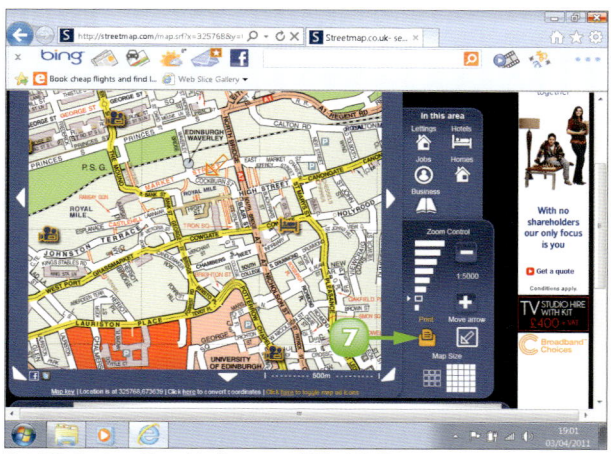

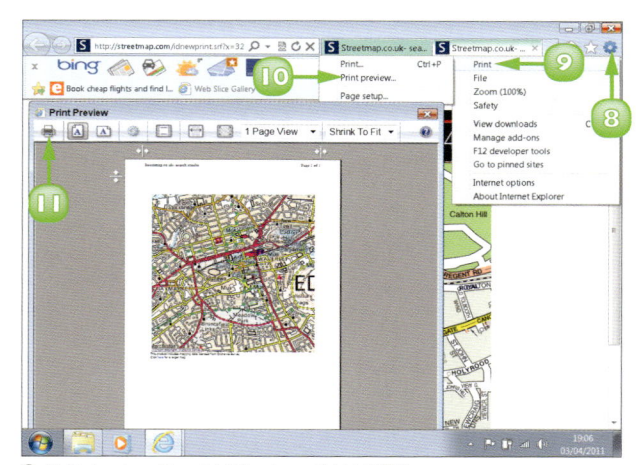

Courtesy of HowStuffWorks.com

CHAPTER 7 DISCOVERING THE INTERNET

SAVE TEXT AND PICTURES

It is possible to save text and pictures to make up a document that contains just the information that you require leaving out the bits that are irrelevant. You can also save pictures to use them in the same way as your own pictures (see Chapter 11).

Save Text to a Document

1. Open Word 2010 and click Minimize (🗕).

   Word appears as an icon on the Taskbar.

2. Open Internet Explorer.

3. Type **kilda.org.uk** into the address bar.

   The St Kilda home page appears.

4. Hover over the start of the text (⇩ changes to I).

5. Hold the left mouse button down and drag the cursor to the bottom of the text.

6. Release the mouse button.

7. Right-click the highlighted text.

8. Click **Copy**.

9. Click the Word icon on the Taskbar to bring Word to the foreground.

10. Click **Paste** (📋).

    The text appears in the document.

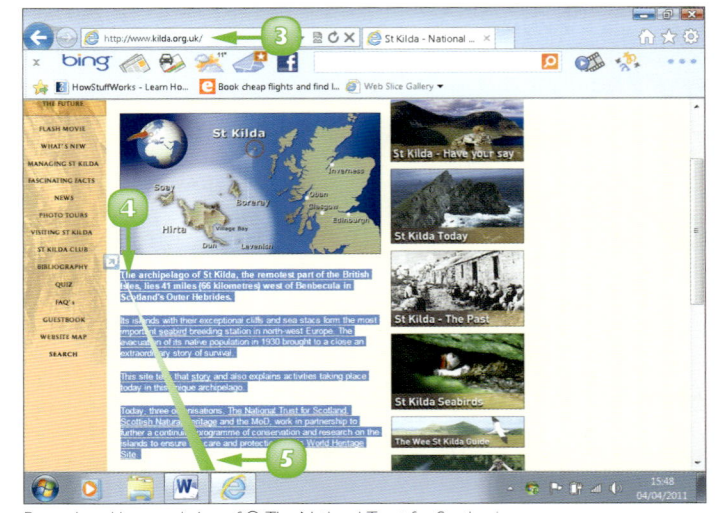

Reproduced by permission of © The National Trust for Scotland

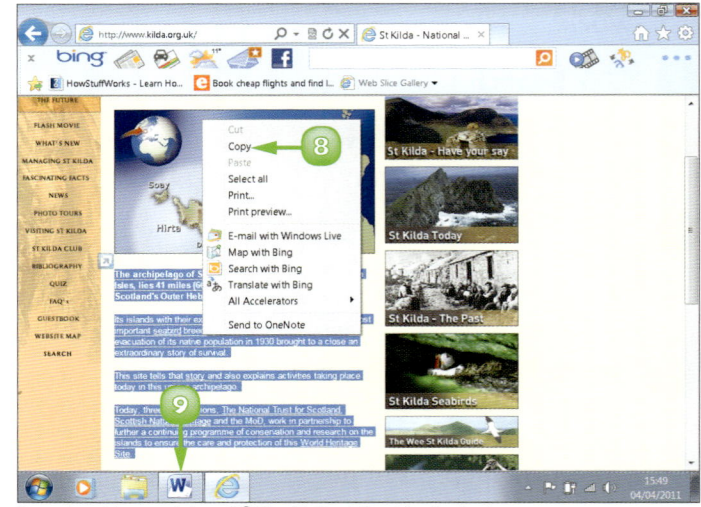

Reproduced by permission of © The National Trust for Scotland

CHAPTER 7 DISCOVERING THE INTERNET

Save a Picture to a Document

1. Click the Internet Explorer icon on the Taskbar.
2. Right-click the picture.
3. Click **Copy**.
4. Click the Word icon on the Taskbar to bring Word to the foreground.
5. Click **Paste** ( ).

   The picture appears in the document.
6. Save the document.

Save a Picture as a JPEG File

1. Click the Internet Explorer icon on the Taskbar.
2. Right-click the picture.
3. Click **Save Picture As**.

   The Pictures library appears.
4. Double-click the **Sample Pictures** folder.
5. Click **Save**.

   The picture is saved on your computer.

> *Use the Picture Tools menu to make changes to the picture. See the "Add a Picture" section in Chapter 4.*

> *You can go back to the website and add as much text and as many pictures as you wish to your document.*

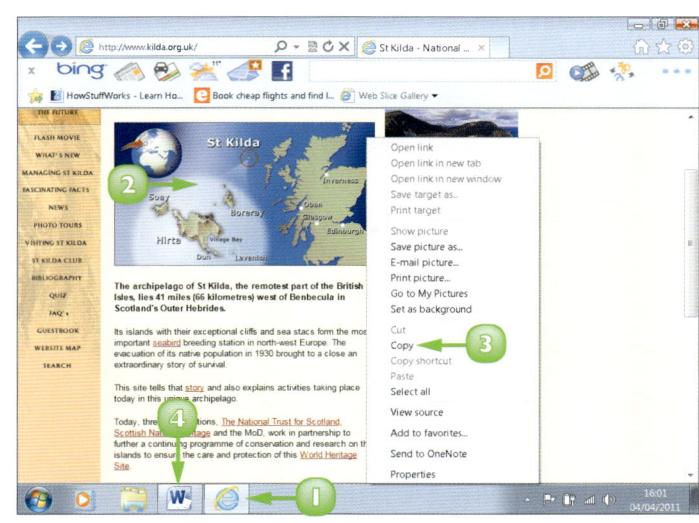

Reproduced by permission of © The National Trust for Scotland

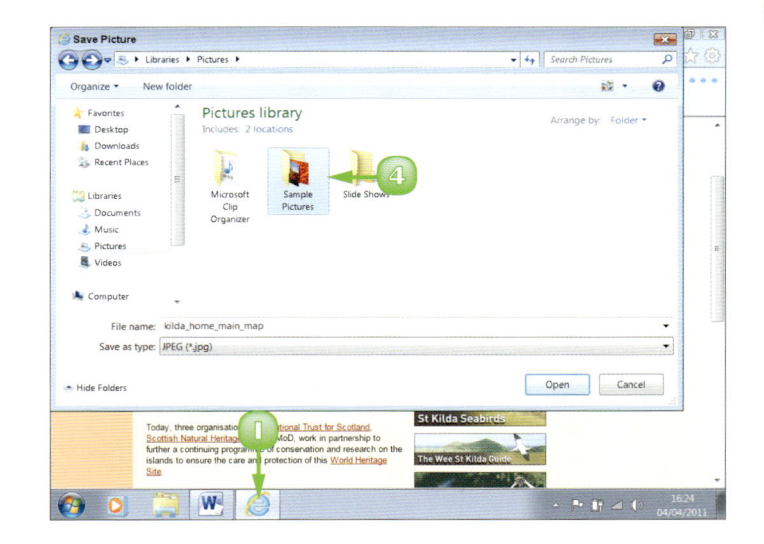

CONTENTS

100	Shop Online
104	Explore Travel Sites
106	Book Tickets and Holidays
108	Buy and Sell on eBay
110	Use Online Banking
113	Add Skype to Your Computer
114	Use Skype

8

USING THE INTERNET

From the comfort of your armchair, it is now possible to do your shopping, organise travel, book holidays and theatre tickets and keep an eye on your finances. In this chapter, we also look at how to buy and sell on the Internet and download a useful free program to the computer.

SHOP ONLINE

Shopping online couldn't be easier. If you cannot get to the shops you would like to use, you will find the Internet can satisfy all your needs. Buying online is convenient in terms of time, there is a vast range of products to choose from and comparing prices to get the best value for money couldn't be simpler.

Search for a Book

1. Open Internet Explorer.
2. Type **wiley.com** into the address bar.

   The Wiley home page opens.
3. Type **simply** into the search bar near the top of the screen.
4. Click **Search**.

   Courtesy of www.wiley.com

   A list of results appears.
5. Click **Simply Office 2010**.

   Courtesy of www.wiley.com

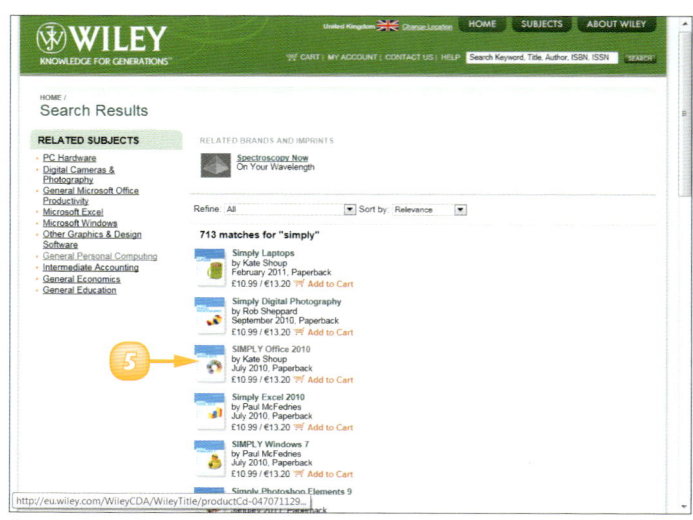

The book's description is shown.

6. Scroll down to read a description of the book.

7. Click the **Table of Contents** tab to see the book's contents.

8. Click **Read Excerpt 1** to read some of the book.

9. Click **Add to Cart** to tell the website that you'd like to buy the book.

Courtesy of www.wiley.com

Your shopping cart is displayed, showing the book you selected.

10. Click **quantity**, enter a number and click **Update** to buy more copies.

   Ⓐ *You can click **Remove** to take items out of the shopping cart.*

11. Click **Continue Shopping** to find more books.

   Ⓑ *You can click **Checkout Now** to buy the items in the shopping cart.*

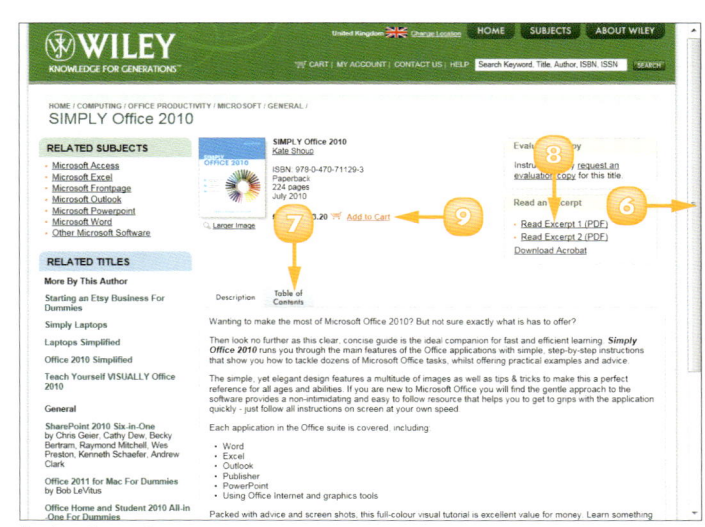

Courtesy of www.wiley.com

continued ➜

SHOP ONLINE (continued)

There are some things that you should bear in mind when shopping online: you cannot physically examine products before buying; goods may get damaged during transit or may not arrive; and, most importantly, you must be aware of Internet security. You can compare prices and features of products and read customer reviews without revealing any personal information but you need to register with the shopping site and provide credit or debit card details to pay for goods.

Buy a Book

When you click Checkout Now, the Billing Information screen appears.

1. Click the **Title** and select your title.
2. Click **Initials** and enter your initials.
3. Click **Last name** and enter your name.
4. Enter your email address, twice.
5. Enter your postal address.
6. Click **Ship my order to this address**.
7. Click **Continue Secure Checkout**.

The Setup an Account window opens.

A. *The padlock shows that the website is secure.*

8. Type in a password.
9. Repeat your password.
10. Click **Create an Account and Continue**.

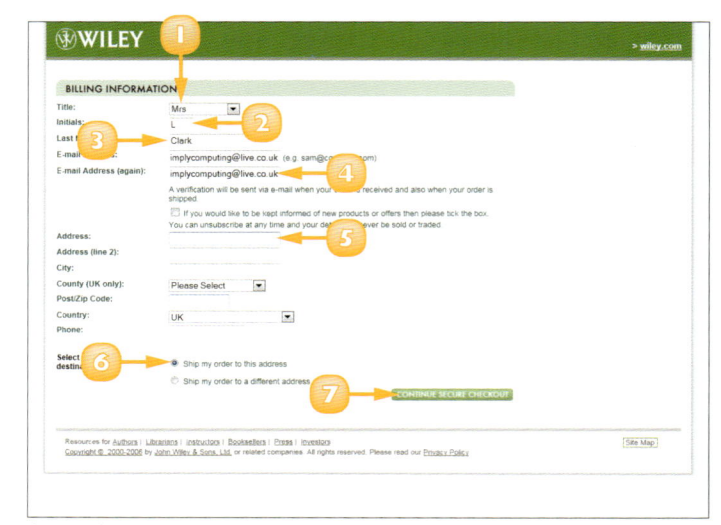

Courtesy of www.wiley.com

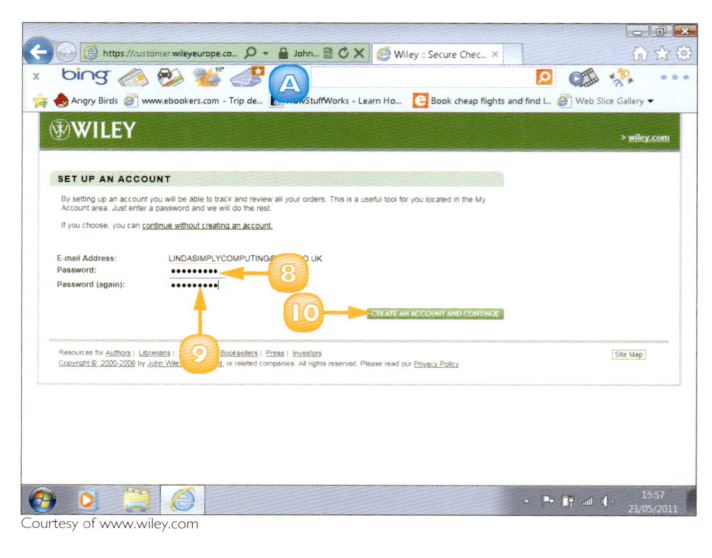

Courtesy of www.wiley.com

CHAPTER 8 USING THE INTERNET

11 Check that your order is correct.

    A *If you have a promotion code, you can enter it and click **Apply Code**.*

    B *If you want to change the delivery method, select it from the drop-down list and click **Update**.*

12 Click **Continue Secure Checkout.**

The Payment Information screen appears.

Courtesy of www.wiley.com

13 Click **Card Type** and select your card.

14 Enter your **Card Number**.

15 Click the month and year to select the **Expiration Date** of your card.

16 Enter the **Security Digits** from the back of your card.

    C *If you are using a Maestro card, enter the issue number and Start Date.*

17 Click **Submit Your Order**.

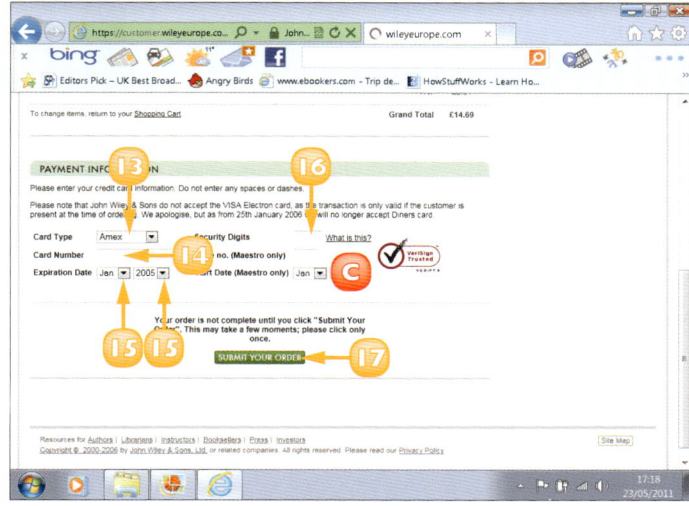

Courtesy of www.wiley.com

The order is not processed until you click Submit Your Order.

A confirmation email is sent to the email address you gave when registering.

CHAPTER 8 USING THE INTERNET

103

EXPLORE TRAVEL SITES

Going to visit a friend, organising a weekend break or planning the holiday of a lifetime? Travel websites can help you work out the best itinerary for you. Train, bus and plane sites allow you to look up timetables and check the cost without committing to buying tickets. This means that you can compare the options and decide which suits you best.

A couple of example sites are shown here but the search facility (see Chapter 7) will throw up many alternatives. Travel websites usually offer hotel and car hire deals.

UK Train Travel

1. Open Internet Explorer.
2. Type **thetrainline.com** into the address bar.
3. Type in the details of your trip.
4. Click **Get times & tickets**.

   The timetable is displayed.
5. Click **Show prices**.
6. Click on your choice of outward train.
7. Click on your choice of return train.

   A. The total cost is shown.

   B. You can click **Next** if you want to buy the tickets.

Note: You can print the page.

Reproduced by permission of thetrainline.com

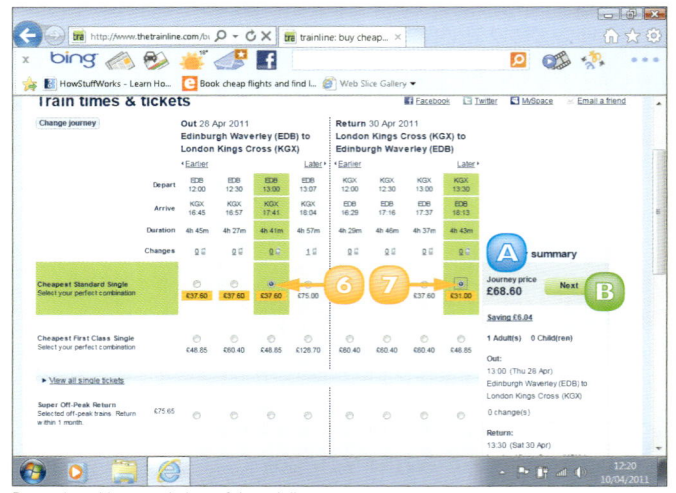

Reproduced by permission of thetrainline.com

thetrainline.com is often the cheapest way to buy tickets.

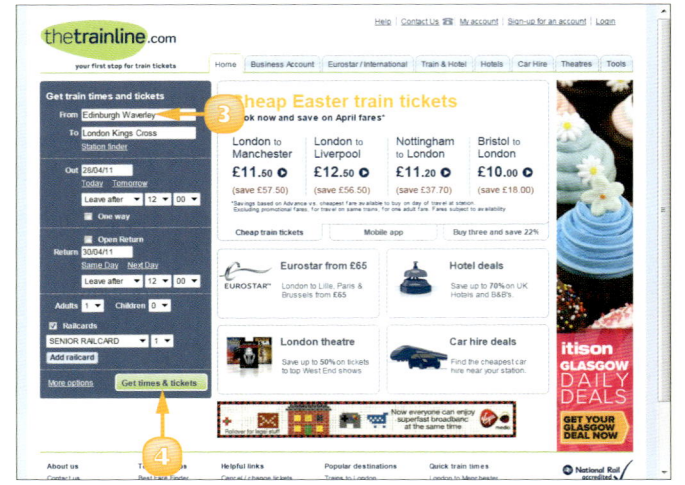

CHAPTER 8 USING THE INTERNET

Air Travel

1. Type **expedia.co.uk** into the Internet Explorer address bar.

    The Expedia home page opens.

2. Click **Flight only**.

3. Complete the airport and date details.

    Note: *Clicking in a date box produces a calendar that allows you to choose the date.*

4. Click **Search**.

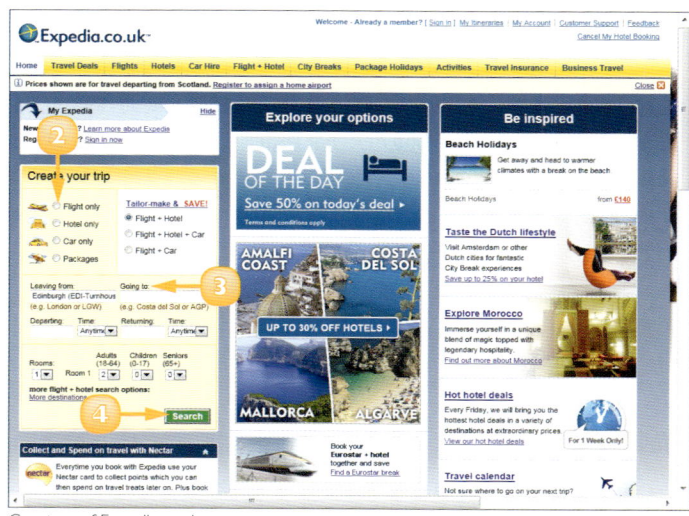

    A list of available flights is displayed in order of price.

    Ⓐ *You can change the order to display by duration, departure time or arrival time.*

    Note: *You can print the page.*

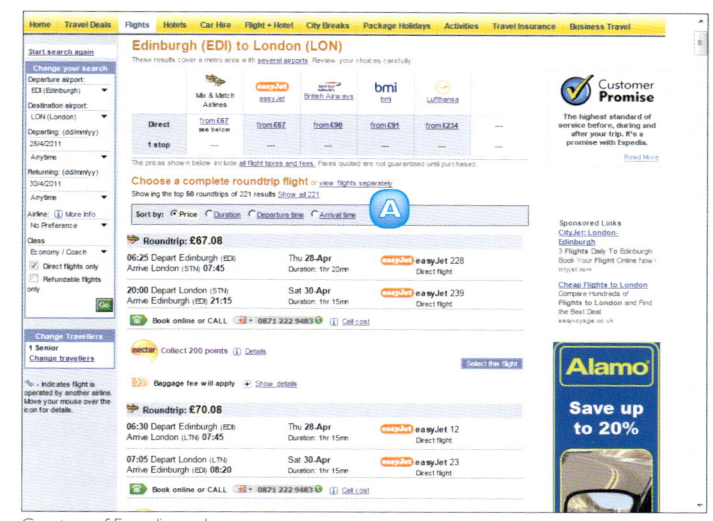

Courtesy of Expedia.co.uk

Courtesy of Expedia.co.uk

🛑 ***Read through the details carefully, especially departure and arrival times and airports, before buying tickets.***

CHAPTER 8 USING THE INTERNET

BOOK TICKETS AND HOLIDAYS

To book tickets and holidays online, you need to sign up with a website and own a credit or debit card to make the payment. (See the "Shop Online" section.) Most websites give you the option of phoning to place an order but you still need to have your credit or debit card handy. We use two specific websites as examples but you will find that other websites have similar features.

For a small fee you can usually get cinema and theatre tickets sent out in advance of the performance. Alternatively, you can pick them up at the box office but you must present the card you used for the purchase.

Book Tickets

1. Type **www.domeonline.co.uk** into Internet Explorer.
2. Click **Create an Account**.
3. Complete the registration form and click **Save**.
4. Click the time of your chosen screening.

Reproduced by permission of Worthing Dome Cinema

5. Choose the number of tickets.
6. Click **2. Add to Order**.

   The tickets and price are totalled (note the booking fee).
7. Click **Continue**.
8. Click the tick box to agree to the Terms and Conditions.
9. Complete the credit or debit card details.
10. Click **Confirm and Pay**.

Reproduced by permission of Worthing Dome Cinema

CHAPTER 8 USING THE INTERNET

Book Holidays

1. Type **www.vjv.com** into the Internet Explorer address bar.

   The Voyages Jules Verne home page opens.

2. Click **Click to Open**.

3. Click **Africa and the Indian Ocean**.

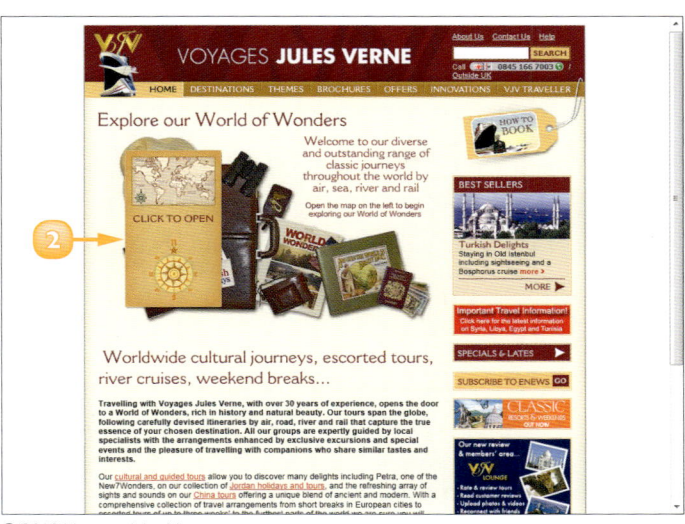

© 2010 Voyages Jules Verne

4. Click **South Africa**.

5. Click **A Taste of South Africa**.

   ✓ *You can use the search engine to decide where you would like to go.*

   A description appears.

6. Click the tabs to check on the Itinerary, Accommodation, Departures and Prices, and Reviews.

7. Click **Book Now** to view the hotels and departure dates.

© 2010 Voyages Jules Verne

🛑 *Do not complete the credit or debit card details unless you intend to take the holiday.*

🛑 *There may be a surcharge for credit card bookings.*

CHAPTER 8 USING THE INTERNET

BUY AND SELL ON EBAY

If you want to grab a bargain or sell some stuff that you no longer need, eBay is the website for you. You need to register with the site to carry out transactions. There is a lot of help available on how to buy and sell securely on eBay.

Register

1. Type **ebay.co.uk** into the Internet Explorer address bar.
2. Click **Register**.
3. Complete the registration form.
4. Click **Continue**.

   A confirmation email will be sent to you.

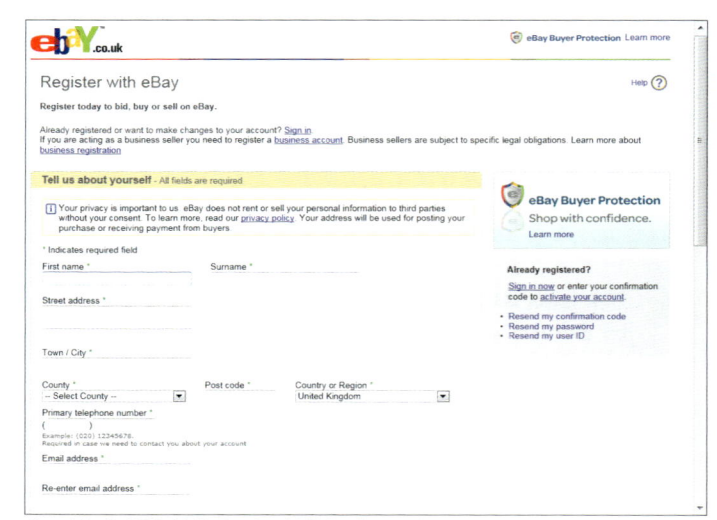

Copyright © 1995–2011 eBay Inc. All Rights Reserved

Buy an Item

1. Log in to eBay.
2. Hover over **Electronics**.
3. Click **Photography**.
4. Click **Fujifilm**.

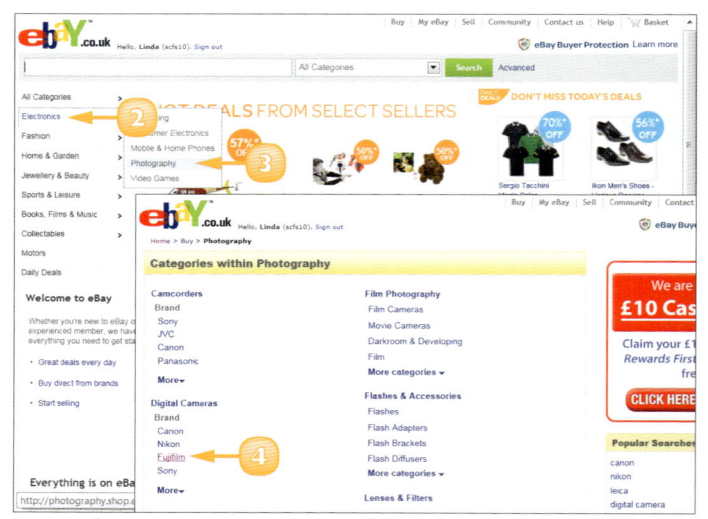

Copyright © 1995–2011 eBay Inc. All Rights Reserved

CHAPTER 8 USING THE INTERNET

The buying screen opens.

Ⓐ *You can narrow the search by choosing options.*

5 Click the **picture** or **text** of the item you'd like to buy.

6 Type an amount into the box.

7 Click **Place bid**.

8 Click **Confirm bid** in the Review and confirm bid menu.

✓ *At the close of bidding, eBay sends an email to say if you have been successful or not.*

Sell an Item

1 Hover over **Sell**.

2 Click **Sell an item**.

3 Click **Browse categories**.

✓ *A* How to Sell *guide is available on the Sell menu.*

4 Click to choose the categories and sub-categories for your item.

5 Click **Continue**.

The **Create your listing** screen appears.

6 Enter details and click **Continue**.

🛑 *For secure transactions on eBay, you need to sign up for PayPal.*

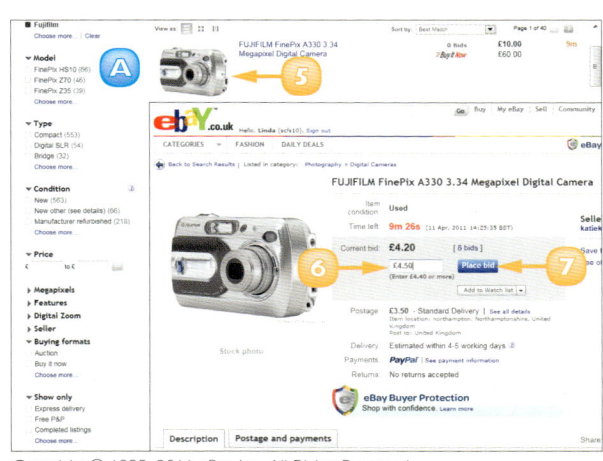

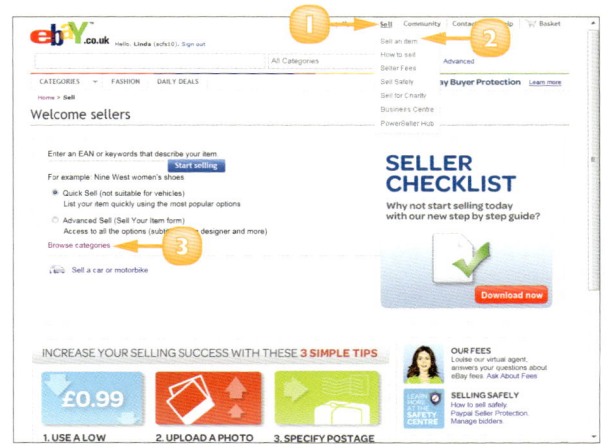

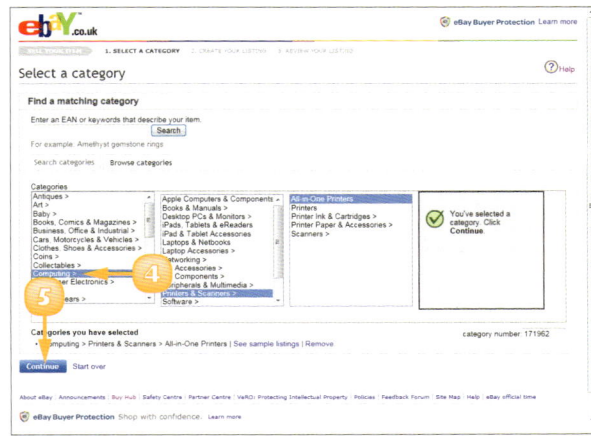

USE ONLINE BANKING

Online banking means that the bank is open 24 hours a day and 7 days a week. You can check your balance and make payments at any time. Should you need it, there is usually a telephone number to call to reach helpful staff. You need a bank account before you can set up online banking.

Help and Registration

1. Type **Halifax.co.uk** into the Internet Explorer address bar.
2. Click **Help Centre**.
3. Click **Online Banking demo**.

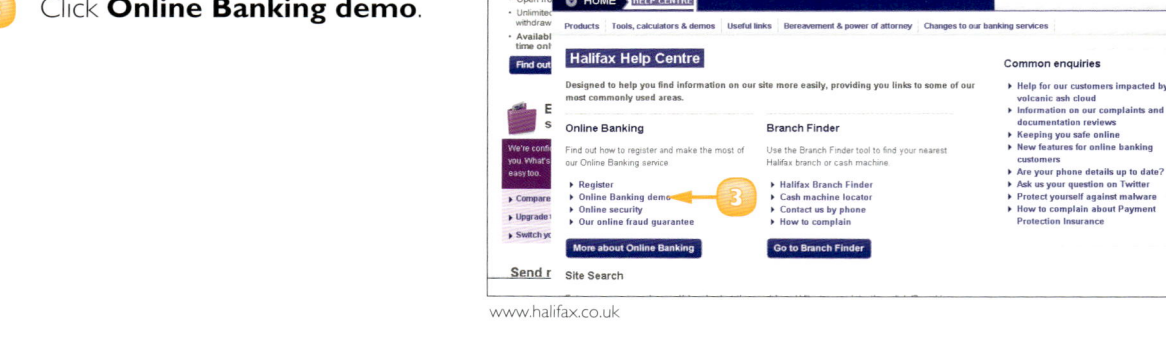

www.halifax.co.uk

4. Click **Register for online banking now**.
5. Complete the registration form.

   You will be sent a password by post to activate the account.

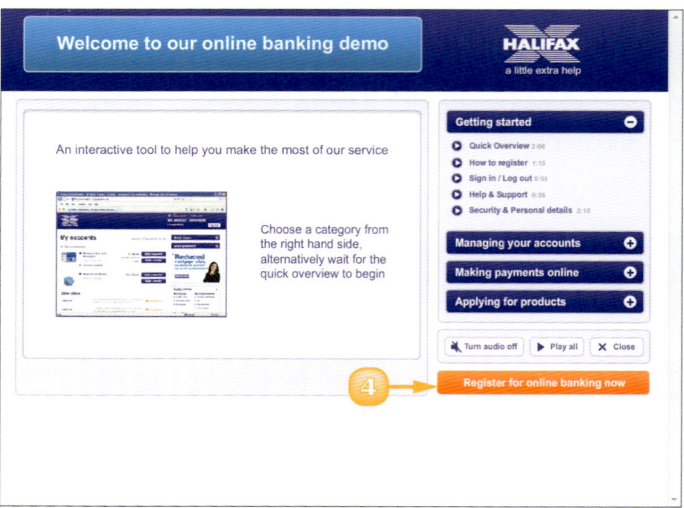

www.halifax.co.uk

CHAPTER 8 USING THE INTERNET

Check Your Balance

1. Enter your username.
2. Enter your password.
3. Click **Continue**.

   The balance on your online account is displayed.

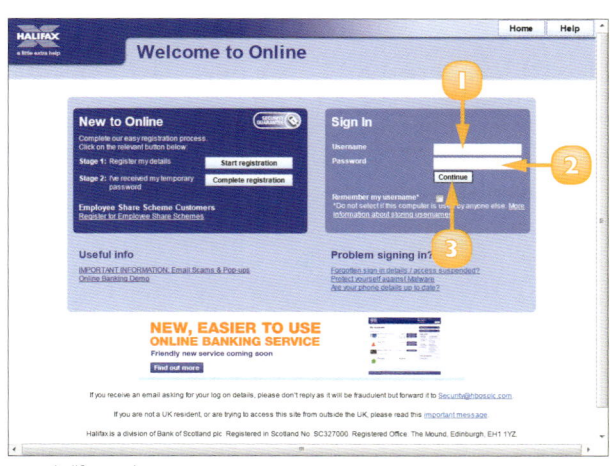

www.halifax.co.uk

4. Click an account name or image to view a statement.

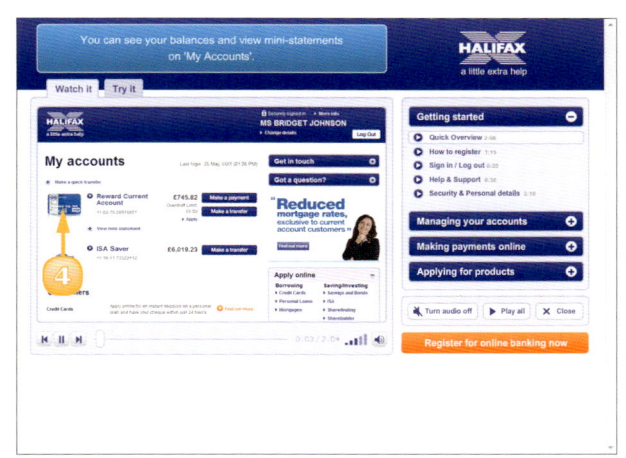

www.halifax.co.uk

Make a Payment

1. Click **Make a payment**.

   The Make a payment to a company or person page opens.

2. Fill in the details.
3. Click **Confirm**.

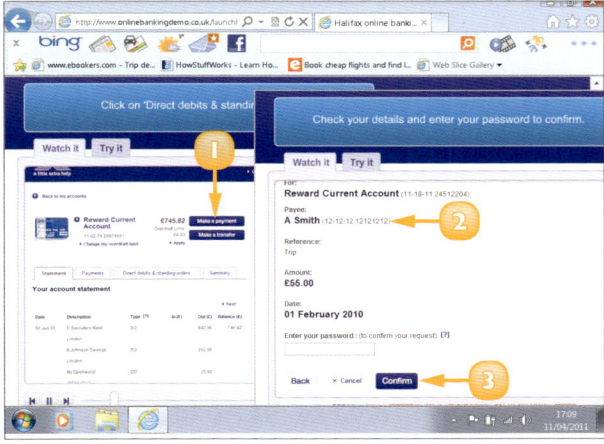

www.halifax.co.uk

continued →

CHAPTER 8 USING THE INTERNET

USE ONLINE BANKING (continued)

You can make payments to people in other countries. You can also set up and amend direct debits and standing orders.

Make an International Payment

1. Click the **Payments** tab.
2. Click **International Payments**.
3. Click **Create a new recipient**.
4. Click **Send money to an international bank**.
5. Click **Next**.
6. Complete the recipient and payment details and click **Submit**.
7. Print the confirmation page.

Set up a Standing Order

1. Click the **Direct debit and standing orders** tab.
2. Click **Set up standing order**.

   A *You can also cancel or modify direct debits.*

STOP *Remember to log out at the end of the session to maintain security on your account.*

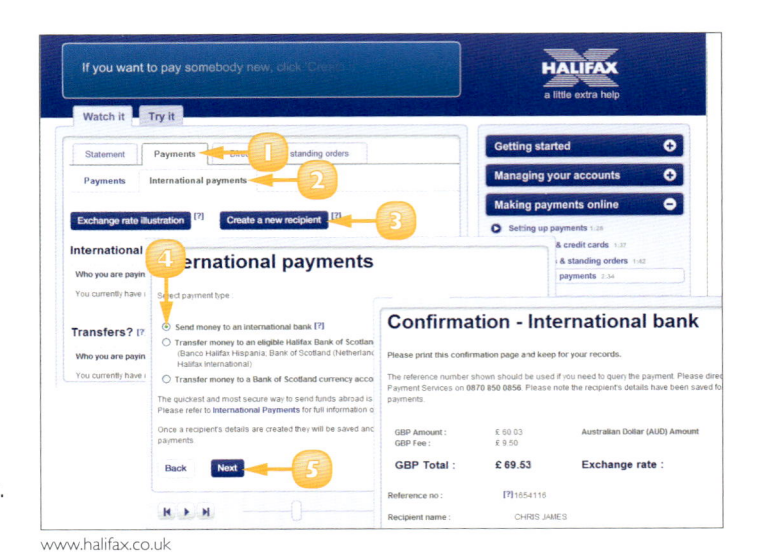

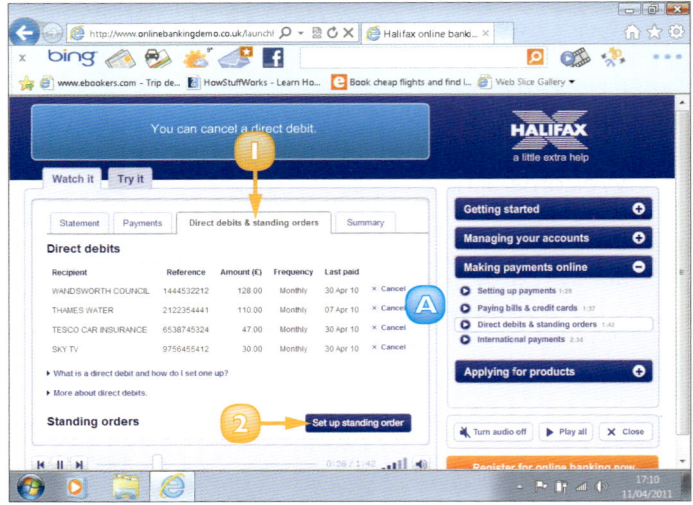

www.halifax.co.uk

www.halifax.co.uk

CHAPTER 8 USING THE INTERNET

ADD SKYPE TO YOUR COMPUTER

There are hundreds of free programs, called freeware, available on the Internet that can be downloaded to your computer. One of the most useful is Skype, which allows you to make free phone calls, with video if you wish, over the Internet to anybody else in the world who also has Skype.

In Chapter 6, we covered how to download antivirus software. Now we look at downloading Skype.

1. Type **skype.com** into the address bar of Internet Explorer.
2. Hover over **Get Skype**.
3. Click **Windows**.

© 2011 Skype Limited

4. Click **Download Skype**.
5. Click **Run**.

   After a few minutes, the Welcome Screen appears.

6. Click **Close this welcome screen and start using Skype**.
7. Register to use the Skype service.

© 2011 Skype Limited

CHAPTER 8 USING THE INTERNET

USE SKYPE

To make a phone call over the Internet, you need speakers, a microphone (and a webcam if you want to make video calls). It is also possible to make cheap calls to people who do not have Skype on their computer.

Before making a call, we add a contact and check the sound settings.

Add a Contact

1. Type a name in the **Search box**.
2. Click **Find this person**.

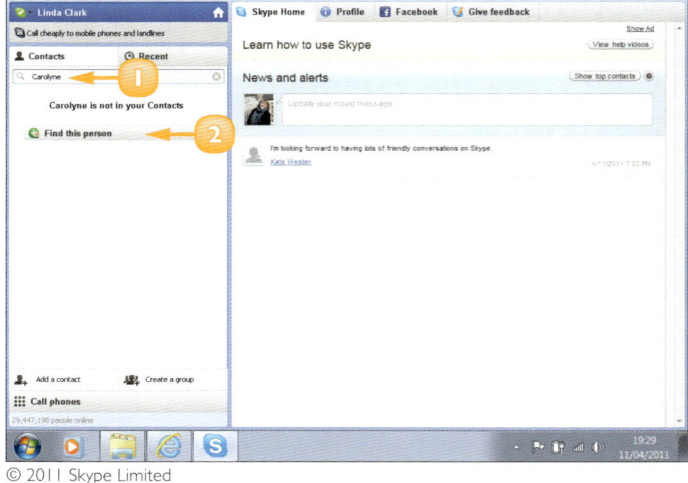

© 2011 Skype Limited

3. Click **Add contact** beside the correct person.

   You can write a personal message that Skype sends when it asks them to agree to be your contact.

✓ *To find out more about Skype, click* **View help videos**.

© 2011 Skype Limited

CHAPTER 8 USING THE INTERNET

Check Sound Settings

1. Click **Echo/Sound Test Service** in the Contact list.
2. Click **Call**.
   - Ⓐ The call window opens and you are guided through the sound test.

Check Video Settings

1. If you have a webcam, click on a contact who also has a webcam.
2. Click **Check settings**.
3. Click the **Webcam** tab to check that the webcam is working.

Make a Call Online

1. Click a person shown in the Contact list as online.
2. Click **Call** or **Video call**.
3. Click **End Call** to close the call.

Make a Call to a Phone

1. Click **Call phones**.
2. Key in the number.
   - Ⓐ You can click the buttons instead of typing.
   - Ⓑ You have to pay to call a phone.
3. Click **Call**.

✓ *Your first call to a phone is free.*

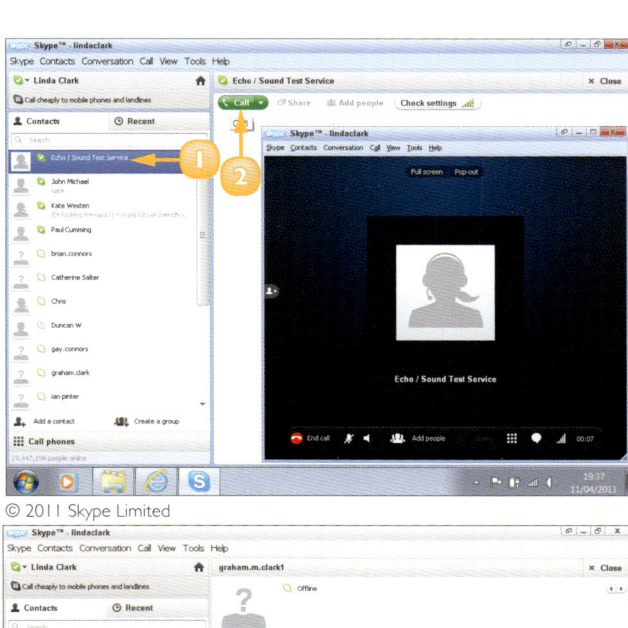

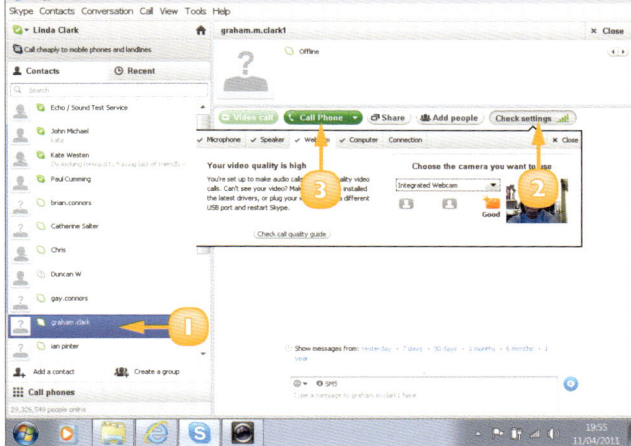

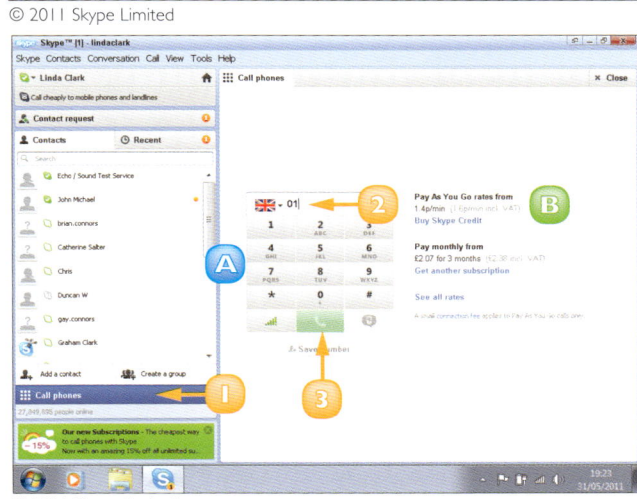

© 2011 Skype Limited

© 2011 Skype Limited

© 2011 Skype Limited

CHAPTER 8 USING THE INTERNET

CONTENTS

- **118** Choose and Set Up an Email Account
- **120** Access Your Email Account
- **122** Read and Respond to an Email
- **124** Write and Send an Email
- **126** Delete an Email
- **127** Deal with Junk Mail

9

SETTING UP AND USING EMAIL

One of the main reasons for wanting to get online is to keep in touch with family and friends wherever they live in the world. After working through this chapter, you should have the confidence to keep in touch and up-to-date with your loved ones and have learnt how to deal with unwanted emails. This chapter covers how to set up a free email account, how to access it and send and receive messages.

CHOOSE AND SET UP AN EMAIL ACCOUNT

Email – short for electronic mail – is quick, reliable and easy to use. If you worked through the "Windows Live Essentials" section (Chapter 6), you will have an email account and one will have been provided by your Internet Service Provider (ISP). If not, or if you would like to have more than one account, there are several options available. For example, free email accounts are available from Hotmail and Google.

1 Type **hotmail.co.uk** into the Internet Explorer address bar.

2 Click **Sign Up**.

The registration screen appears.

3 Enter the first part of the email address you would like.

4 Click **Check availability**.

A Your first choice may not be available.

B Hotmail may suggest some alternatives. You can click one of them to select it.

5 Close the list and repeat Steps 3 and 4 until a name you would like is available.

✓ *Make a note of your final choice of email address and password to keep in a secure place until you have memorised them.*

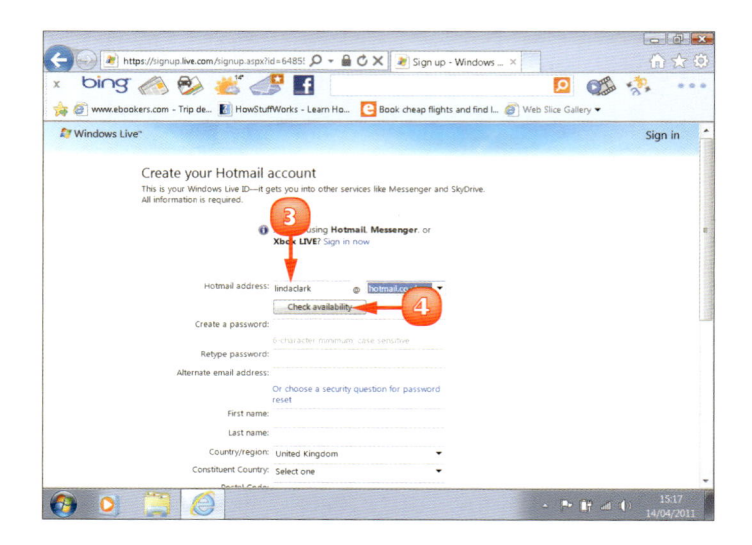

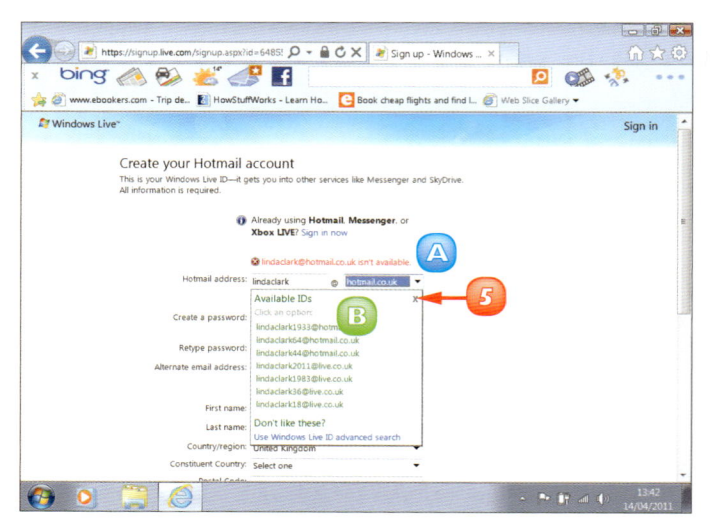

CHAPTER 9 SETTING UP AND USING EMAIL

6 Type in your chosen password.

The Help box next to the window shows how "strong" (difficult to guess) your password is.

7 Re-type your password (to ensure that you can type it later – it will not work if you have mis-spelled it).

8 Type in an additional email address (if you have one).

This will allow you to recover your Hotmail account if you forget your password.

9 Enter the rest of your personal details.

C *Letters and numbers are displayed.*

10 Type the displayed letters and numbers into the box to prove that a person is completing the form.

11 Unclick the box if you do not wish to receive promotional offers.

12 Click to read Microsoft's **service agreement**.

13 Click **I accept** to agree to the terms and conditions.

The Windows Live home screen is displayed.

D *The first message is a welcome from Hotmail.*

E *You can go straight to your inbox to read emails.*

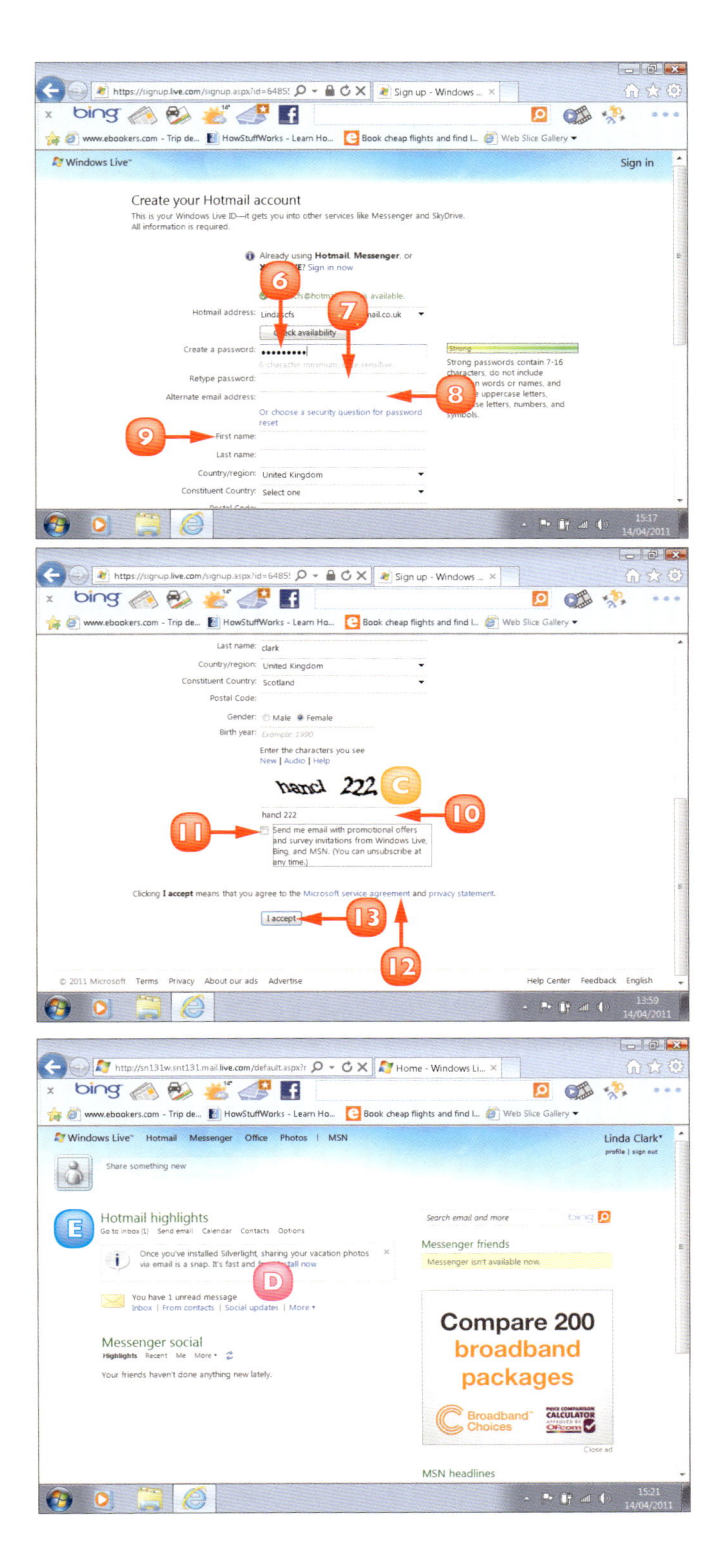

CHAPTER 9 SETTING UP AND USING EMAIL

ACCESS YOUR EMAIL ACCOUNT

As long as you can remember your user name (usually your email address) and password you can access your email account from anywhere in the world where you have access to the Internet.

Sign In

1. Type **hotmail.co.uk** into the Internet Explorer address bar.
2. Type in your email address.
3. Type in your password.
4. Click **Remember me** to unselect it.
5. Click **Sign in**.

The Windows Live home screen is displayed.

6. Click **Inbox**.

Your email inbox is displayed.

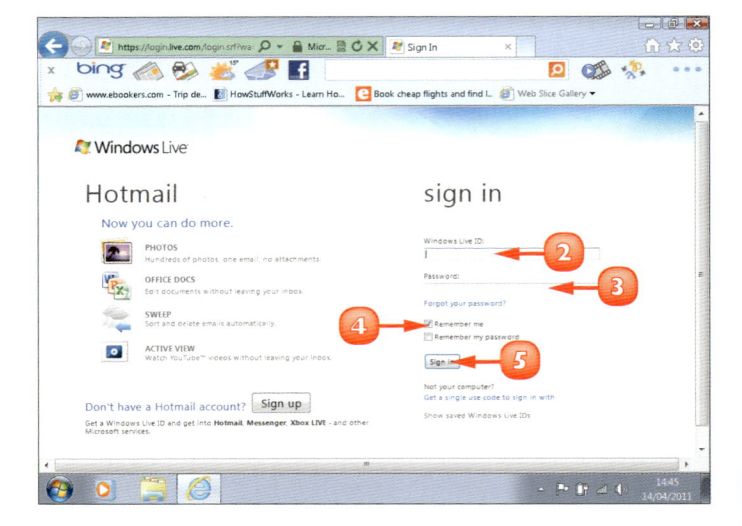

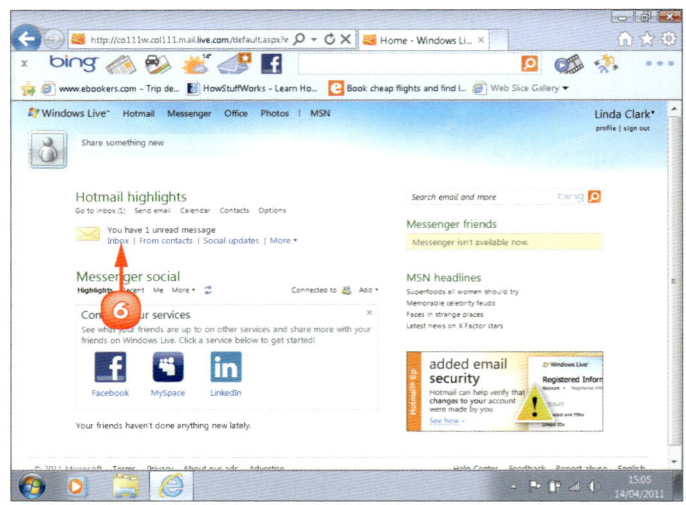

CHAPTER 9 SETTING UP AND USING EMAIL

The Hotmail Inbox

A **Inbox menu**

B **Select All check box**

Click this check box to select (or deselect) all messages.

C **Select check box**

Click a message's check box to select (or deselect) a single message.

D **Delete**

Click to delete selected messages.

E **New**

Create a new message.

F **Junk**

Send selected messages to the Junk folder.

G **Sweep menu**

A list of tools for cleaning up groups of messages.

H **Mark as menu**

A list of options for read status of messages.

I **Move to menu**

A list of the folders to which you can move the selected messages.

Note: *You can also move a message by clicking a folder in the Inbox menu.*

J **Print**

Print selected messages.

K **Sign out**

Click to close Hotmail.

Remember to sign out when you are finished. This is especially important if you are accessing email in a public location.

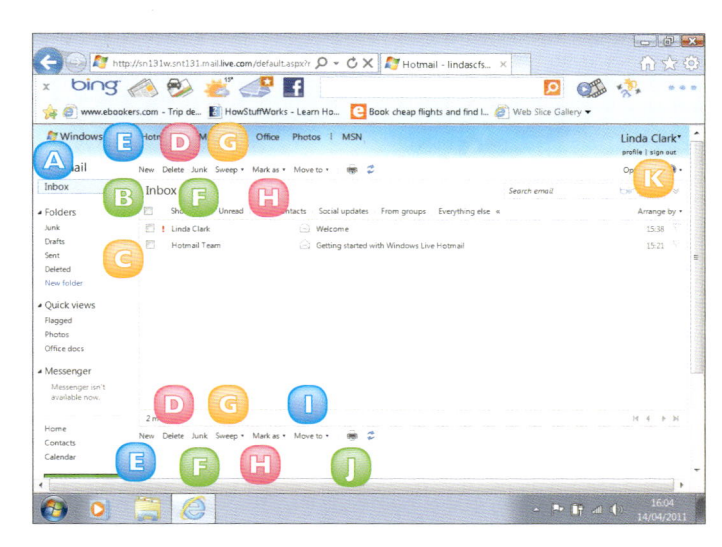

CHAPTER 9 SETTING UP AND USING EMAIL

READ AND RESPOND TO AN EMAIL

Now that you have an email account, you can read emails and reply to them. You can use the reading pane or open an email to read it in a full screen.

Read an Email in the Reading Pane

1. Sign in to your Hotmail account and click **Inbox**.

2. Click **Options**.

3. Click **Bottom**.

   A reading pane opens at the bottom of the screen.

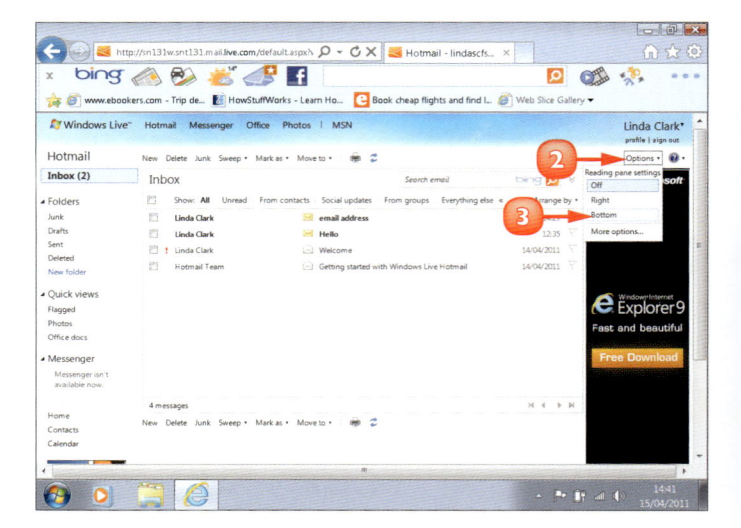

4. Click a message in the Inbox.

   A You can read the message in the reading pane.

   ✓ *You can flag a message as a reminder. Click ⚑. The flag turns red.*

5. Double-click a message in the Inbox to open it.

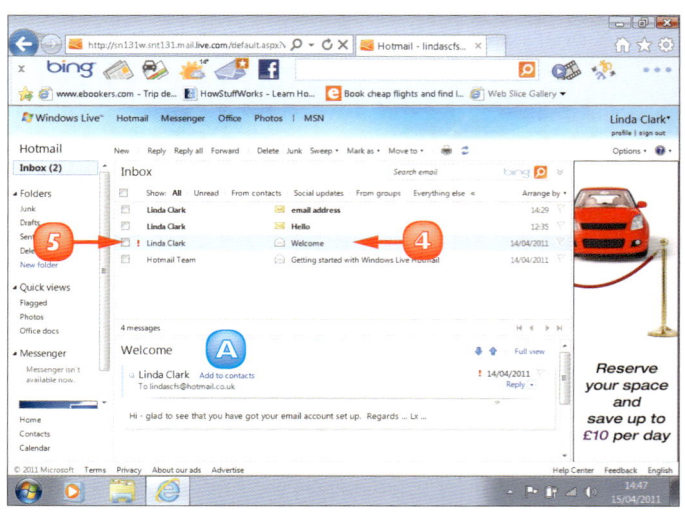

CHAPTER 9 SETTING UP AND USING EMAIL

Respond to an Email

1 Read the message.

- **A** You can scroll to see the end of the message, if it is long.
- **B** You can click **Back to messages** to return to the Inbox.

2 Click **Reply**.

The reply message appears.

3 Type a reply in the space provided.

Note: As you type more text the space gets bigger.

4 Click **Send**.

You may be asked to type in some characters, to verify your identity.

5 Click **Send** again or click the message and follow the onscreen instructions.

The "message sent" screen appears and gives you the chance to add the recipient to your contact list.

6 Type in the name of the contact.

7 Click **Add to contacts**.

The Inbox appears.

> ***To remove the advertisements, scroll to the bottom and click Close ad. The ads keep returning unless you upgrade and pay for Hotmail Plus.***

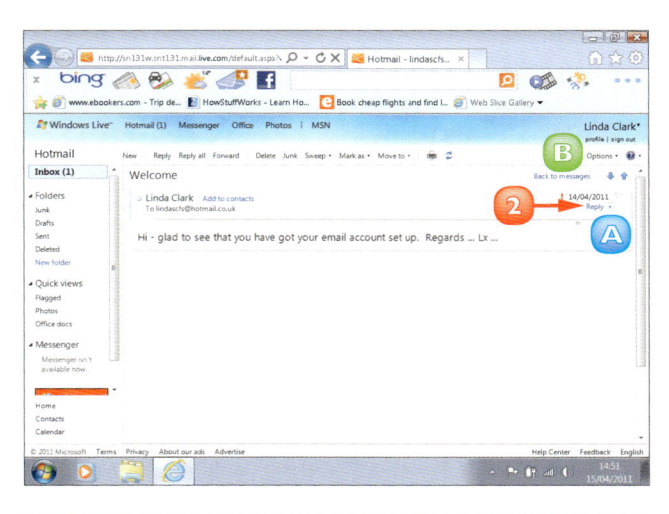

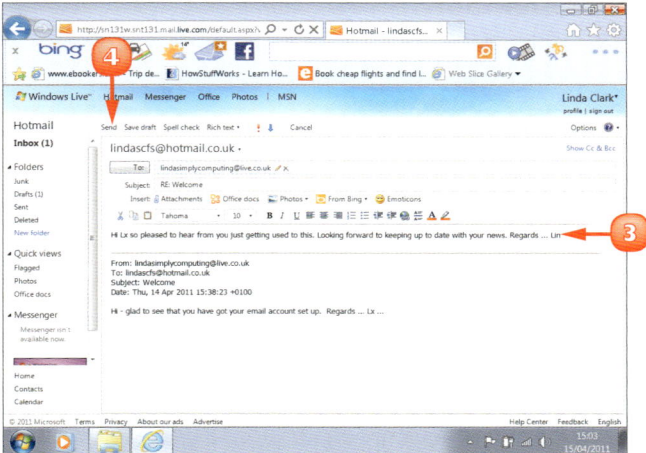

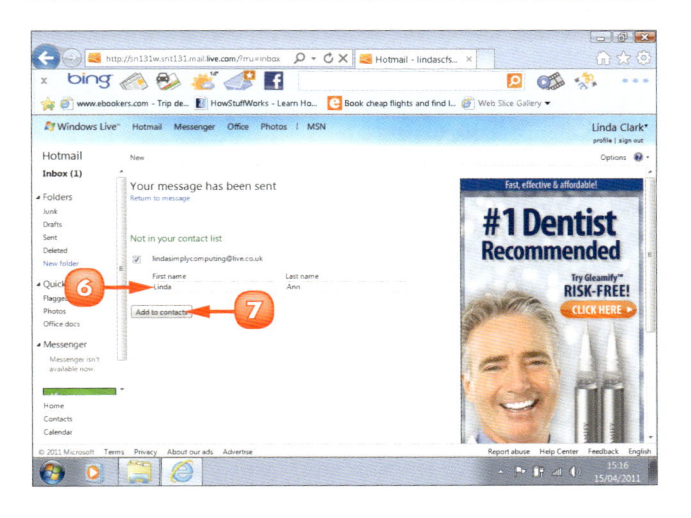

CHAPTER 9 SETTING UP AND USING EMAIL

WRITE AND SEND AN EMAIL

When you respond to an email, you use the email address on the received message. Before sending a new message, you need to know the email address for the person you are contacting. Many organisations provide an email address, such as info@sending.com or secretary@writing.net. It is important to write down the precise email address of somebody you wish to contact. Misplacing a dot or an @ or transposing a letter in the name means that your message will not get through.

Create a New Message

1. Open your email account.
2. Click **New** (see "The Hotmail Inbox" if you need help finding it).
3. Type the email address.
4. Type the subject.

Note: Some email providers do not allow messages without a subject heading.

5. Type the message.

   A. You can change the font, size and enhancements of the selected text.

Check the Spelling

1. Click **Spell check**.
2. Click a word underlined in red.

   A drop-down menu appears with alternative spelling suggestions.

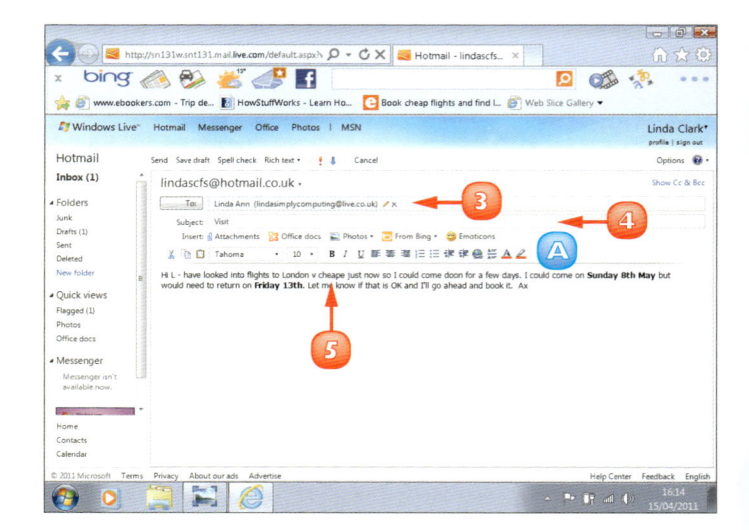

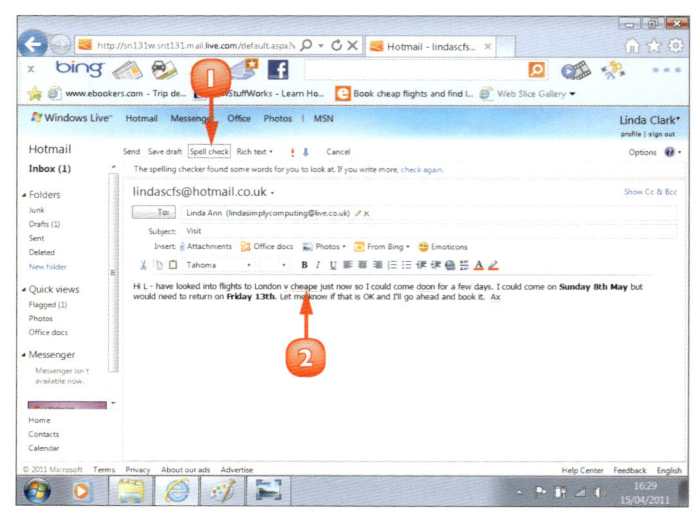

CHAPTER 9 SETTING UP AND USING EMAIL

Send to Several People

1. Click the space next to the first email address in the **To:** bar.
2. Type in the additional address.
3. Click **Show Cc and Bcc**.

4. Type an address into the **Cc:** bar so that everyone can see to whom the message is copied.
5. Type an address into the **Bcc:** bar so that this address is concealed from the other recipients.
6. Click **Send**.

   You are invited to add the new email addresses to your contact list.

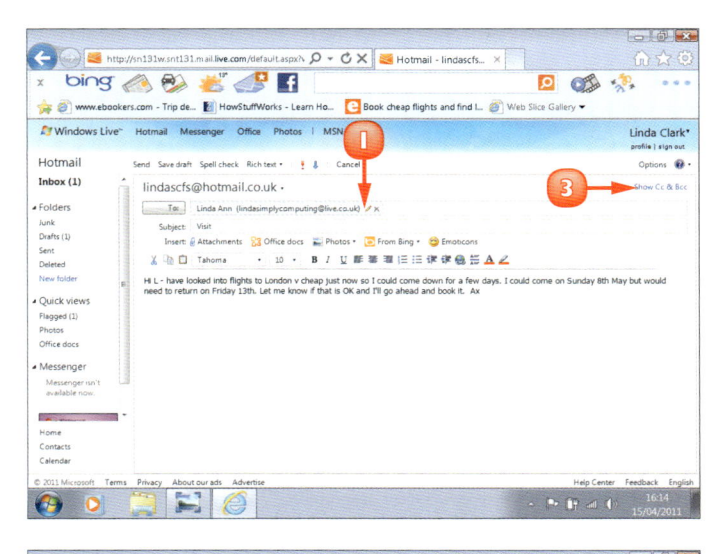

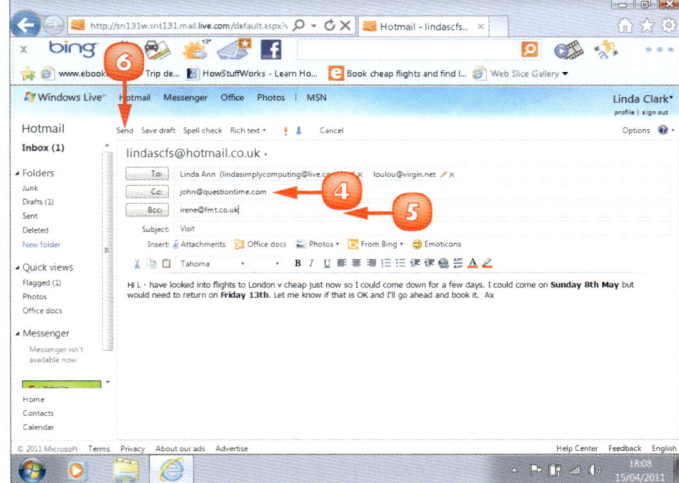

> ✓ *You can click* **Save draft** *to save a message in the Drafts folder for later.*
>
> ✓ *To work on a saved message, click* **Drafts**. *Click the message. Click* **Continue working on this message**.

CHAPTER 9 SETTING UP AND USING EMAIL

DELETE AN EMAIL

Your Inbox will very quickly fill up. There is usually a generous allowance of space, but a full Inbox results in emails not being delivered.

Delete Messages

1. Open your Inbox.
2. Click the check box beside each email to be deleted.
3. Click **Delete**.

   A *The emails are sent to the Deleted folder.*

Retrieve a Deleted Message

1. Click the **Deleted** folder.
2. Click the check box beside the email to be retrieved.
3. Click **Move to**.
4. Click **Inbox** from the drop-down menu.

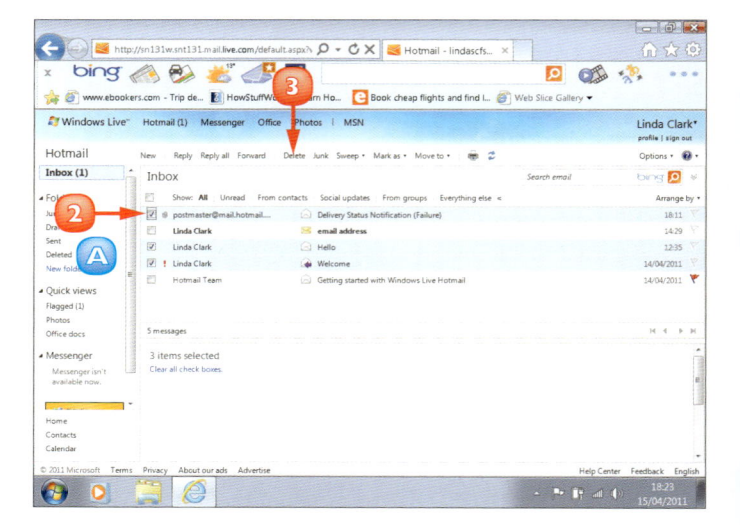

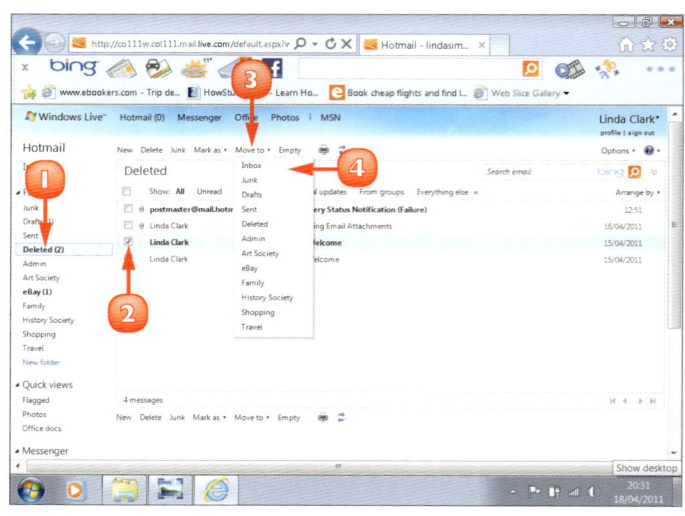

CHAPTER 9 SETTING UP AND USING EMAIL

DEAL WITH JUNK MAIL

Junk mail, also known as spam, is unsolicited email. It can clog up your Inbox and is usually trying to sell you something or get your personal details to steal either your money or your identity. Most email providers offer a junk mail filter. Occasionally, genuine emails that you wanted to receive are consigned to Junk so it is worth knowing how to retrieve them.

Retrieve Messages from Junk

1. Open your email account.
2. Click the **Junk** folder.

   The Junk folder opens.

3. Click the check box next to the email to be retrieved.
4. Click **Not junk** to move email back to the Inbox.

Send Messages to Junk

1. Click the check box next to the unwanted email.
2. Click **Junk**.

   The email is moved to the Junk folder.

If the Junk folder is empty, you receive a congratulations message.

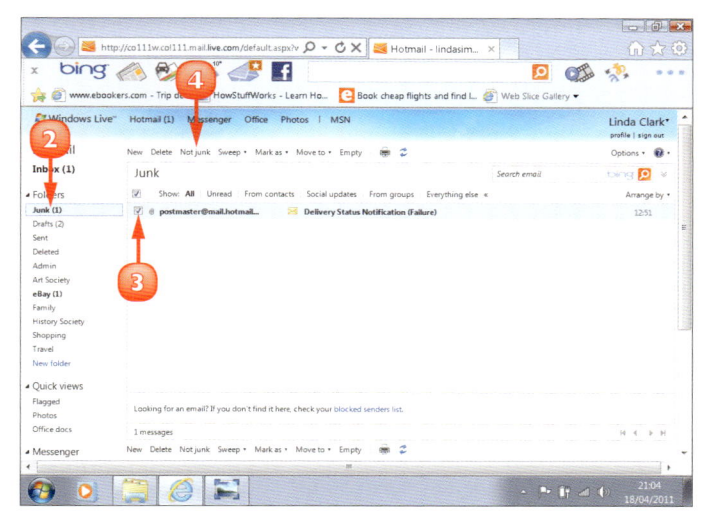

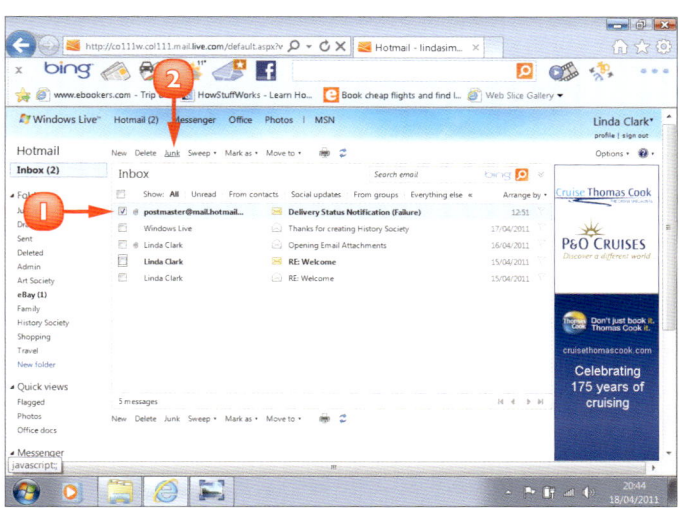

CHAPTER 9 SETTING UP AND USING EMAIL

CONTENTS

- **130** Open Email Attachments
- **132** Save Attachments
- **134** Send Attachments
- **136** Store Messages in Folders
- **138** Add People to a Contact List
- **140** Find People in a Contact List

10. ORGANISING EMAIL

Using the email account set up in Chapter 9, we look at organising emails and contact lists, find out how to attach documents and pictures to emails and create and use folders to store emails.

OPEN EMAIL ATTACHMENTS

An attachment to an email can be a document or a picture. Do not open an attachment if you are unsure who it is from or if the email looks in any way suspicious. The consequences could be a virus or a worm getting into your computer and corrupting it.

Open an Attached Document

1. Open your email account.

2. Click a message with an attachment.

    A *The paperclip indicates an attachment.*

    B *The email opens.*

    C *The type of attachment is shown by an image.*

3. Click **View online**.

    D *You can also Download an attachment (see "Save Attachments").*

    The document appears after a few seconds.

4. Click ◄ and ► to view other pages.

5. Click **Close** (✖) to go back to the email.

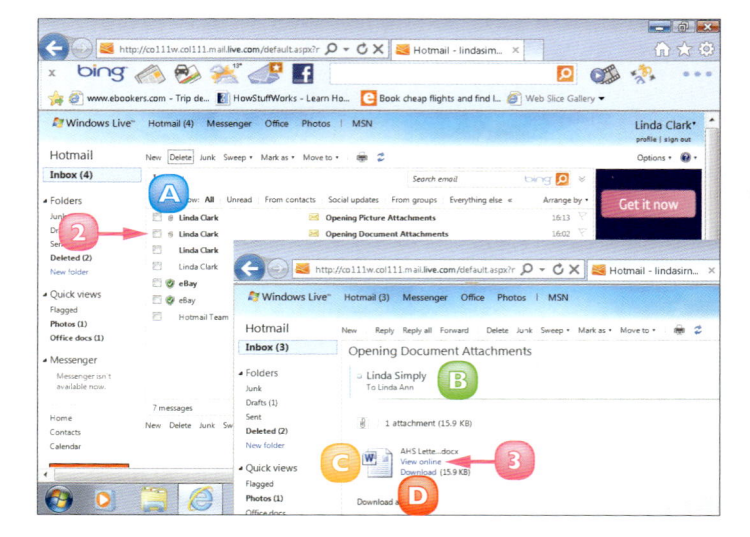

CHAPTER 10 ORGANISING EMAIL

Open an Attached Picture

1. Click a message with an attachment.

   The email opens.

   A *Small thumbnail images of the pictures are displayed.*

2. Click **View slide show.**

   B *The figure in brackets tells you how many pictures are in the slide show.*

   The picture is enlarged.

3. Click another thumbnail image to see the next picture.

   The menu bars disappear.

4. Hover near the top or bottom of the slide show screen.

   The menu bars reappear.

   A *You can click **Full screen** to see a larger image. Press Esc or click **Exit full screen** to return to the previous view.*

5. Click ❌ to close the slide show and return to the message.

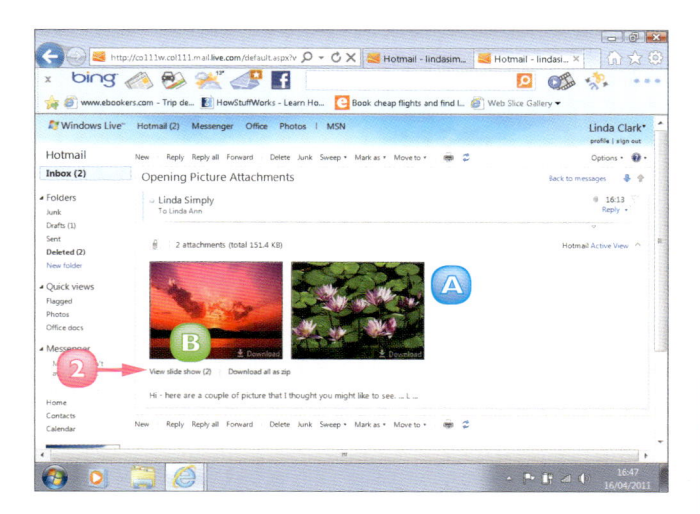

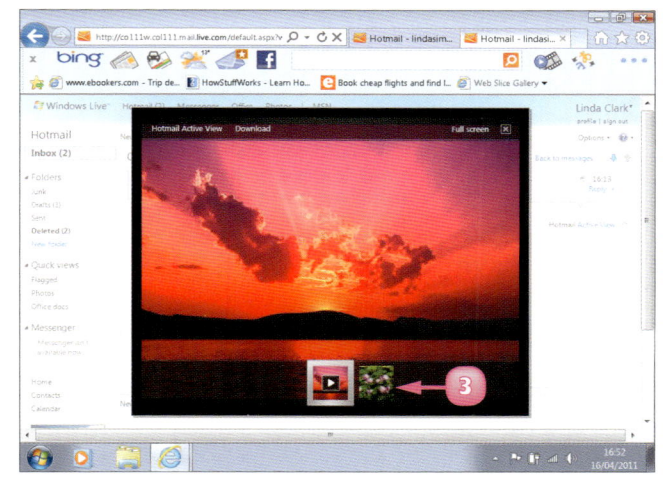

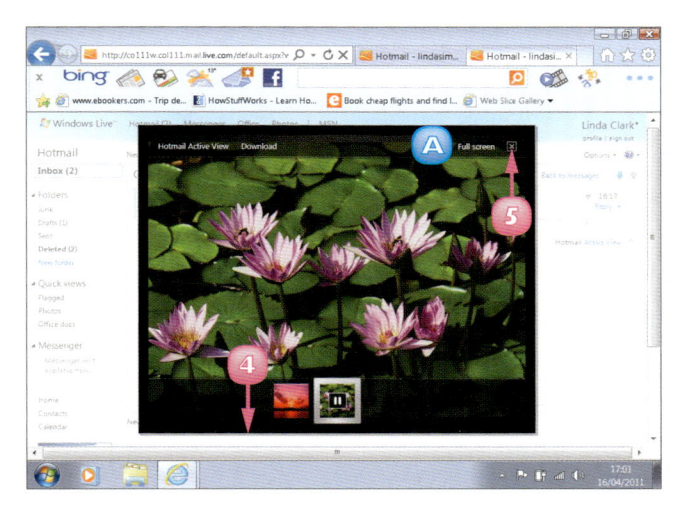

CHAPTER 10 ORGANISING EMAIL

SAVE ATTACHMENTS

As an alternative to opening an attachment, you can save it to your computer. You can then edit it and use it in many ways.

Save a Document

1. Open your email account and click a message with an attachment.

2. Click **Download**.

   A menu appears at the bottom of the screen.

3. Click **Save**.

4. Click **Open folder**.

5. Double-click the document title.

   The document opens in protected mode.

6. Click **Click for more details**.

   The Protected Mode Word 2010 window opens.

7. Click **Enable Editing**.

   A *You can click the Home tab to continue to view the document in Protected Mode.*

8. Click Internet Explorer to return to the Inbox.

   B *You can click ✖ to close Word.*

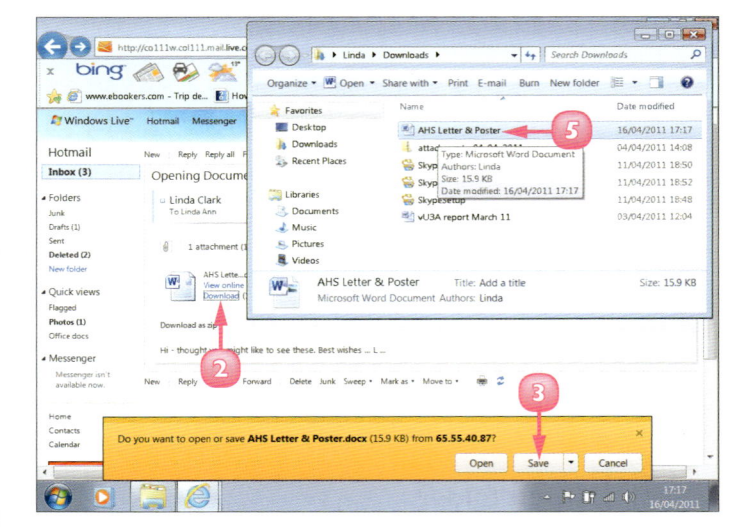

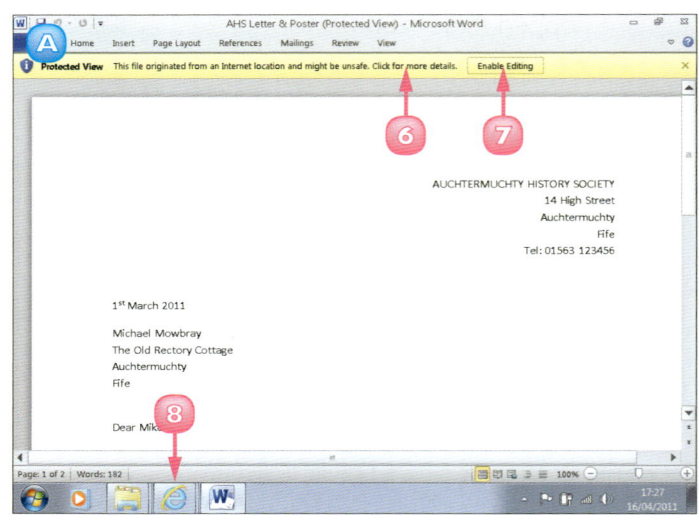

CHAPTER 10 ORGANISING EMAIL

Save an Individual Picture

1. Open your email account and click a message with attached pictures.

2. Click **Download** on the picture.

   A menu appears at the bottom of the screen.

3. Click **Save**.

   The image is saved and the Downloads folder opens.

Save Several Pictures

1. Click **Download all as zip**.

Note: *A zip file contains one or more files that are compressed to reduce file size.*

   A menu appears at the bottom of the screen.

2. Click **Save**.

3. Click **Open folder**.

   The zipped folder appears in the **Downloads** folder.

4. Double-click the zipped folder.

5. Double-click a picture to view it.

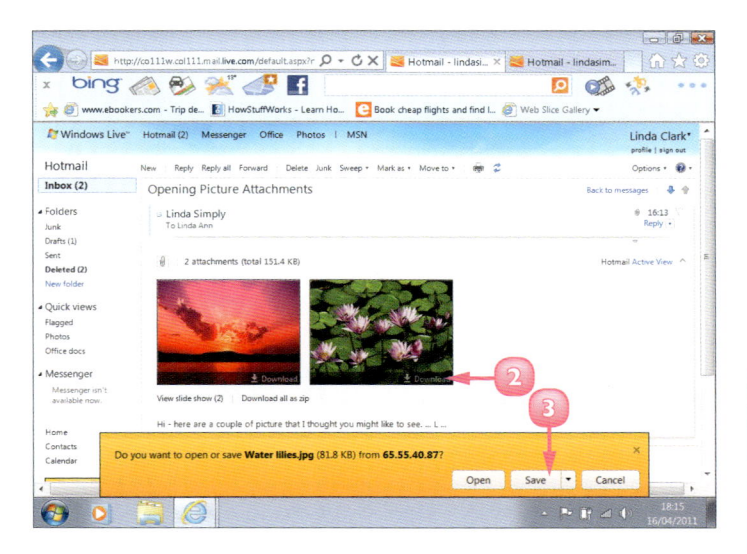

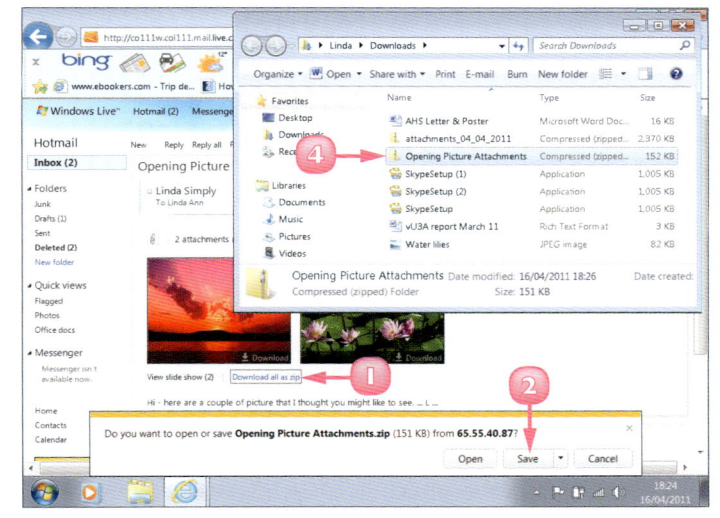

SEND ATTACHMENTS

Now we look at how you can send documents and pictures as attachments to email messages. Make a mental note of where your document or picture is saved so that you can find it easily when it comes to attaching it to your email.

Send a Document

1. Open your email account and click **New**.

2. Type a message.

3. Click **Attachments**.

   The **Documents library** appears.

4. Click the folder that contains the document you want to attach.

5. Click the document name.

6. Click **Open**.

   A copy of the document is attached to the email.

7. Click **Send as an online doc**.

   A You can click **No thanks** to simply attach the document.

8. Click **Send**.

   Your email is sent.

   ✓ *Click the Sent folder to check that your email has gone.*

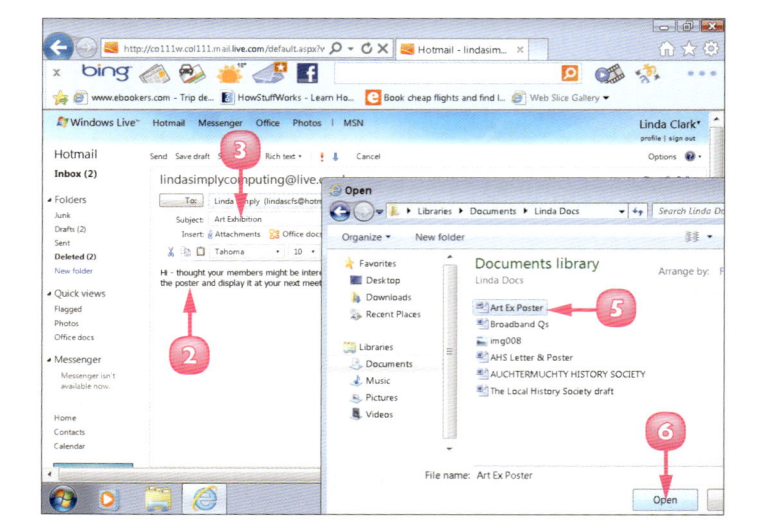

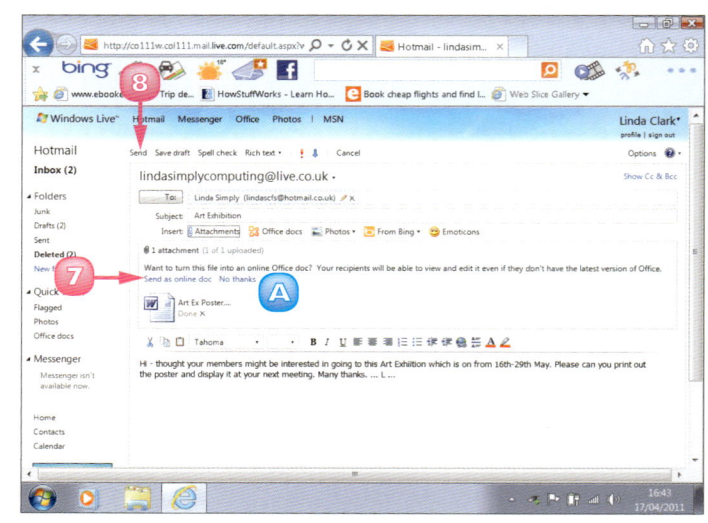

Send a Picture

1. Open your email account and click **New**.
2. Type a message.
3. Click **Photos**.

   The Pictures library appears.
4. Click the folder where the pictures are stored.
5. Click **Open**.

   The pictures are displayed.
6. Click a picture and click **Open**.

   Wait for a copy of the picture to be attached to your email.
7. Click the **Photo size**.
8. Click **Medium** to reduce the size of the picture.

Note: Large pictures take a long time to send and receive. The quality of the reduced size picture is good enough for viewing on the computer but too poor to print out well.

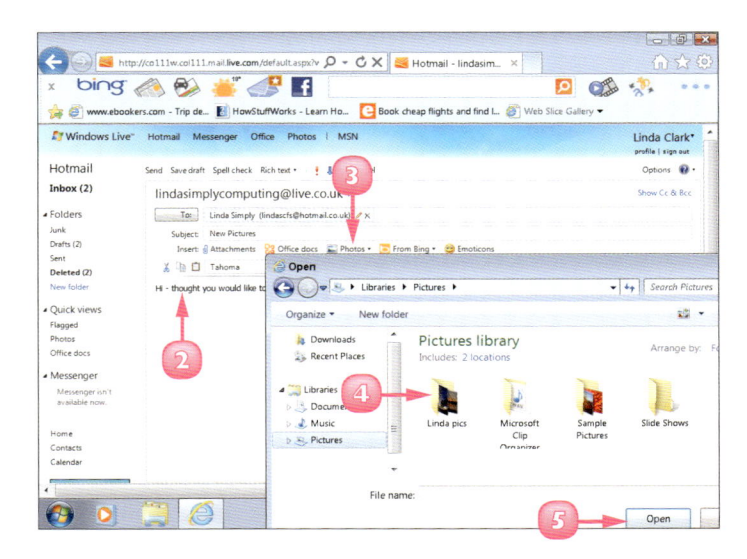

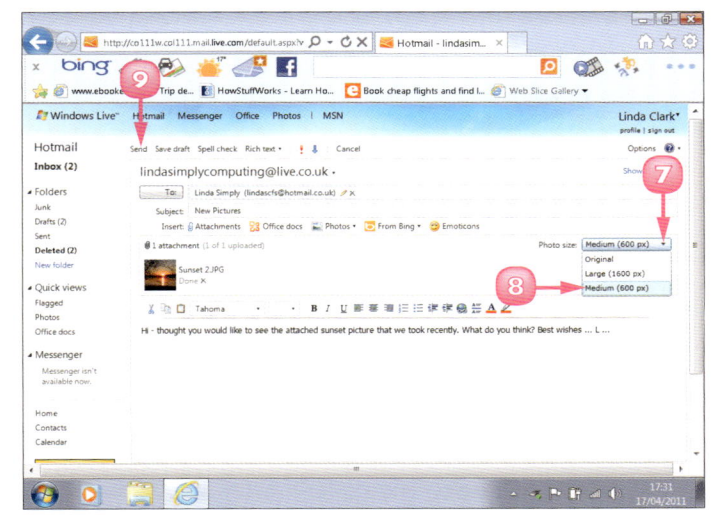

9. Click **Send**.

✓ *If you attached the wrong picture, click ✕ (next to Done) to remove it and try again.*

STORE MESSAGES IN FOLDERS

Your Inbox will eventually start to look a little untidy and begin to fill up. You now need a filing system that allows you to move emails from your Inbox and store them for future reference.

Create a Folder

1. Open your email account.
2. Click **New folder**.
3. Type in a name.
4. Click the **Create in**.
5. Click **Inbox** to place the new folder inside the Inbox.
6. Click **Save**.

   The new folder is created.

7. Click **Inbox** to return to your emails.

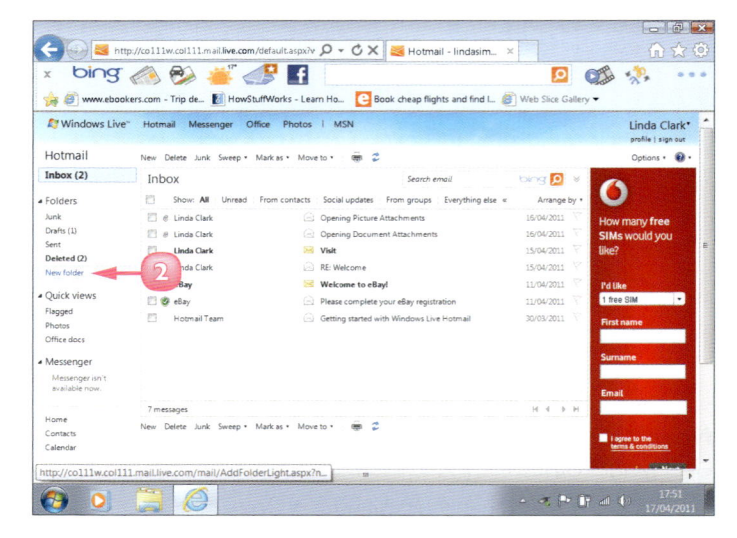

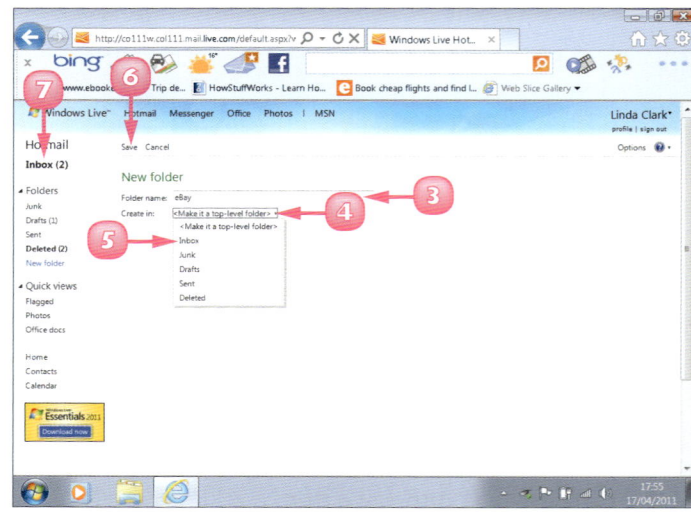

CHAPTER 10 ORGANISING EMAIL

Move Emails to a Folder

1. Click the check boxes of emails to be put in the new folder.
2. Click the **Move to** .
3. Click the folder's name.

   The emails are moved to the new folder.

Drag Emails to a Folder

1. Point to the message to be moved.
2. Hold down the left mouse button.
3. Drag the message to the folder.

Manage Folders

1. Point to **Folders**.
2. Click the **Actions** icon ( ).
3. Click **Manage folders** to go to the Folders menu and organise your folders.

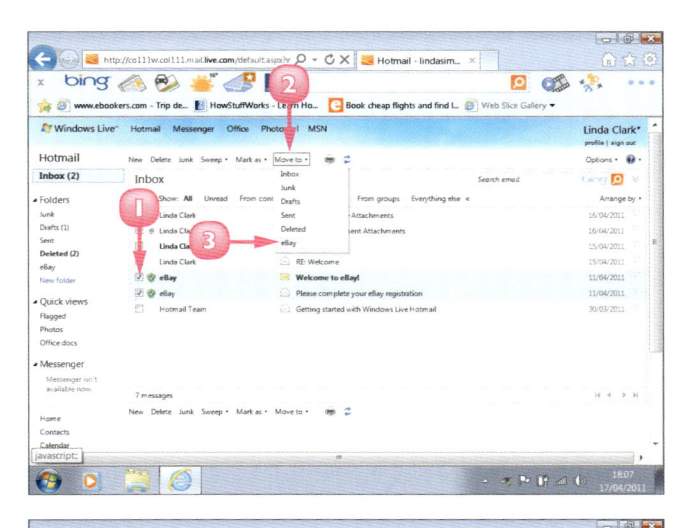

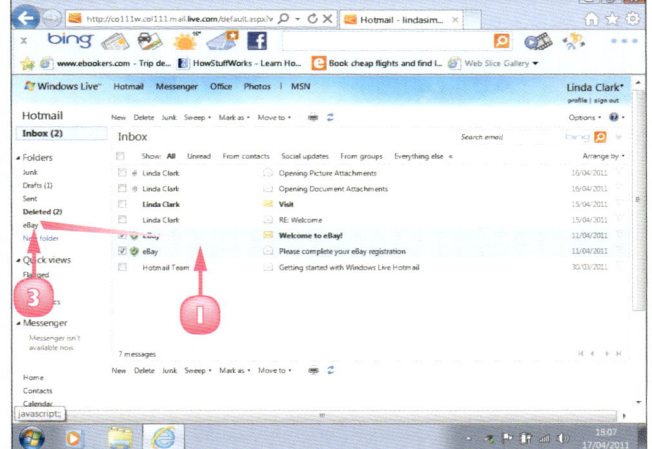

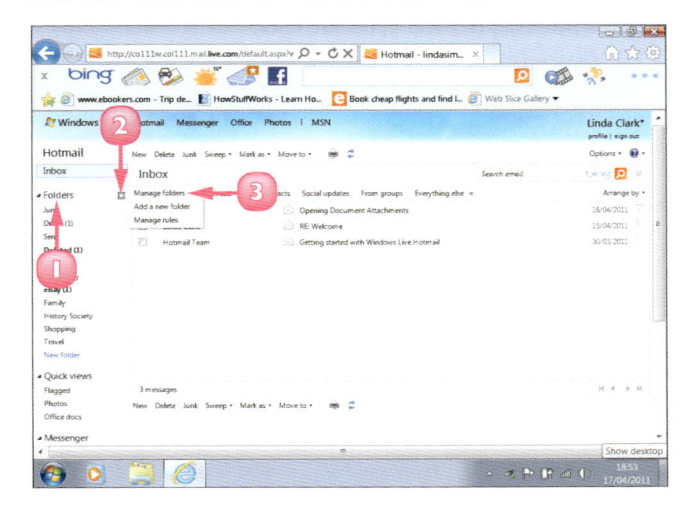

CHAPTER 10 ORGANISING EMAIL

ADD PEOPLE TO A CONTACT LIST

It is very useful to keep a record of all your contacts. When you want to send them an email you will not have to remember their email addresses or run the risk of mis-spelling them. You can also amend your contact list and set up a group email list.

1. Open your email account and click **Contacts** in the menu.

   The Contacts menu appears.

2. Click **Add people**.

   The Add People page appears.

3. Type in the email address of your contact.

   A *Click **Select from your contact list** to include people that you have already emailed.*

4. Click **Next**.

5. Click the **Make this person a favorite** check box.

   The name is shown near the top of your contacts list.

6. Click **Invite**.

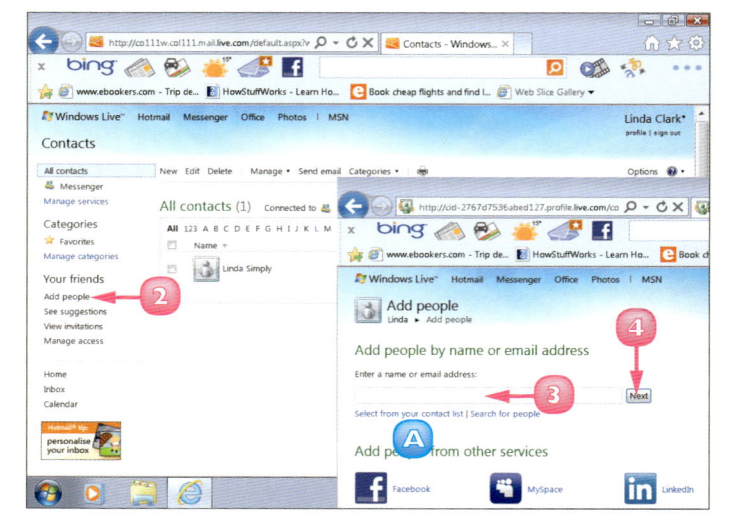

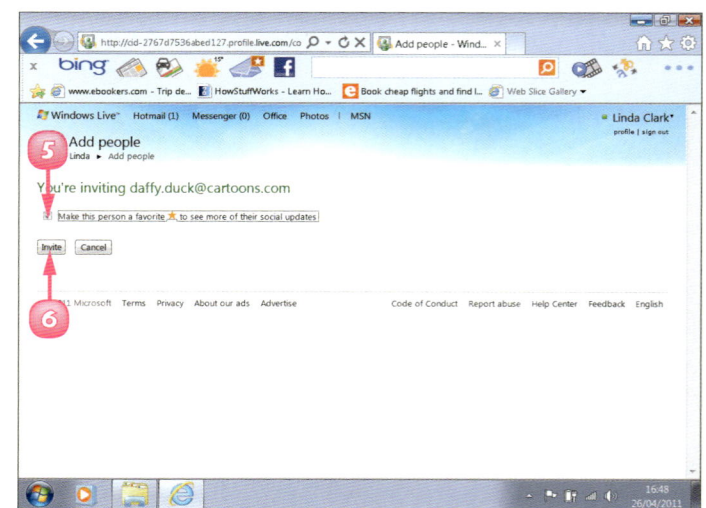

CHAPTER 10 ORGANISING EMAIL

Amend the Contact List

1. On the Inbox screen, click **Contacts**.
2. Click a **contact**.
3. Click **View details**.
4. Click **Edit** to change the contact's details.

Set Up a Group Email

1. On the Contacts screen, click **View Invitations**.
2. Click **Create a Group**.
3. Type in the name of your group.
4. Click **Check availability**.
5. Type in the email addresses of the members of the group.

Note: You can also click **Select from your contact list.**

6. Click **check boxes** to select email addresses.
7. Click **Create**.

   A welcome message appears.

Click **Hotmail** *and then click* **Inbox** *to return to your Inbox.*

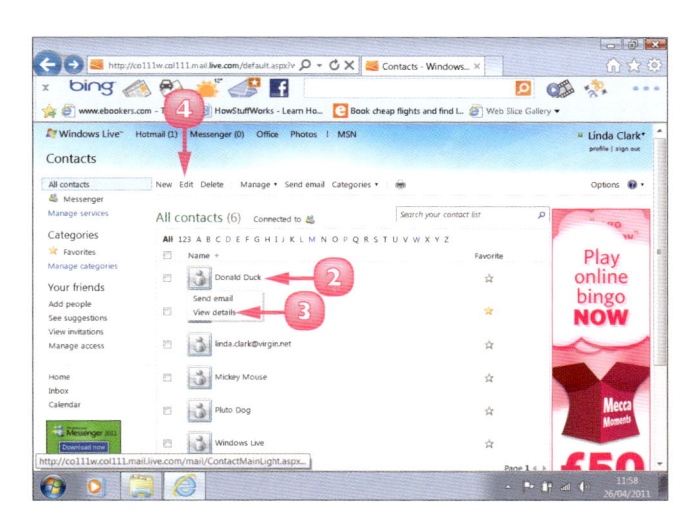

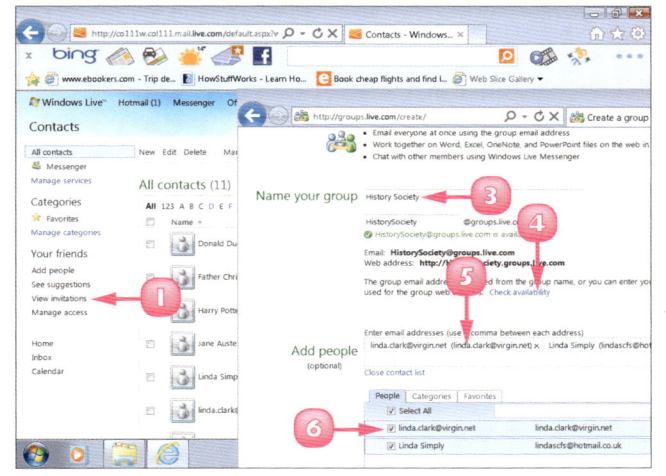

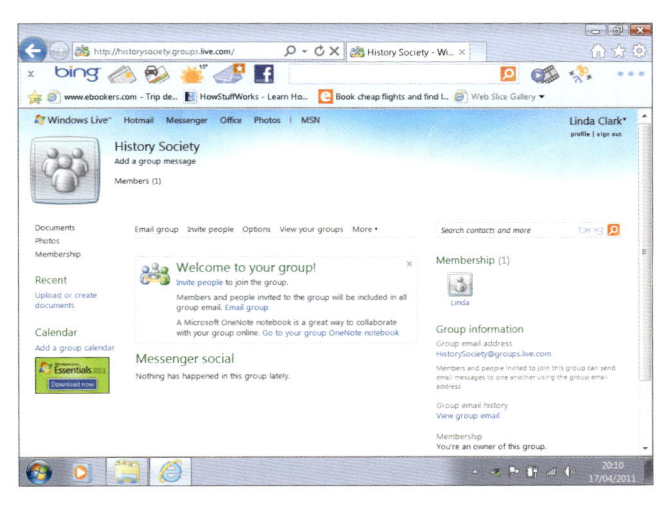

CHAPTER 10 ORGANISING EMAIL

FIND PEOPLE IN A CONTACT LIST

Once you have set up a contact list, there are several ways to quickly find an email address when you are creating a message.

Access the Contact List from the To: box

1. Go to your Inbox and click **New**.
2. Click the **To:** button.

   A drop down list appears.

3. Click the check box next to one or more contacts.

   A You can click the **Select All** check box.

4. Click **Close**.

Access the Contact List from the Address Bar

1. Go to your Inbox and click **New**.
2. Type the first letter of the email address in the **To:** bar.
3. Choose an email address from the list.

✓ *If you accidentally click the wrong check box, click again to unselect it.*

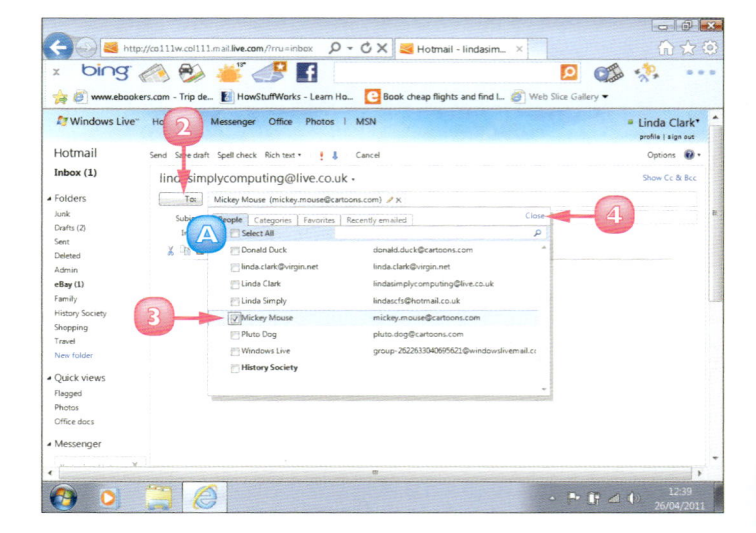

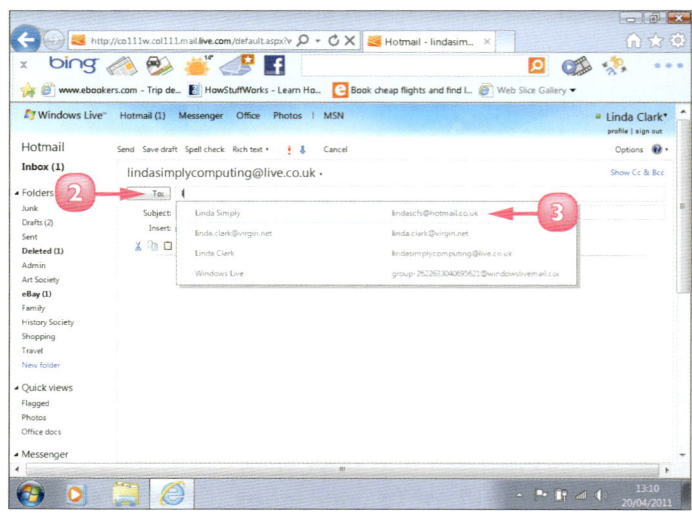

CHAPTER 10 ORGANISING EMAIL

Search for a Contact

1. Go to your Inbox and click **New**.
2. Click the **To:** button.
3. Type the first letter of the name in the **Search box**.

   Possible matches are listed.
4. Click the check boxes to choose addresses.
5. Click **Close**.

Recently Contacted List

1. Go to your Inbox and click **New**.
2. Click the **To:** button.
3. Click the **Recently emailed** tab.

   A drop down list appears.
4. Click the check boxes to choose addresses.
5. Click **Close**.

View the Contact List

1. On the Inbox screen, click **Contacts**.

   All Contacts are displayed.
2. Click a letter to view a list of contacts beginning with that letter.

Note: *Blue letters contain email addresses. Black letters are empty.*

   Ⓐ Click **All** to return to the complete list.
3. Click check boxes to choose addresses.

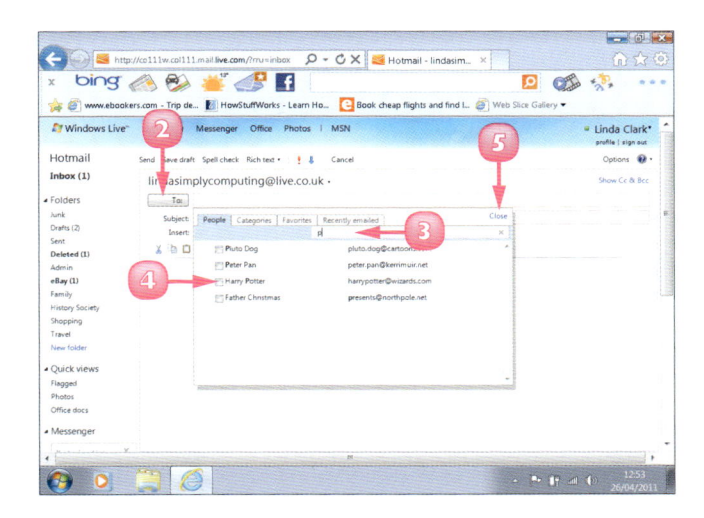

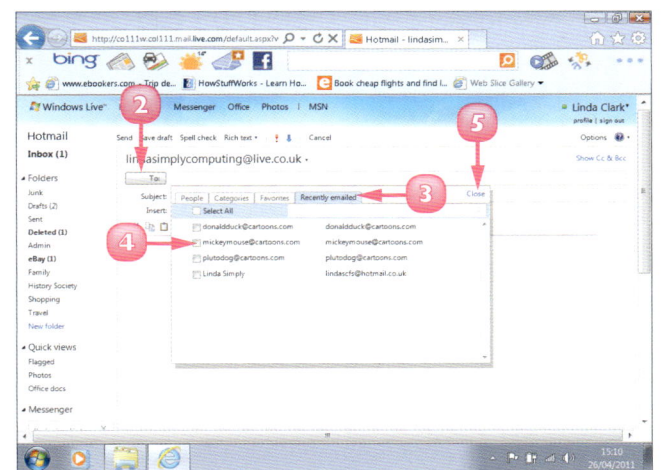

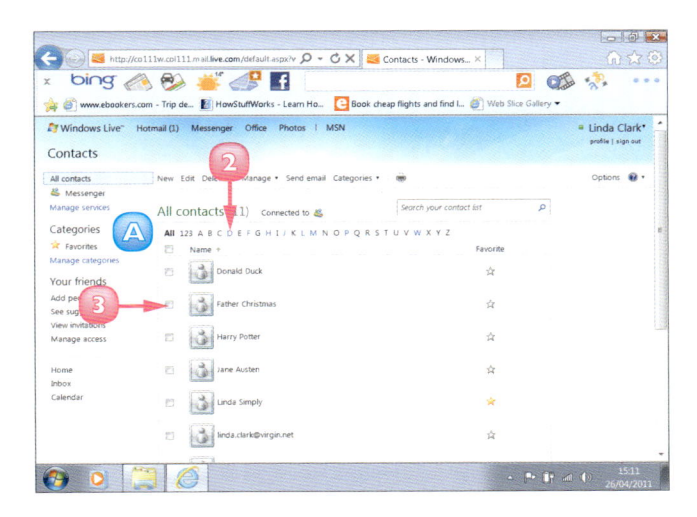

CHAPTER 10 ORGANISING EMAIL

CONTENTS

- **144** Get Pictures from Camera to Computer
- **146** Open and View Pictures
- **148** Organise and Find Pictures
- **150** Improve the Appearance of Pictures
- **152** Save Pictures to a CD or Flash Drive
- **154** Share Pictures on the Internet

MANAGING PICTURES

Digital cameras hold a lot of pictures but eventually you will have to consider downloading them to free up space. Windows Live Photo Gallery is ideal for organising and enhancing digital pictures. We also look at saving pictures to a removable device and how to share your pictures with others online.

GET PICTURES FROM CAMERA TO COMPUTER

There are two ways of getting pictures from a camera onto a computer. One is to use a card reader. The second and simplest method is to use the cable (and some cameras also use a cradle) that came with your camera.

Connect the Camera to the Computer

1. Connect one end of the cable to the camera and the other end to a USB port on your computer.

   The Autoplay window appears.

2. Click **Import pictures and videos**.

3. Click **Review, organize, and group items to import**.

4. Click **Next**.

   The Import Settings dialog appears.

Import Pictures

1. Click **Enter a name** and type in a name.

   A You can type a name.

2. Click **Add tags** and type a description.

   B You can type short descriptions.

3. Click **Import**.

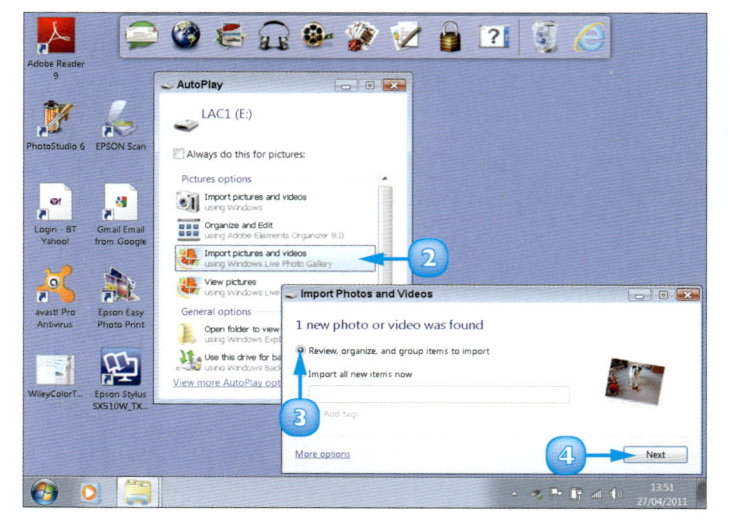

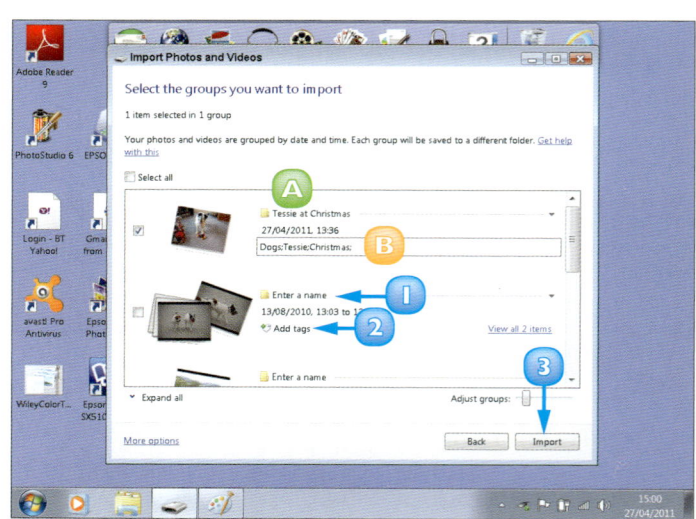

CHAPTER 11 MANAGING PICTURES

The pictures are imported to your Pictures Library and are recorded in the Windows Live Photo Gallery as thumbnails or small icons.

4 Click the **Windows Explorer folder** on the Taskbar, double-click the **Pictures library**. Double-click your new folder to open it and check that the pictures are all there.

Delete Pictures from the Camera

1 Click **Removable Disk** and navigate down to the folder that holds the pictures.

2 Click on the first picture.

3 Press Ctrl + A to select all the pictures.

4 Click **Organize**.

5 Click **Delete**.

The pictures are deleted.

Note: *You can also press* Del *to delete the pictures.*

✓ **To disconnect the camera, click the removable device icon (🔌), click Eject and wait for the "Safe to Remove" message.**

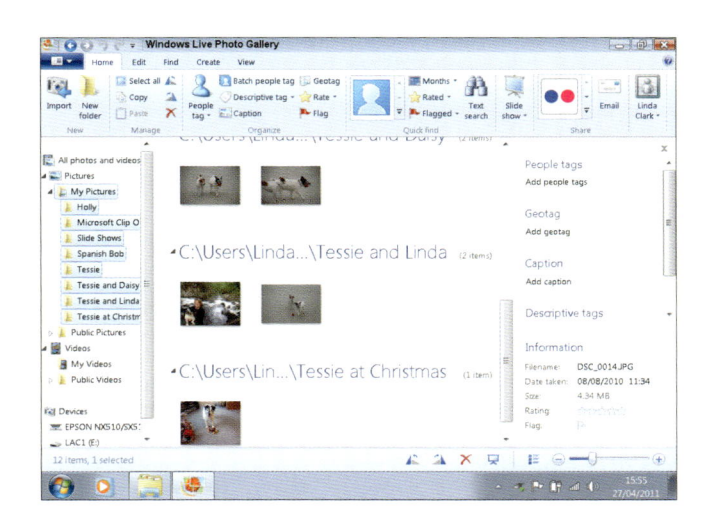

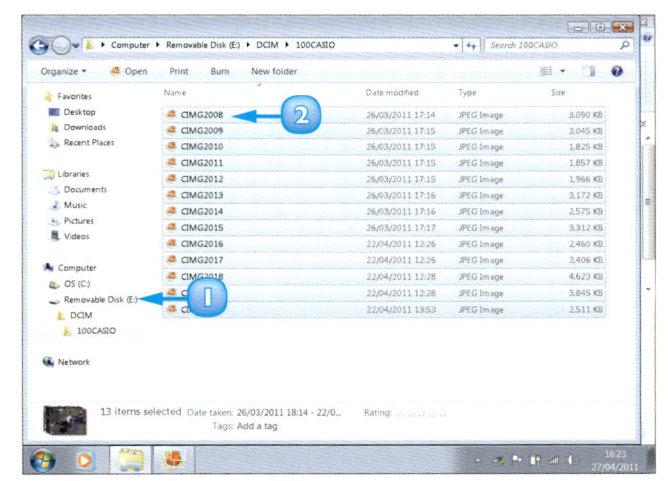

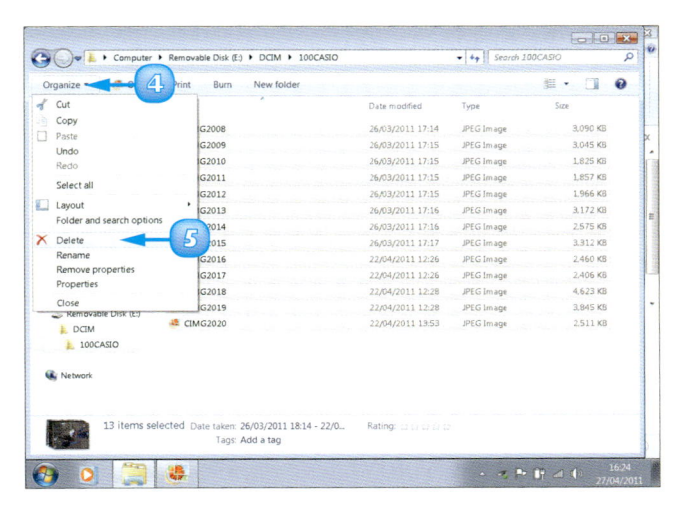

CHAPTER 11 MANAGING PICTURES

OPEN AND VIEW PICTURES

You can open and manage your pictures in the Pictures library.

You can also view and manage your pictures in Windows Live Photo Gallery.

Open Pictures

1. Click the **Windows Explorer folder** on the Taskbar.
2. Click **Pictures**.

    The Pictures library opens.

3. Double-click the folder you want to view.

    The Pictures are displayed.

4. Click the View ▾.

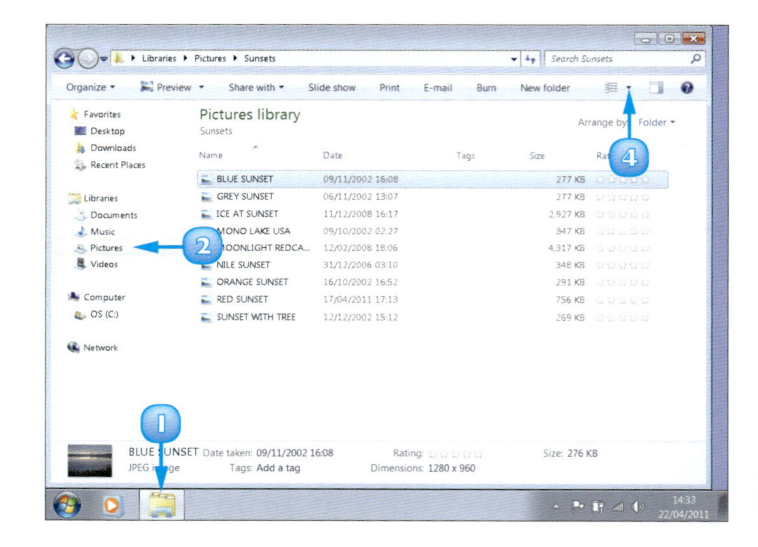

5. Drag the slider to change the size of the picture images.
6. Double-click a picture.

    Windows Live Photo Gallery opens.

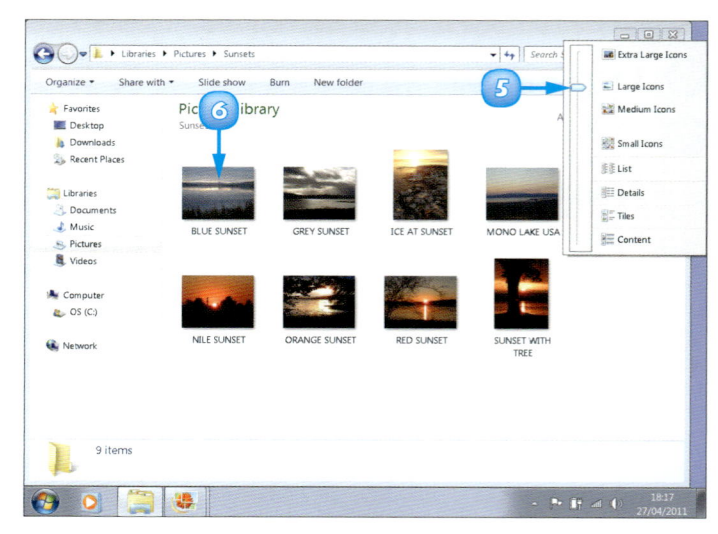

CHAPTER 11 MANAGING PICTURES

View Pictures

1. Click ◄ and ► to view other pictures.

2. Click ⬈ or ⬉ to rotate the image.

3. Click ✛ to view the image at its actual size.

4. Point to the picture (✋ appears). Hold down the left mouse button and move the mouse to view parts of the picture more closely.

Note: *Click ⛶ to return to the view images screen.*

5. Use the slider to zoom in and out.

6. Click **Slide show** (or 🖵) to view pictures in a slide show.

7. Shake the mouse to open the Slide Show menu.

8. Click **Back to Photo Gallery** or `Esc` to return to Windows Live Photo Gallery.

Delete a Picture

1. Click ✗ to delete a picture.

   The Delete File window appears.

2. Click **Yes** and the picture is deleted and sent to the Recycle bin.

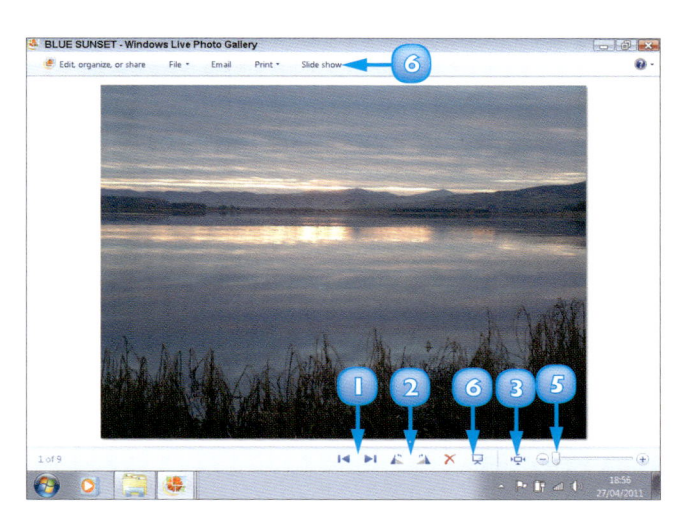

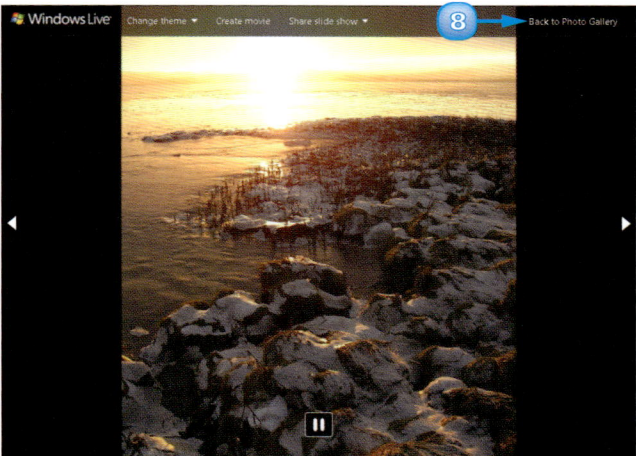

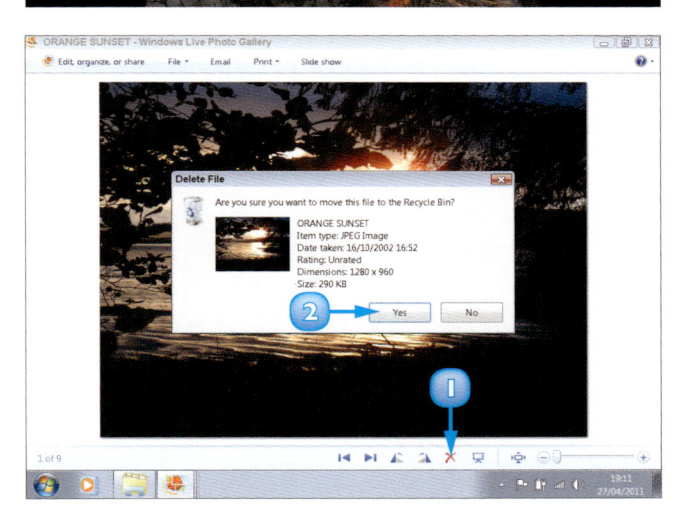

> **STOP** *Clicking* `Del` *also removes the picture from the Picture library and sends it to the Recycle bin.*

CHAPTER 11 MANAGING PICTURES

147

ORGANISE AND FIND PICTURES

Windows Live Photo Gallery saves small copies in icon form and keeps a record of where your pictures are stored. This could be on your computer, a CD, a flash drive or another type of storage device. When you are looking for a picture of the barbecue you had last summer out of the hundreds you have downloaded, Windows Live Photo Gallery finds it fast and you do not have to trawl through a whole summer's worth of pictures with obscure names such as CMG0599.

Tag People

1. Click **Start** and click **Windows Live Photo Gallery**.

   Note: You may have to click All Programs.

   Windows Live Photo Gallery opens at the Home menu.

2. Click a picture to be tagged.

   Ⓐ *Information about the picture is displayed.*

3. Click **Add people tags**.

4. Click the **Who is this?** .

5. Click **Assign a name** and type in a name.

Note: You can also choose a name from the drop-down list.

   Ⓐ *You can rate the picture on a scale of 1 to 5.*

   Ⓑ *You can flag pictures to find them quickly.*

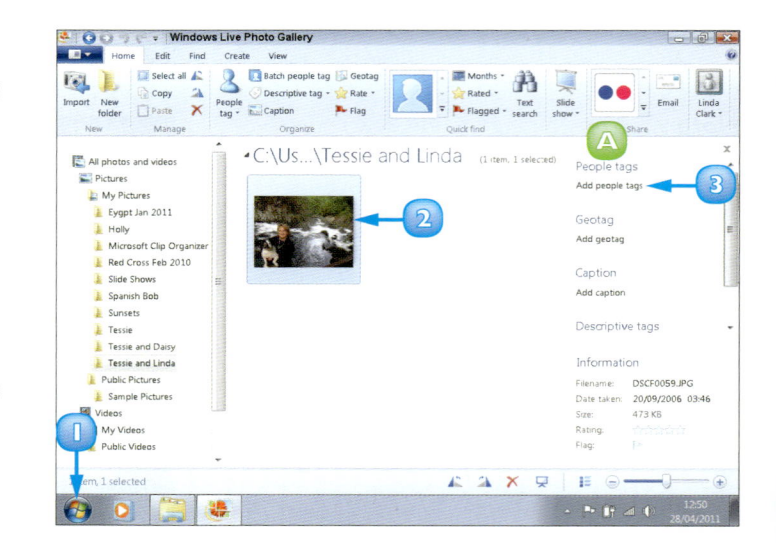

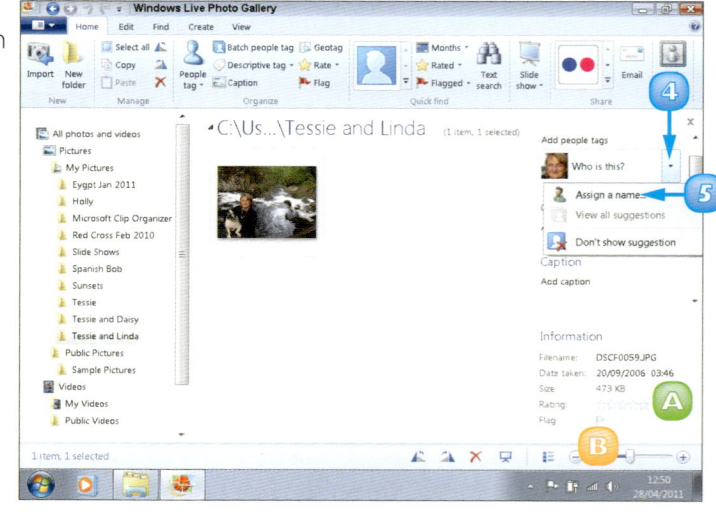

CHAPTER 11 MANAGING PICTURES

Add a Descriptive Tag

1. Click a picture to be tagged.
2. Click **Add descriptive tags**.
3. Type in the tags or choose tags from the drop-down list.

   - **A** *You can add a location using Geotag.*
   - **B** *You can add a caption.*

Find Pictures Using Text Search or People Tags

1. Click **All photos and videos**.
2. Click **Text search** in the Quick find menu.
3. Type in the name you want to find.

   The pictures are displayed.

4. Click ▼.

5. Click to choose a person.

   The pictures you have tagged for that person are displayed.

> ✓ *You can also search on Date, Rating and Flag to help you to find that elusive picture.*

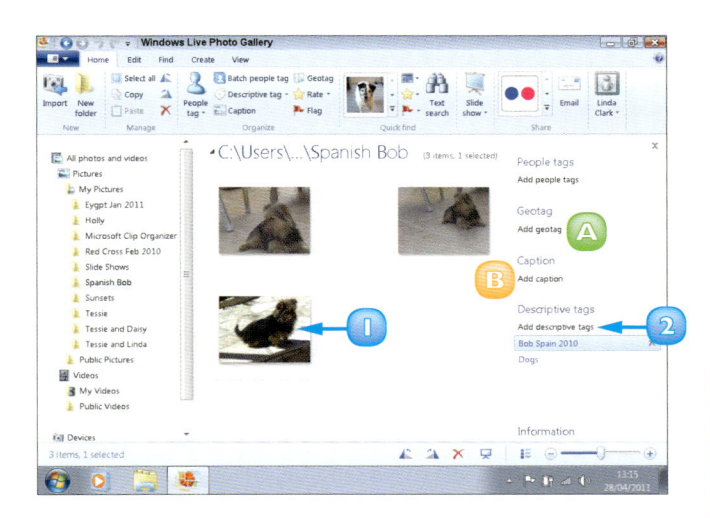

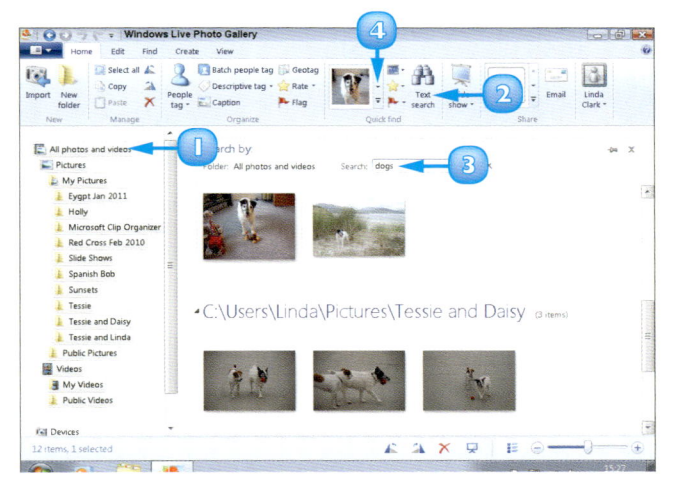

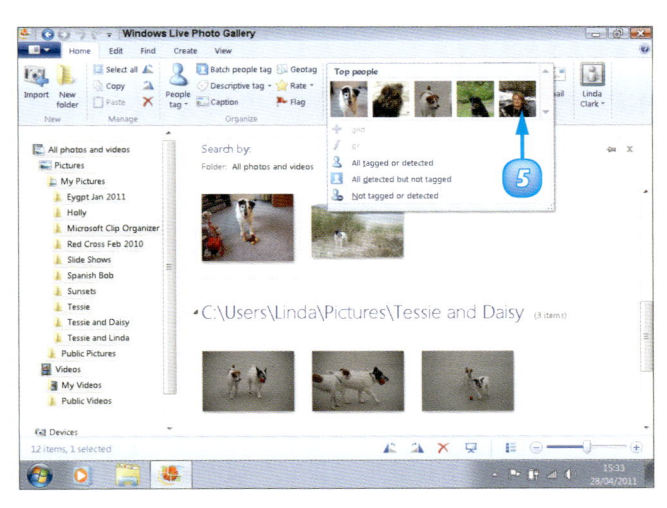

CHAPTER 11 MANAGING PICTURES

IMPROVE THE APPEARANCE OF PICTURES

Perhaps your picture is not straight, there is too much background or the picture is just too dark or light. Windows Live Photo Gallery provides some simple tools for improving the quality of your pictures.

Crop a Picture

1. Click the **Edit** tab.

   The Edit menu opens.

2. Double-click the icon of the picture to be edited.

   The picture opens.

3. Click the **Crop** icon.

   A drop-down menu appears.

4. Click **Proportion**.

5. Click **Custom**.

   A cropping mask appears over the picture.

6. Point to the mask, hold down the left mouse button and move the mouse around. When you are happy with the picture, release the mouse button.

7. Double-click the **Crop** icon.

   The picture is cropped.

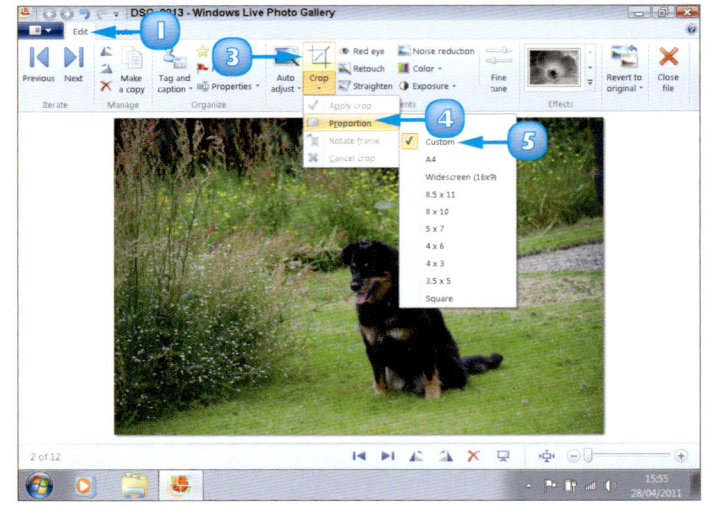

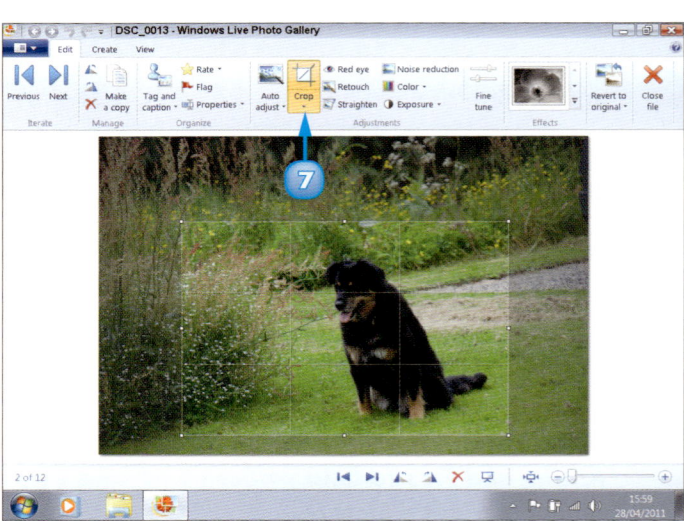

Auto Adjust a Picture

① Click the **Auto adjust** ▾.

Note: *You can straighten the picture, reduce noise, and correct colour and exposure.*

Manually Adjust a Picture

② Click **Fine Tune**.

The Manual Adjustments menu appears.

Straighten a Picture

③ Click **Straighten photo**.

④ Drag the slider until the picture is straight.

⑤ Click ✓.

Adjust Exposure

① Click **Adjust exposure**.

② Drag the slider to adjust the **Brightness** of the picture.

③ Drag the slider to adjust the **Contrast** of the picture.

④ Drag the slider to adjust the **Shadows** in the picture.

⑤ Drag the slider to adjust the **Highlights** in the picture.

⑥ Click **Close file** to return to the picture organiser menu.

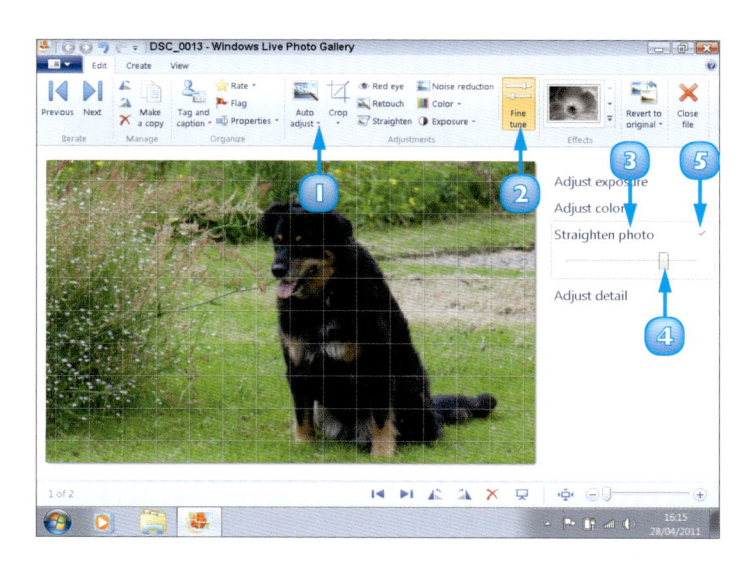

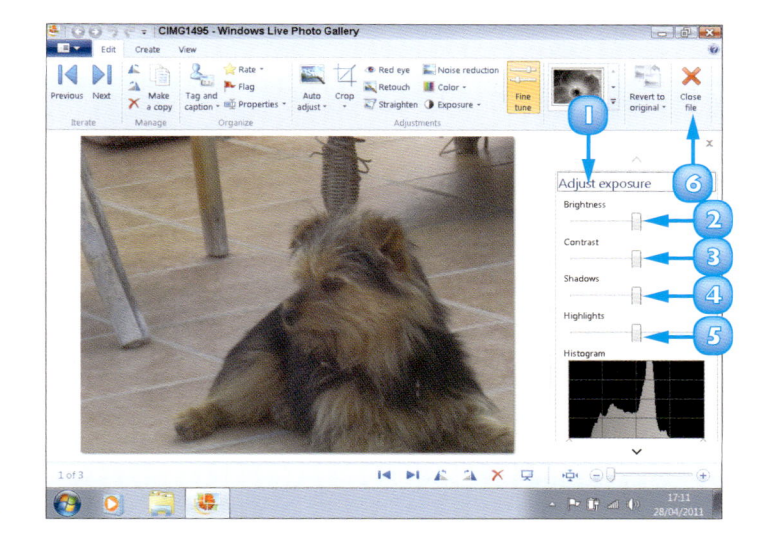

> *You can also adjust the colour and detail from the Fine Tune menu.*

CHAPTER 11 MANAGING PICTURES

SAVE PICTURES TO A CD OR FLASH DRIVE

You may want to send copies of your pictures to a friend or keep a copy in a safe place. You can burn pictures to a CD or DVD through Windows Live Photo Gallery. Windows 7 can also be used to burn a CD or DVD. We use this method to copy pictures to a flash drive or memory stick. You can also use these methods for copying other types of file.

Burn Pictures to a CD

1. Open Windows Live Photo Gallery.
2. Put a CD into the CD or DVD drive of your computer.
3. Find the pictures to be copied.
4. Click the check box at the left corner of pictures to be copied.
5. Click the **File** menu.

6. Click **Burn**.
7. Click **Burn a CD**.
8. Click **With a CD/DVD player**.
9. Click **Next**.
10. Click **Burn to disc** and **Next**.

When it is finished, the disc is ejected.

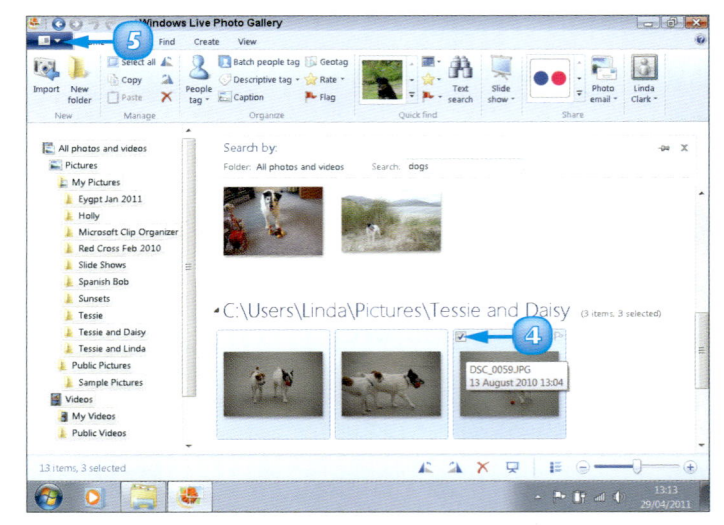

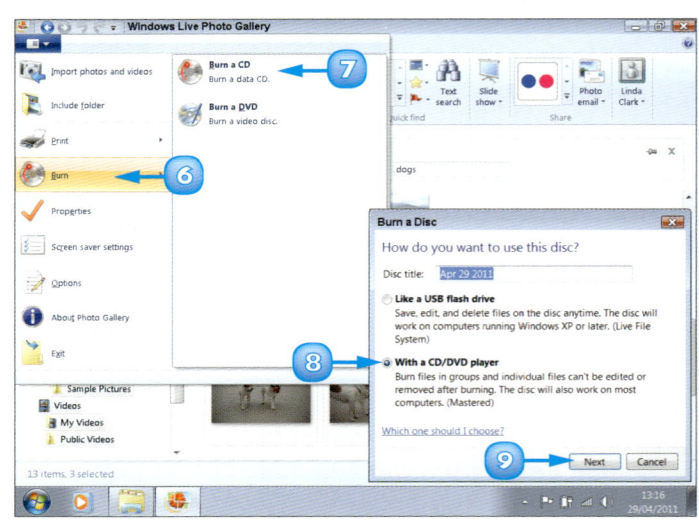

CHAPTER 11 MANAGING PICTURES

Copy Pictures to a Flash Drive

1. Insert a flash drive into a USB port.

   The Autoplay menu appears.

2. Click ✖.

3. Click **Windows Explorer**.

4. Click **Pictures**.

   The Pictures Library opens.

5. Double-click the folder you want to copy from.

   The folder opens and the pictures are displayed.

6. Press and hold down `Ctrl` and click to choose the pictures.

7. Click **Organize**.

8. Click **Copy**.

9. Click the **flash drive**.

10. Click **Organize**.

11. Click **Paste**.

    Copies of the pictures are transferred to the flash drive.

    ✓ **To disconnect the flash drive, click the removable device icon (▯), click Eject and wait for the "Safe to Remove" message.**

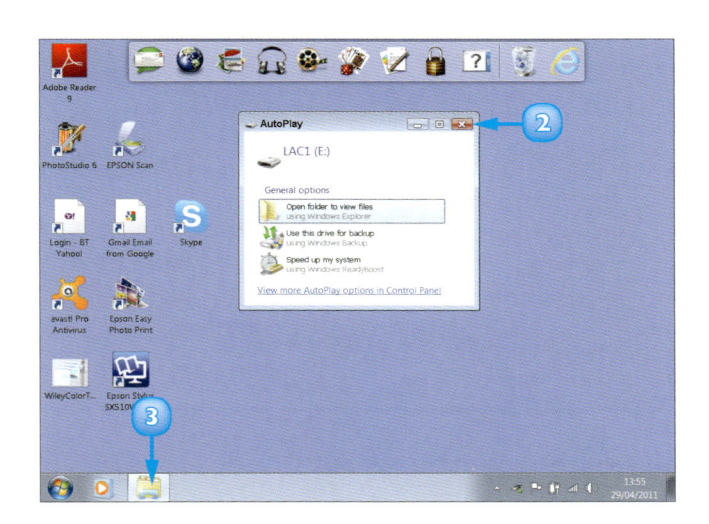

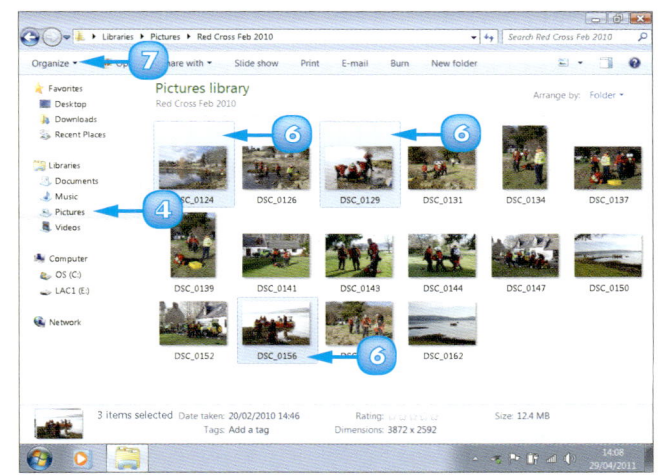

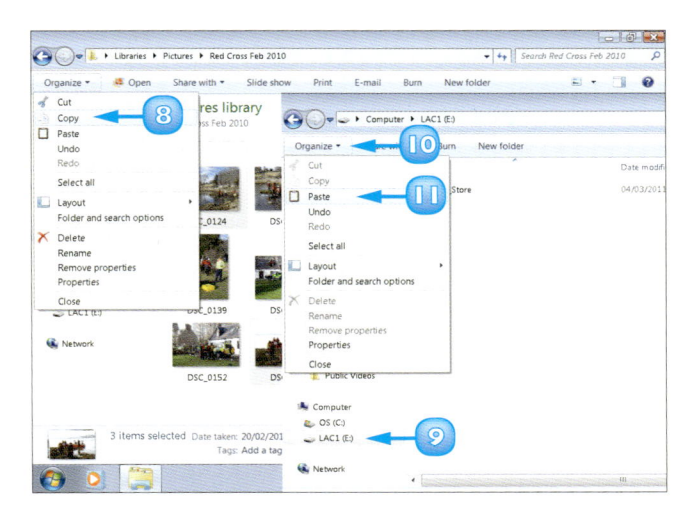

CHAPTER 11 MANAGING PICTURES

153

SHARE PICTURES ON THE INTERNET

One way of sharing your pictures with others is to put them on the Internet. There are various websites to choose from depending on whether you wish to keep your pictures private within a small group of family and friends or make them public, allowing anybody anywhere in the world to see them. We look at SkyDrive, part of the Windows Live package.

Upload to Windows SkyDrive

1. Open Windows Live Photo Gallery.

2. Find the pictures to be copied.

3. Click the check box at the left corner of pictures to be copied.

4. Click the **Share**.

5. Click **SkyDrive**.

   The Publish on Windows Live SkyDrive menu opens.

6. Type in a name for the folder that will be created.

7. Click and choose **Some friends**.

You can change the level of publication later, if you wish.

When you publish widely on the Internet, anyone can see the images. This could make your data vulnerable to attack.

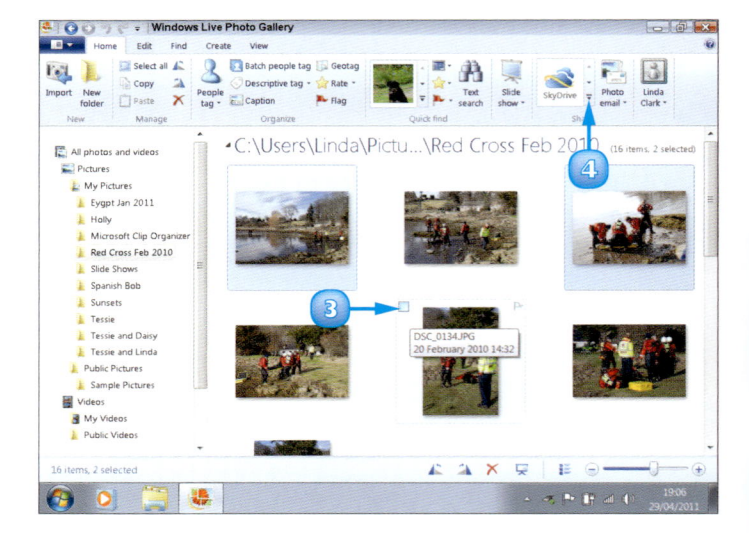

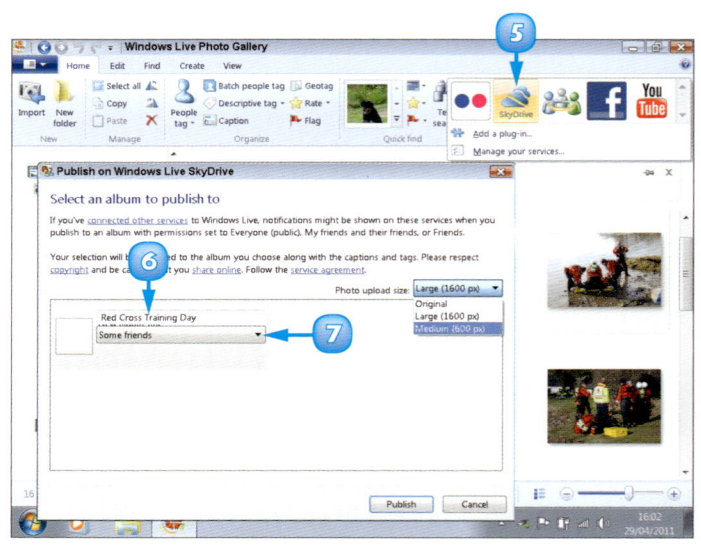

CHAPTER 11 MANAGING PICTURES

⑧ Click the **Photo upload size** ▼.

⑨ Click **Medium**.

⑩ Click **Publish**.

The Uploading information screen opens.

⑪ Click **View online**.

The folder opens in Windows Live SkyDrive.

Share with Friends

① Click **Share**.

② Click **Send a link**.

③ Type in an email address.

④ Click **Send**.

Note: You can send a link to any email address but the recipient needs a Windows Live account or a Hotmail address to access your SkyDrive.

> ✓ **To log in to SkyDrive, type skydrive.live.com into the address bar of Internet Explorer and sign in.**

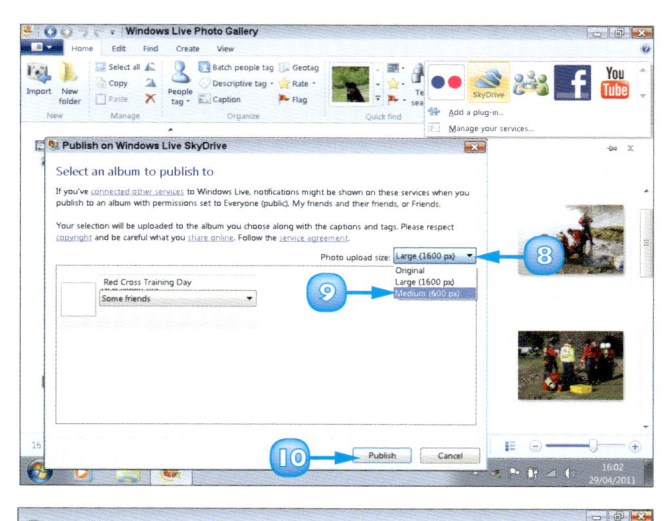

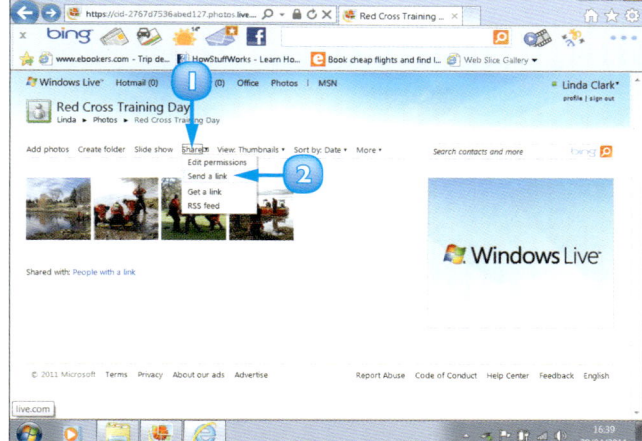

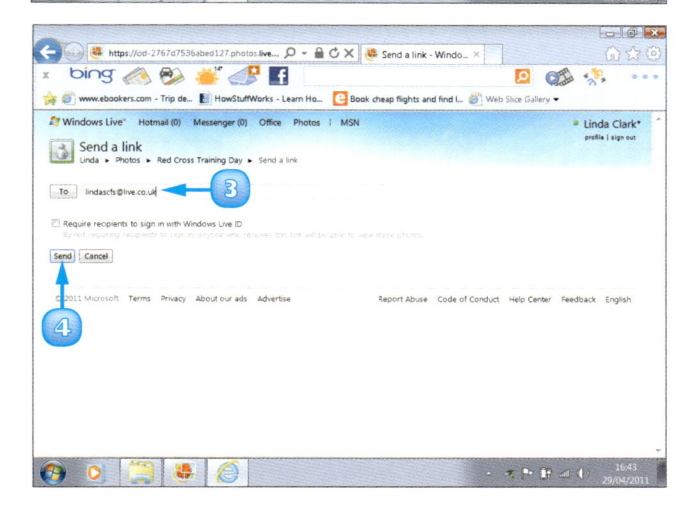

CHAPTER 11 MANAGING PICTURES

CONTENTS

- **158** Start and Explore Excel 2010
- **160** Start Using Excel 2010
- **162** Set Up Columns and Rows
- **164** Add Information and Enhance Cells
- **166** Keep Accounts
- **171** Preview and Print

12
KEEPING RECORDS

We now look at another part of the Microsoft Office 2010 software, Excel. This is a spreadsheet program used for keeping records. These may be the names and addresses of all the people you send Christmas cards to or, if you are a club membership secretary, the contact details of members. You can keep a check on your personal finances or record income and expenditure for an exhibition or other event in which you are involved.

START AND EXPLORE EXCEL 2010

In this section, we open Excel 2010 and get familiar with its interface. Excel has a ribbon menu system, similar to the one in Word 2010. Although some aspects are different, the main features can be found in the same or very similar places. The ribbon is divided into eight menus. This section also introduces an alternative way of opening programs.

Start Excel 2010

1. Click **Start**.

2. Click **All Programs** (it changes to Back).

   The All Programs menu appears.

3. Click **Microsoft Office**.

   The Microsoft Office menu appears.

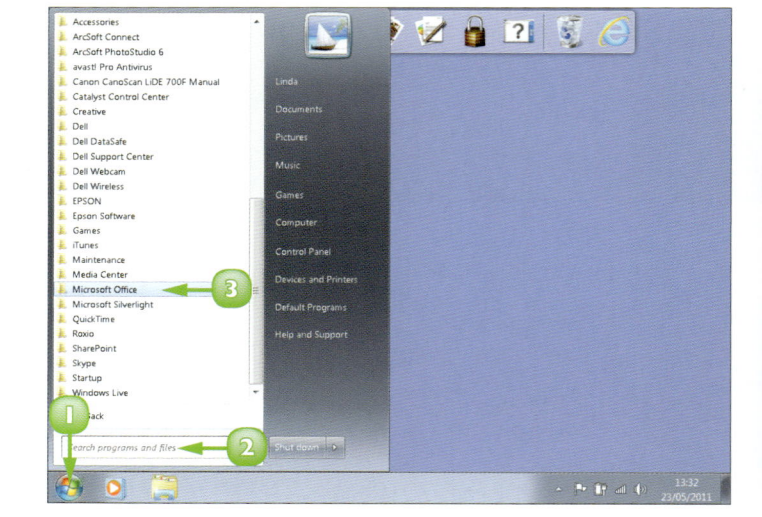

4. Click **Microsoft Excel 2010**.

   The Microsoft Excel 2010 window appears on the desktop.

Note: If your computer has Microsoft Office Starter installed, click **Microsoft Excel Starter 2010**.

✓ *After you have used Excel 2010 a few times, it should appear on the main Start menu.*

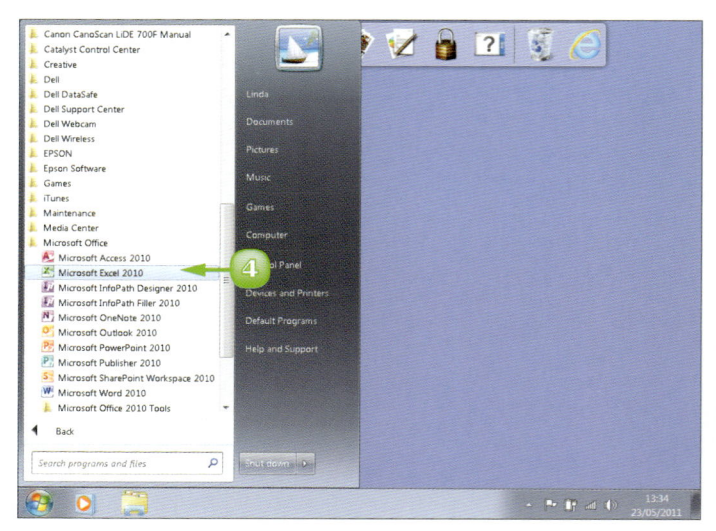

CHAPTER 12 KEEPING RECORDS

A Title Bar

The title bar displays the name of the current workbook.

B Quick Access Toolbar

This area gives you one-click access to a few often-used features. To learn how to customise it, see Chapter 3.

C Window Controls

You use these controls to minimise, maximise, restore and close Excel 2010's application window.

D Workbook Window Controls

You use these controls to minimise, maximise, restore, and close the current workbook window.

E Help Button

Click this button to access help information about Excel 2010.

F Ribbon Minimise Button

Click this button to reduce the size of the Excel 2010 ribbon.

G Ribbon

This area gives you access to all of Excel 2010's commands, options and features.

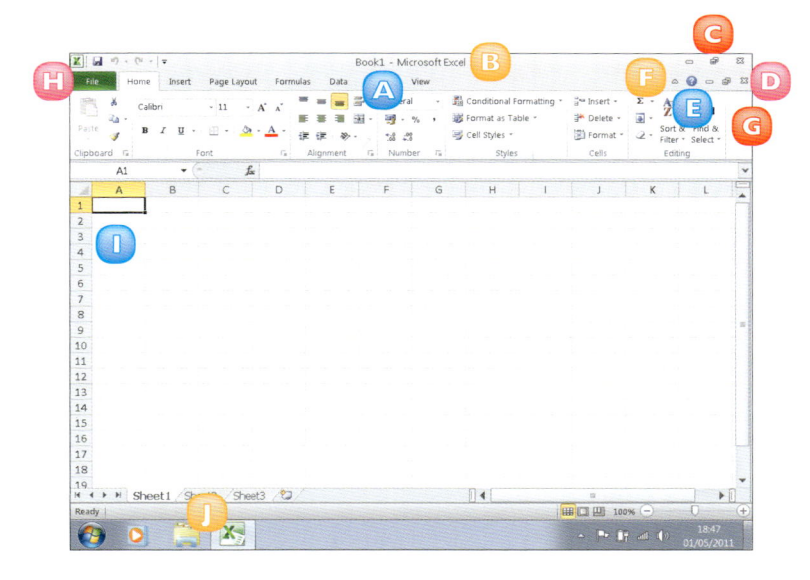

H File Tab

Click this tab to access file-related commands, such as Save and Open.

I Worksheet

This area displays the current worksheet and it is where you will do most of your work.

J Status Bar

This area displays messages about Excel 2010's current status, the results of certain operations and other information.

Note: *If you are using Microsoft Office Starter, the screen may look a little different.*

START USING EXCEL 2010

Excel 2010 is very useful for keeping lists of things, such as names and addresses. We start using Excel 2010 by creating a list of contacts.

Create a Contact List

1 Open Excel 2010.

Note: All the cells have a unique address – the columns across are labelled A, B, C etc. and the rows down are labelled 1, 2, 3 and so on.

2 Click in cell **A1** and enter **name1**.

3 Use **Tab** or → to move to the next cell.

Note: You can also point to the cell and click.

4 Enter **name2** into cell **B1**.

5 Enter **add1** into cell **C1**.

6 Enter **add2** into cell **D1**.

7 Enter **town** into cell **E1**.

8 Enter **postcode** into cell **F1**.

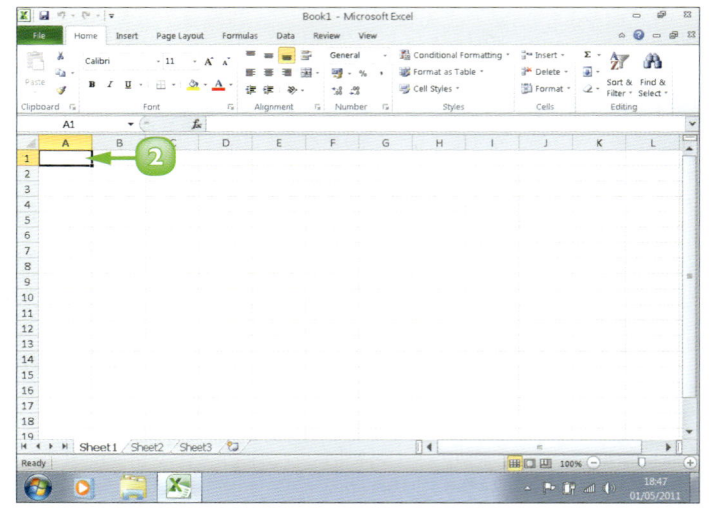

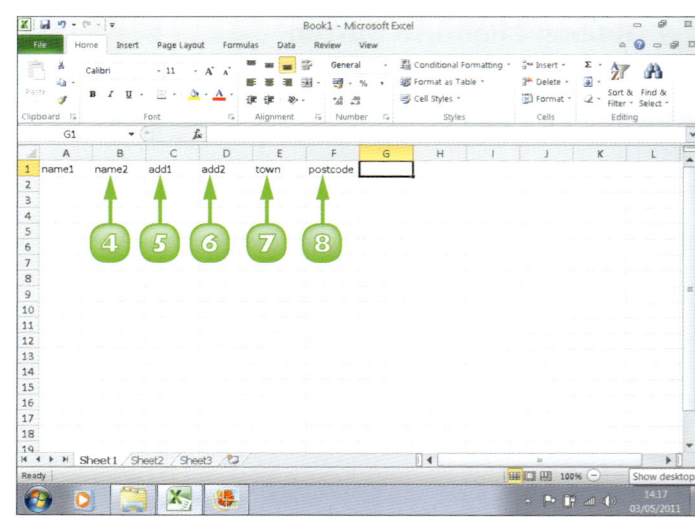

CHAPTER 12 KEEPING RECORDS

9 Click cell **A2** and enter the first name of a contact.

Fill in the rest of the record.

10 Click cell **A3** and add another contact.

A *You can also click in the formula bar and enter a value there.*

Save a Spreadsheet

1 Click the **File** tab.

2 Click **Save As**.

The Save As menu appears.

3 Type in a name for the spreadsheet.

4 Click **Save.**

The file is saved and you can continue changing the spreadsheet.

Correct Mistakes

1 Click on the cell to be corrected.

The formula bar above the cells also shows the cell contents.

2 Click in the formula bar where the mistake is and correct it.

You can also double-click the place in the cell where the mistake has occurred.

3 Use the cursor to move to another cell or press Enter to complete the correction.

You can use ↶ *and* ↷ *to correct errors as they are made.*

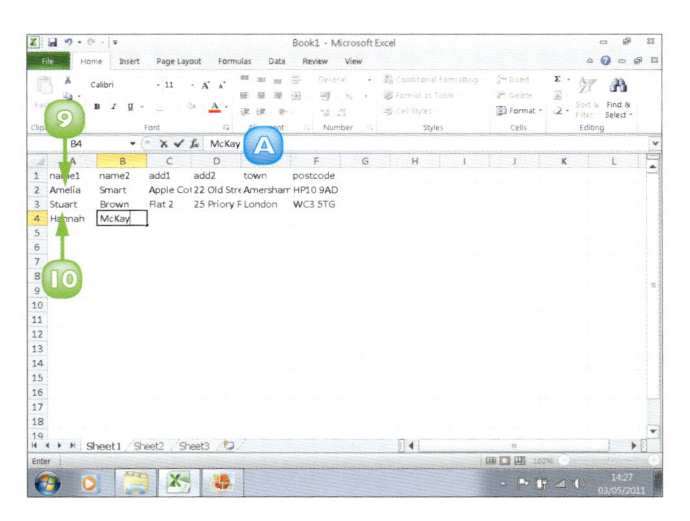

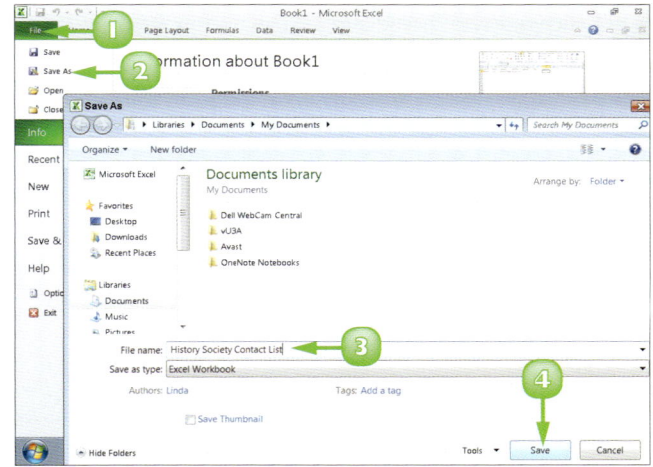

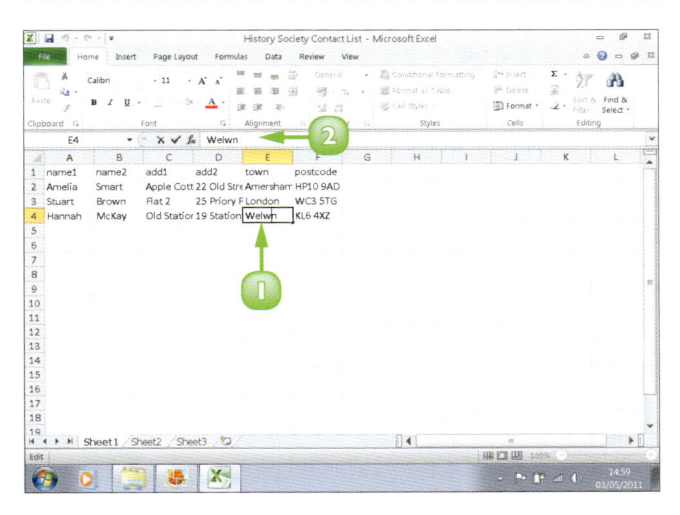

CHAPTER 12 KEEPING RECORDS

SET UP COLUMNS AND ROWS

To make your data easier to read, you can adjust the sizes of the columns and rows. You can also change the styles of cells to distinguish headings from normal data.

Manually Change Column Size

1. Hover over the edge of the column title bar (✥ changes to ↔).

2. Click and drag to the right to make the column wider.

3. Release the cursor when the column is wide enough.

Automatically Change Column Sizes

1. Click cell **A1**.

2. Hold down the left mouse button and drag across the titles. Release the mouse button.

   The titles are highlighted.

3. Click **Format**.

4. Click **Column width**.

5. Enter the required width.

6. Click **OK**.

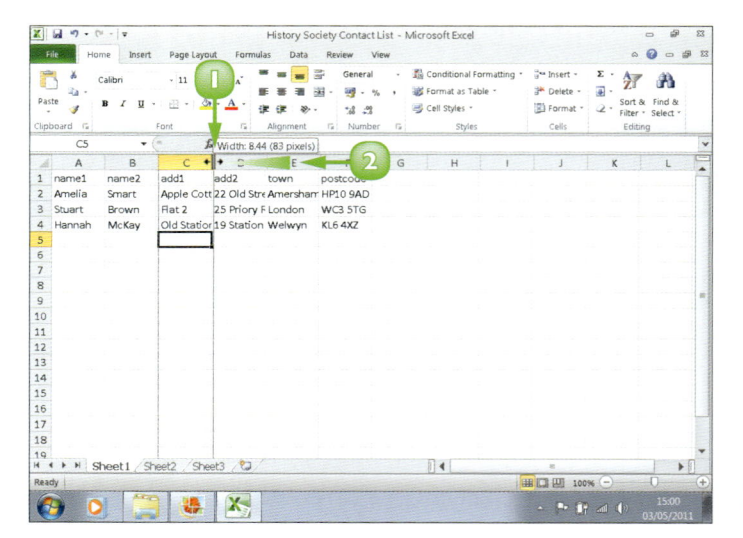

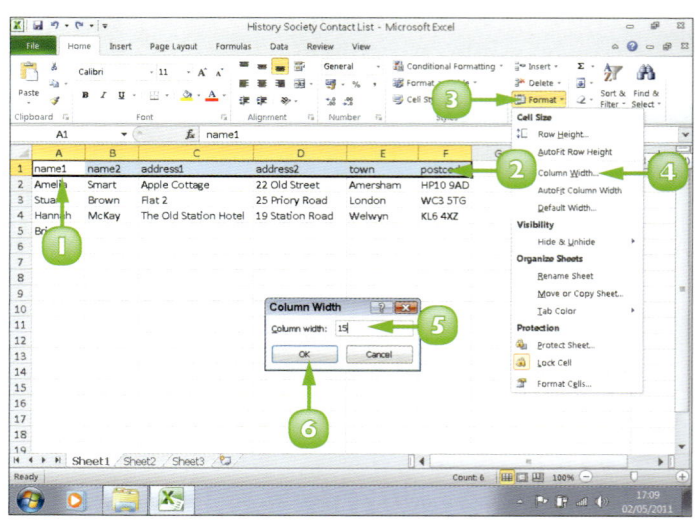

CHAPTER 12 KEEPING RECORDS

Change Row Sizes Automatically

1. Click on cell **A1**.
2. Hold down the left mouse button and drag down the column. Release the mouse button.

    The column is highlighted.
3. Click **Format**.
4. Click **Row height**.
5. Enter the required height.
6. Click **OK**.

Change Cell Styles

1. Highlight the column headings (cells A1 to F1).
2. Click **Cell Styles**.

    The Cell Styles menu is displayed.
3. Click a style to choose it.

    The highlighted text appears in the new style.
4. Click 🖫 to save your work.
5. Click ✖ to close the spreadsheet.

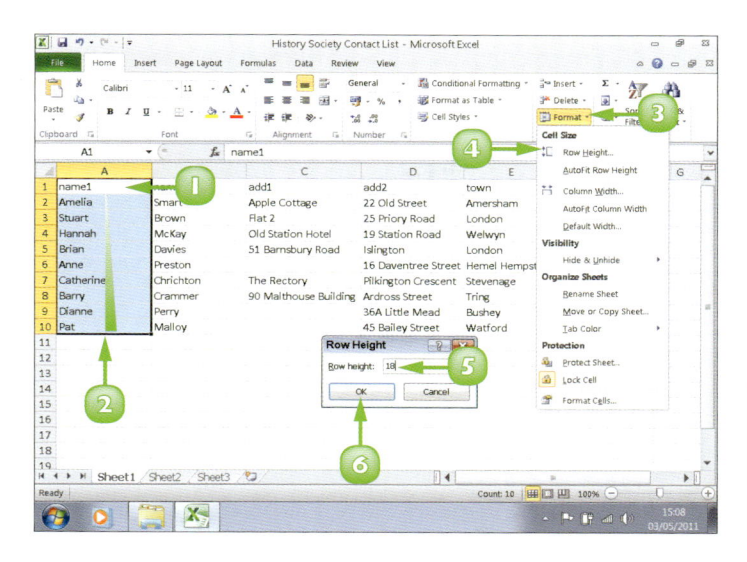

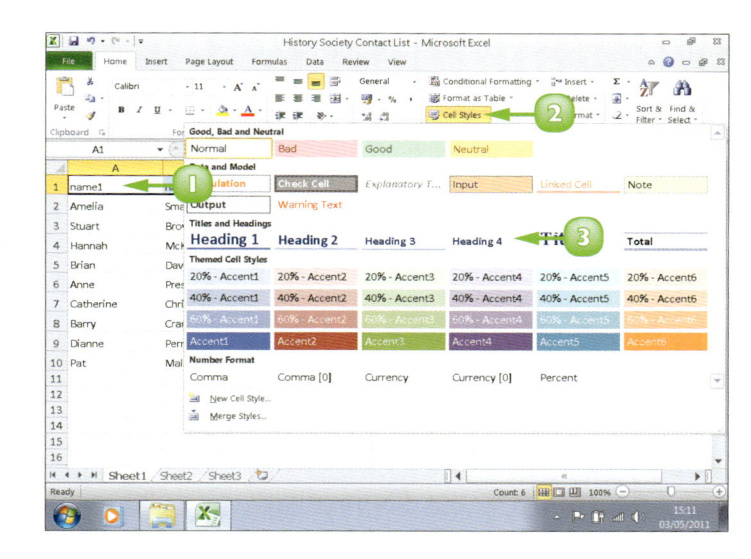

CHAPTER 12 KEEPING RECORDS

ADD INFORMATION AND ENHANCE CELLS

You can open a spreadsheet directly from the Start menu without opening Excel 2010 first. If you decide you need more information in your spreadsheet, you can insert extra rows or columns. You can also add formatting to individual cells.

Open an Existing Spreadsheet

1. Click **Start**.
2. Click **Microsoft Excel 2010**.
3. Click your document on the Recent list.

   A *You can click **Pin to this list** (📌) to ensure your contact list is easily found.*

   The contact list spreadsheet opens.

Insert a Column

1. Click cell **F1**.
2. Click the **Insert** ▾.
3. Click **Insert Sheet Columns**.

   A new column F is inserted to the left of the postcode column, which becomes column G.

4. Click (the new) **F1** and type **county**.
5. Type in the county names to update your contact list.
6. Click 💾.

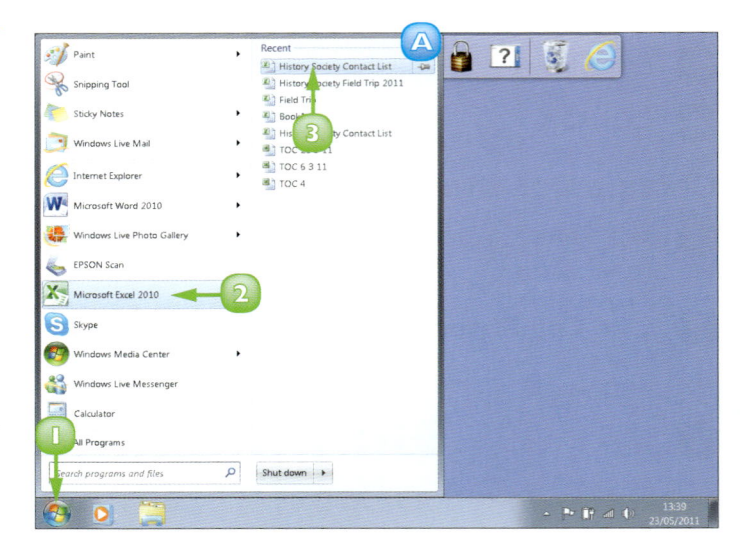

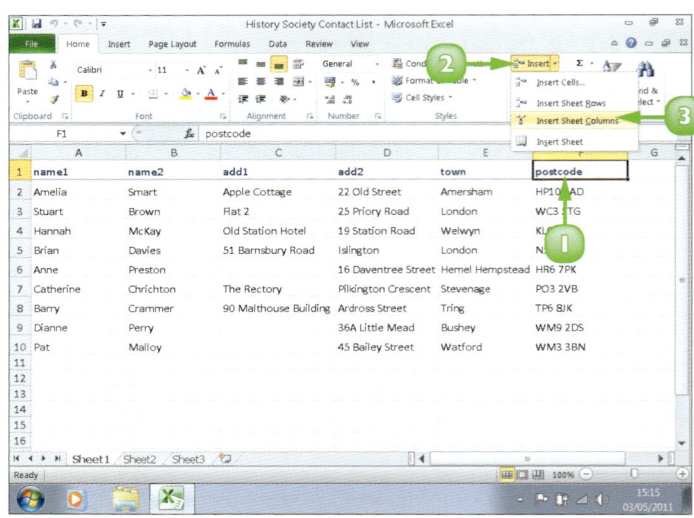

CHAPTER 12 KEEPING RECORDS

Insert Rows

1. Click cell **A1**.
2. Click the **Insert** ▾.
3. Click **Insert Sheet Rows**.

   A row is inserted above the list.
4. Repeat step 2.

Enhance Text

1. Click cell **A1** and type a title for your list.

   The text stretches across cells.

   Note: *The Formula Bar shows that the text appears only in cell A1.*
2. Click **B** to make the title bold.
3. Click **A˙** to make the title text larger.
4. Click **A** to see the colour palette.
5. Click a colour to change the colour of the title text.

   Ⓐ You can click the **Font** ▾ to change the font in the selected cells.

   Ⓑ Click the **Font Size** ▾ to select a font size for the selected cells.

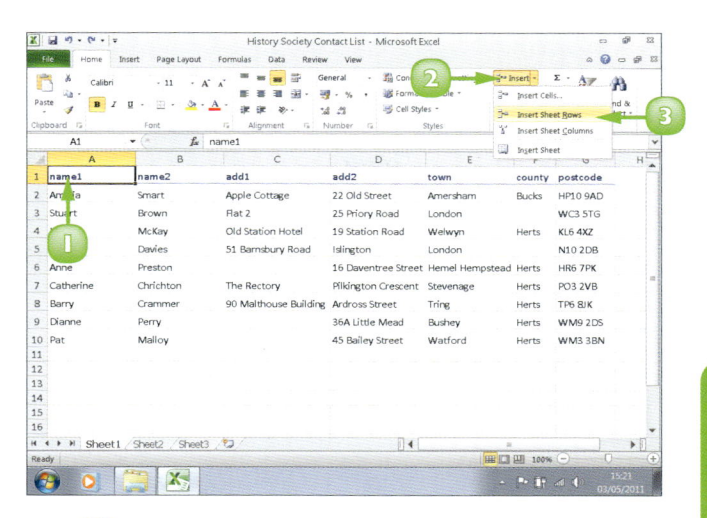

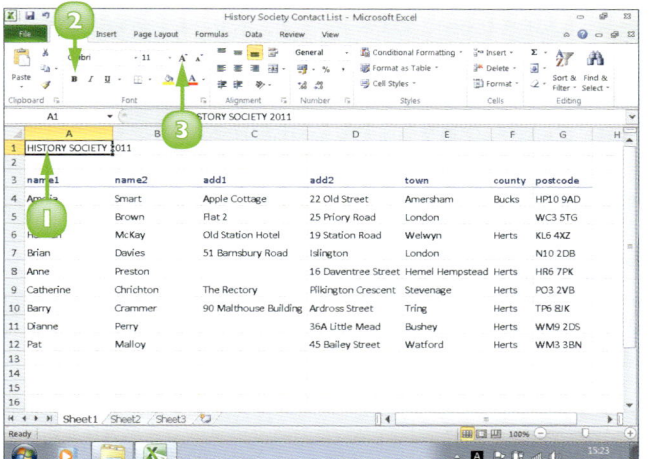

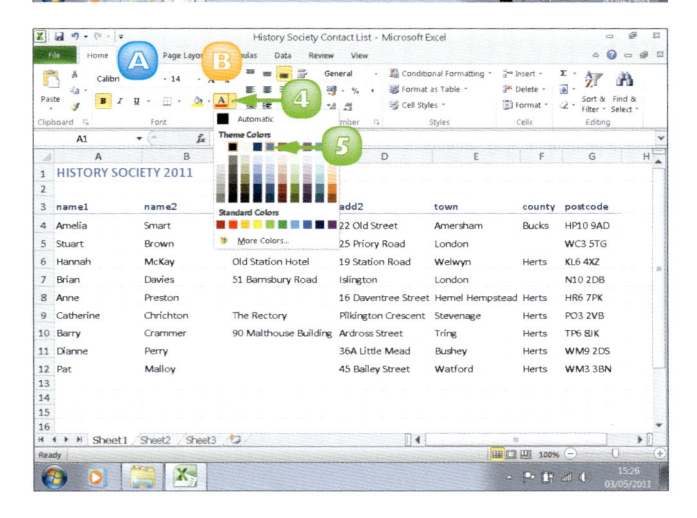

CHAPTER 12 KEEPING RECORDS

KEEP ACCOUNTS

With a simple spreadsheet, you can keep accurate records of your finances. If you are responsible for organising an event, Excel 2010 makes it much easier to keep track. When it comes to reporting back, you can present this spreadsheet to others.

Create an Accounts Spreadsheet

1. Open Excel 2010.
2. Click cell **A1** and type the title.
3. Click cell **A2** and type the date.
4. Click cell **A4** and type **Income**.
5. Click cell **E4** and type **Expenditure**.

Save the Accounts Spreadsheet

1. Click the **File** tab.
2. Click **Save as**.
3. Type in a name for the spreadsheet.
4. Click **Save**.

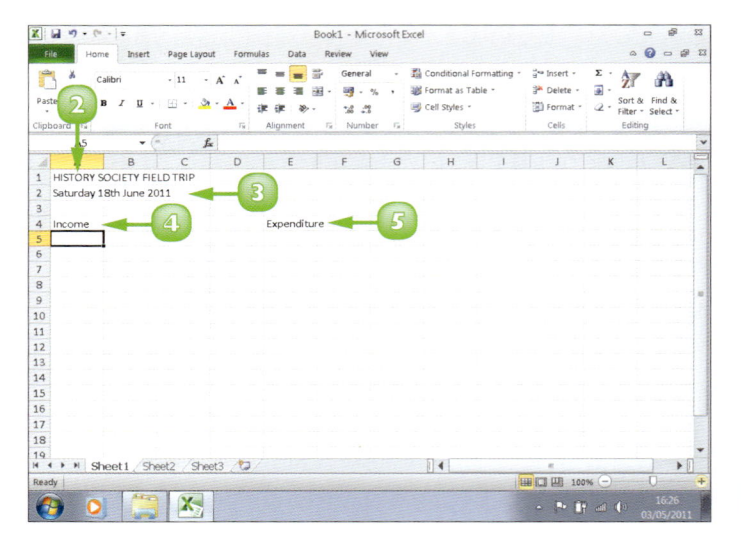

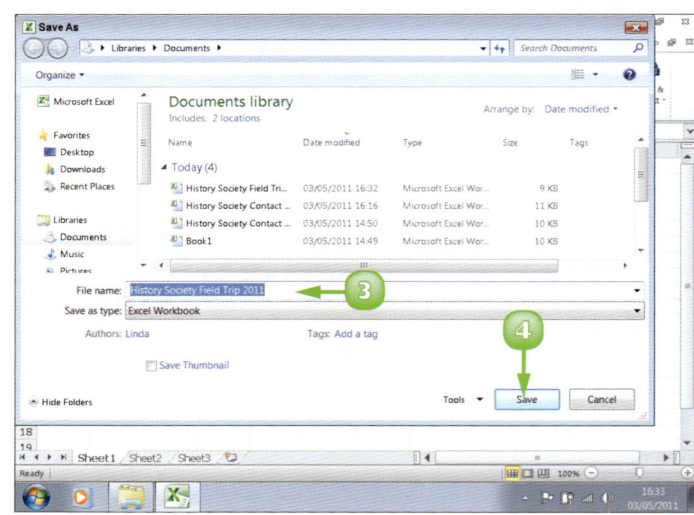

CHAPTER 12 KEEPING RECORDS

Improve the Layout

1. Widen column **A**.
2. Widen column **E**.
3. Click cell **C5** and type **£**.
4. Click ≡ to centre the text.
5. Click cell **G5** and type **£**.
6. Repeat Step 4.

7. Highlight cells **A1** and **A2**.
8. Click A˘.
9. Click cell **A4**.
10. Click **B**.
11. Click cell **E4** and click **B**.

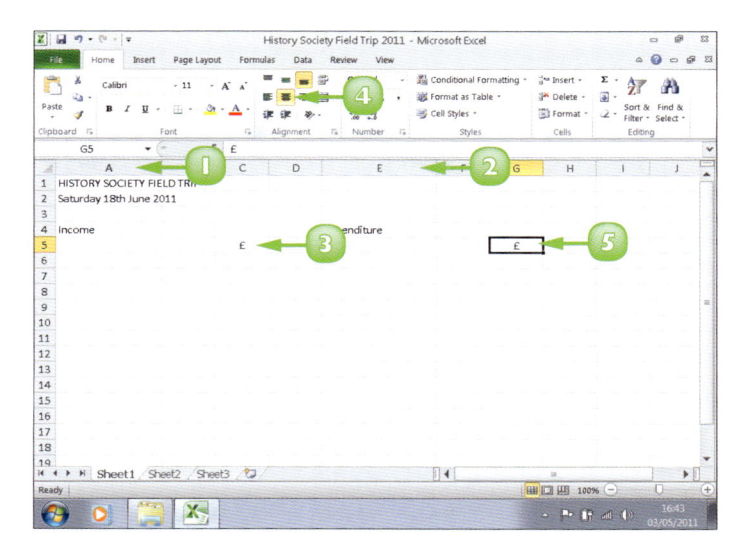

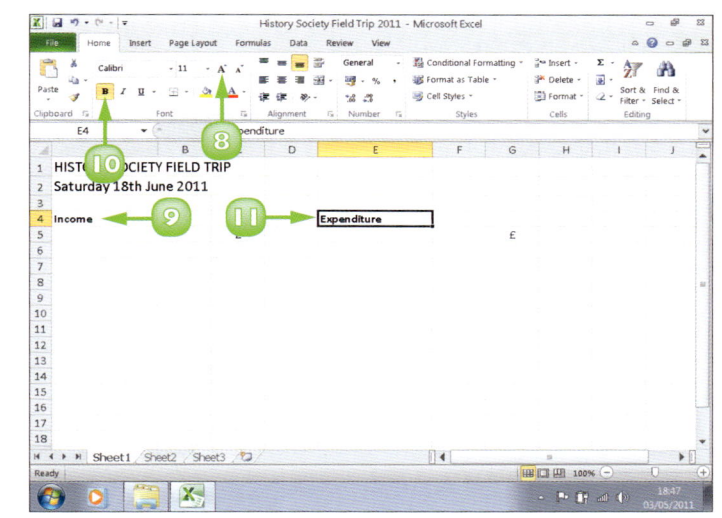

continued →

KEEP ACCOUNTS *(continued)*

When you enter figures into a spreadsheet, you can use formulae to make Excel 2010 calculate totals automatically. You can also format cells containing monetary values so that they automatically show a pound sign and two digits after the decimal point.

Enter Figures and Formulae

1. Type in the income and expenditure details.

2. Click cell **G10** and press ▭.

   The equals sign tells Excel 2010 that this is a formula. What you type appears in the Formula Bar.

3. Type **F8+F9**.

   The sum of the two numbers appears in cell G10.

4. Click cell **G6**.

5. Hold the left mouse button down and drag to **G12**.

6. Release the mouse button.

   The cells are highlighted.

7. Click **Σ** to put the total of the selected cells in cell **G12**.

8. Repeat Steps 4 to 7 for cells C6 to C12.

✓ *If you click the ▼ next to Σ, you can select other functions.*

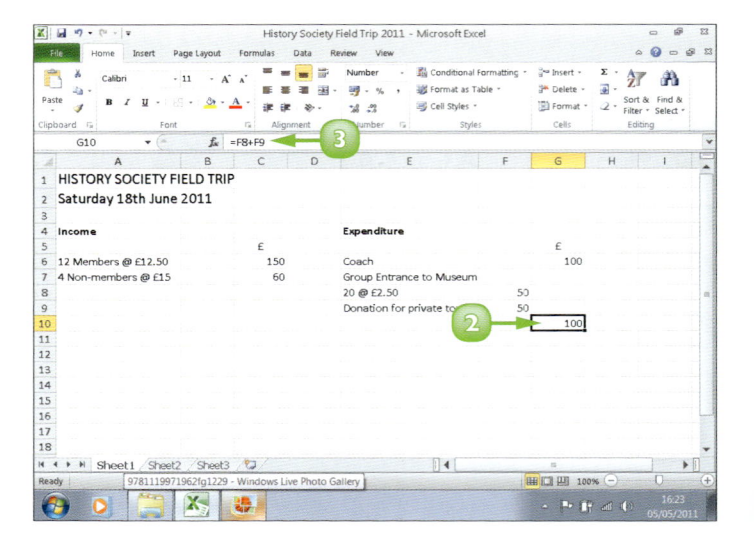

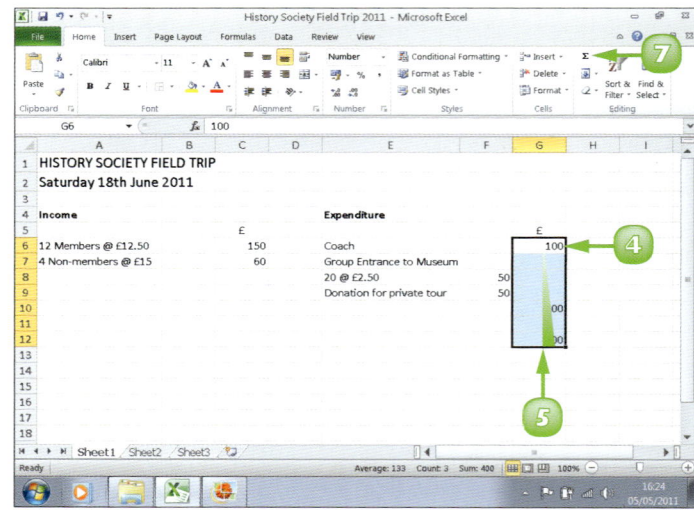

Create a Final Total

1. Click cell **A14** and type **Excess of Income over Expenditure**.

2. Click cell **C14** and type **=C12-G12** to subtract one number from the other.

Format Cells for Currency

1. Highlight cells **C6** to **C14**.

2. Click ⁖⁰⁰ to display the numbers with two decimal places.

3. Highlight cells **F8** and **F9** and click ⁖⁰⁰ .

4. Highlight cells **G6** to **G12** and click ⁖⁰⁰ .

5. Click cell **C12**.

6. Click the **Number ▾**.

7. Click **Currency**.

8. Repeat for cell **G12**.

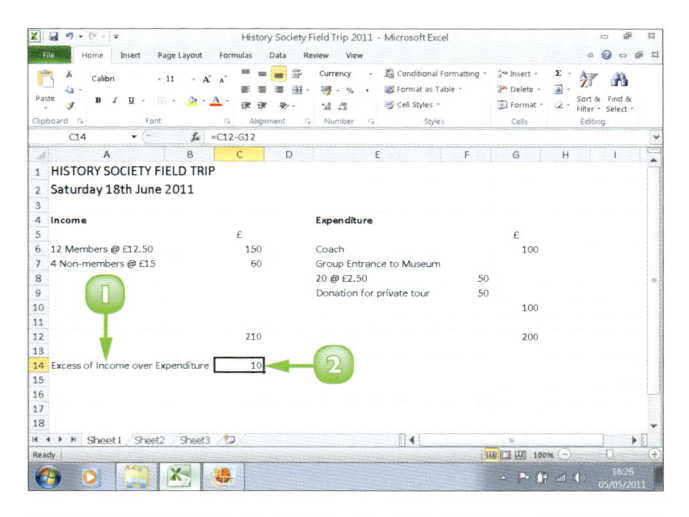

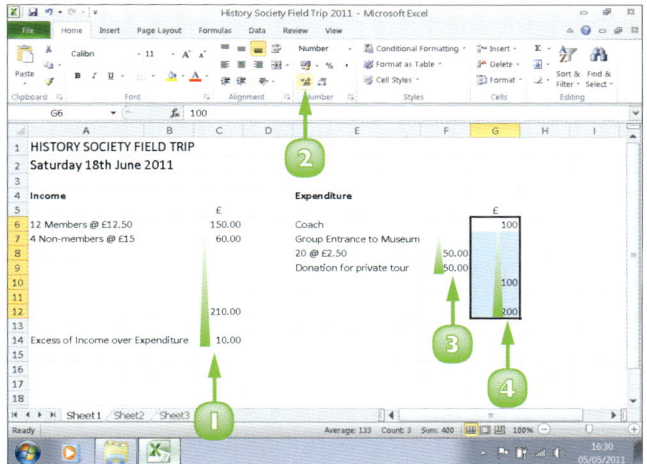

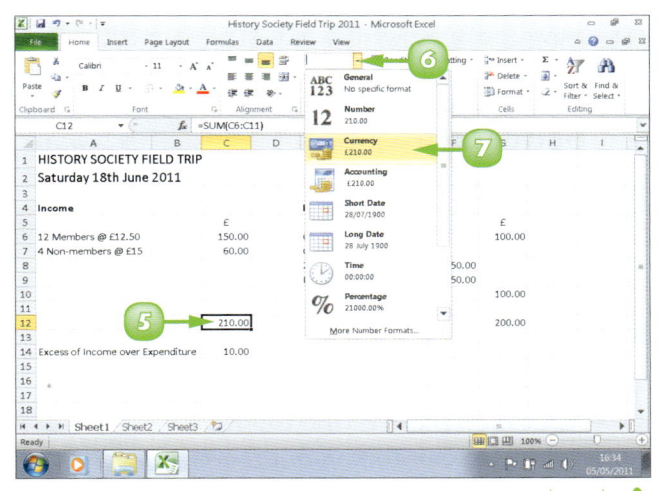

continued ➡

CHAPTER 12 KEEPING RECORDS

KEEP ACCOUNTS (continued)

It can be helpful to put lines under totals, as you would in a paper accounts book. Excel 2010 lets you do this to spreadsheet cells.

Add Lines to Cells

1. Click cell **F9**.
2. Click ⊞.
3. Click **Bottom Border**.

4. Click cell **G12**.
5. Click ⊞.
6. Click on **Top and Double Bottom Border**.
7. Repeat for cell **C12**.

✓ We have used Add, Subtract and Sum but there are many other formulae available. Click the Question mark at the top right of the screen to find out more.

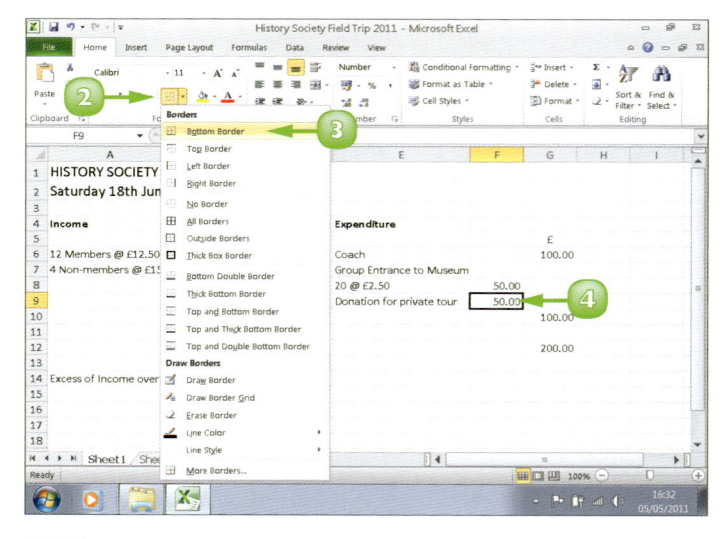

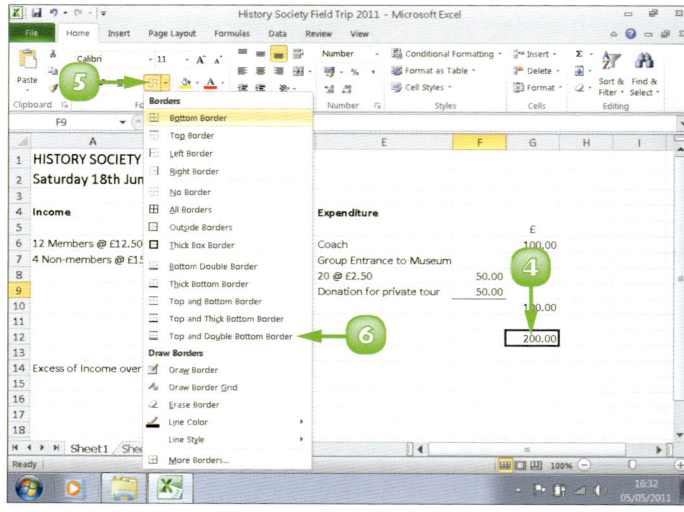

CHAPTER 12 KEEPING RECORDS

PREVIEW AND PRINT

Spreadsheets are working documents and are not meant to be printed out. Occasionally, however, it is useful to be able to do so. For example, you may need to print out your accounts to show someone else.

1. Click the **File** tab.
2. Click **Print**.

   The Print menu appears.

   A You can see the spreadsheet in the Preview window.

3. Scroll down the **Settings** menu and click **Page Setup**.

   The Page Setup dialog appears.

4. Click the **Margins** tab.
5. Click **Top** and type in a number to set the top margin.
6. Click the **Left** and **Right** to change the side margins.

   B You can see the changes in the Preview window.

7. Click **Print**.

   The spreadsheet is printed.

✓ *You can print gridlines. Click* **Page Setup, Sheet.** *Click the* **Gridlines** *check box.*

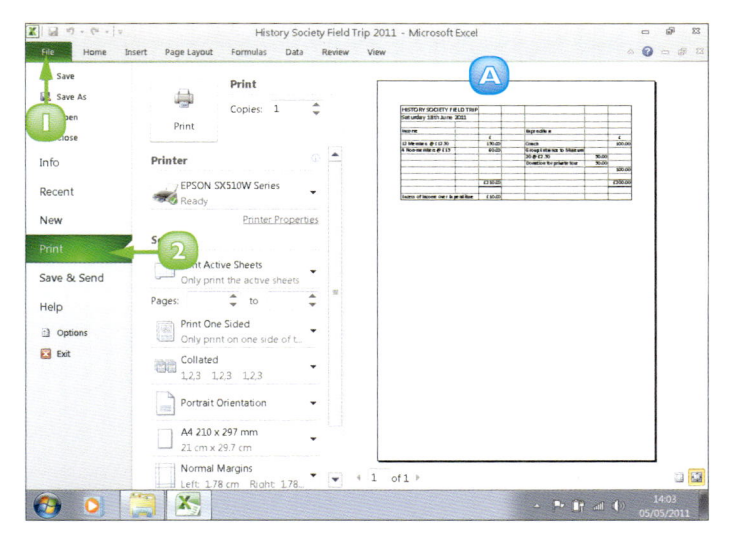

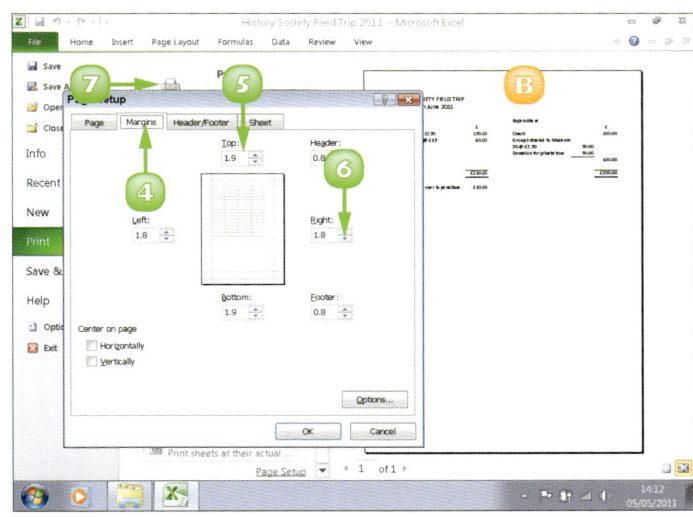

CHAPTER 12 KEEPING RECORDS

CONTENTS

174 Get Started with Windows Explorer

176 Find Files and Folders

179 Rename a File or Folder

180 Create Folders

182 Move and Copy Files

184 Delete and Recover Files

186 Keep Copies of Files

13

ORGANISING FILES AND FOLDERS

If you have been working your way through the book, by now you will have created lots of files and folders. Although Jump Lists and Aero Peek help with finding files, it is useful to set up a filing system. One advantage of doing it now is that you probably have under 50 files; it will not be long before this becomes 1000 or more. In this chapter, we use Windows Explorer to organise files and copy files to a CD so you can back up important files in case your computer crashes.

GET STARTED WITH WINDOWS EXPLORER

We have passed by Windows Explorer on many occasions in previous chapters but now we are going to find out a little bit more about how it can help us manage information on the computer.

In Windows Explorer, you can see files and folders in different layouts and change the order in which files are displayed.

Open Windows Explorer and Change the View

1. Click 📁 in the Taskbar.

   Windows Explorer opens.

2. Click the **Change Your View** ▾.

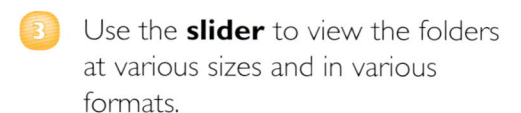

3. Use the **slider** to view the folders at various sizes and in various formats.

> ✓ In list view, you can change the size of a column. Hover over the column edge in the title bar (⇔ appears) and drag left or right.

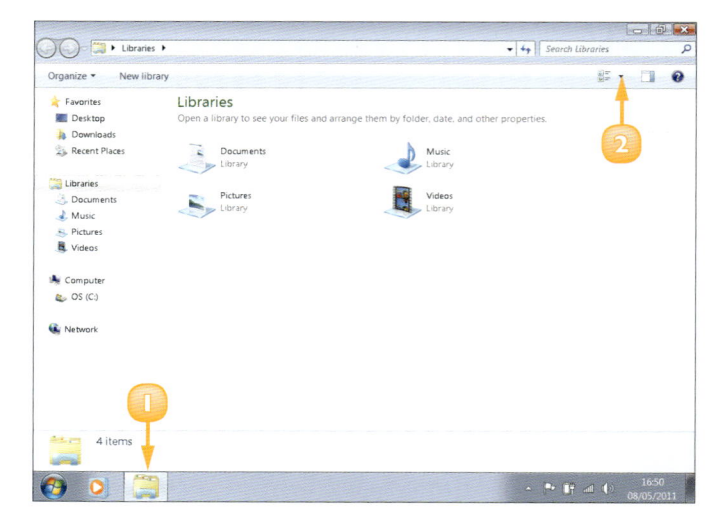

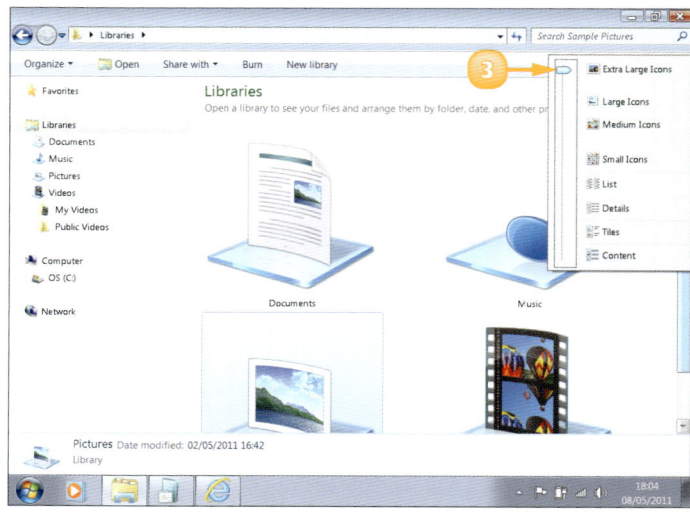

CHAPTER 13 ORGANISING FILES AND FOLDERS

Preview Pane

① Click **Show the preview pane** (□).

A pane opens to show the contents of a file you have clicked on.

② Double-click **Pictures**.

③ Double-click **Sample pictures**.

④ Click on a picture.

Ⓐ *The picture opens in the Preview pane.*

⑤ Click the **Preview Pane** icon again to hide it.

Change the Order of Files

① Double-click **Documents**.

The Documents library opens listing all folders and files in alphabetical order.

② Click **Name**.

The file order is reversed.

③ Click **Name** again to revert to A–Z.

Ⓑ *You can click* **Type** *to order by file type.*

✓ *You can click on any column header to order by that column.*

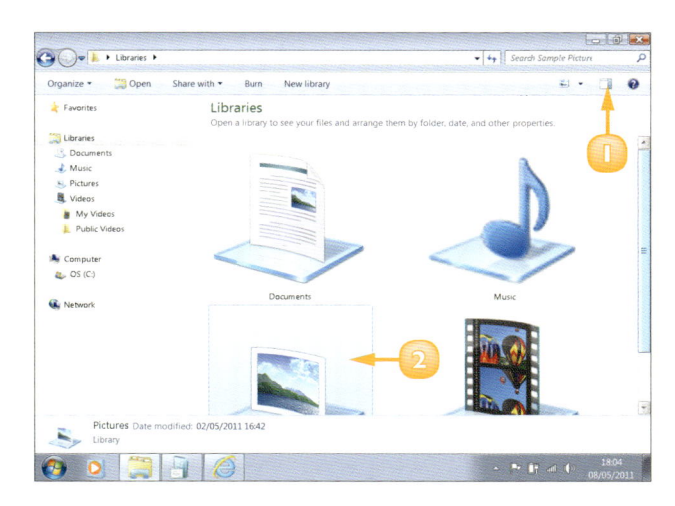

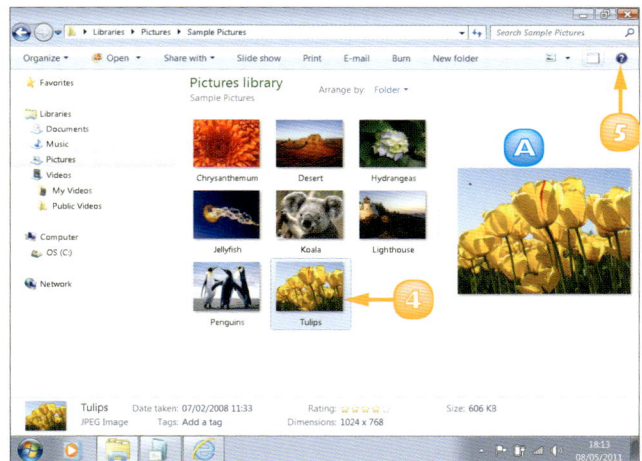

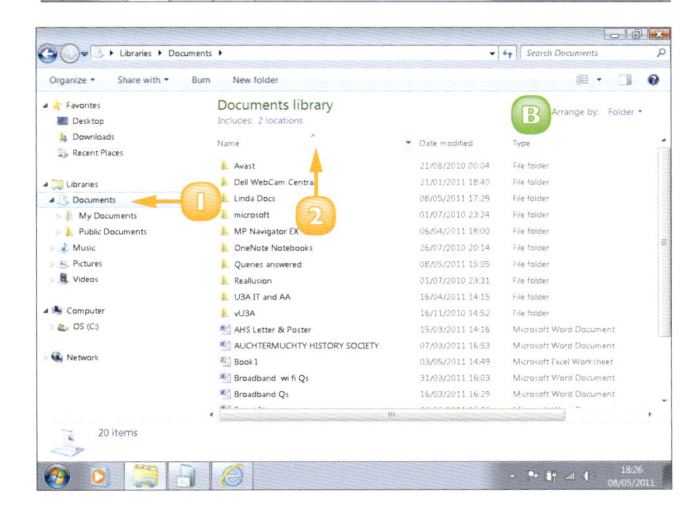

CHAPTER 13 ORGANISING FILES AND FOLDERS

175

FIND FILES AND FOLDERS

You can use Windows Explorer to search for a file or folder if you do not know where it is.

Search for Files and Folders

1. Click the **Date modified**.

   The date menu appears.

2. Click **Select a date or date range**.

3. Click a date to display files modified on that date.

   A You can click **Today** to display files modified today.

4. Click the **Type**.

5. Click **Microsoft Word Document** to display only Word files.

   B Click **File folder** to display only folders.

   C Click **Microsoft Excel Worksheet** to display only spreadsheets.

Note: You can also restrict the display by Name and Size.

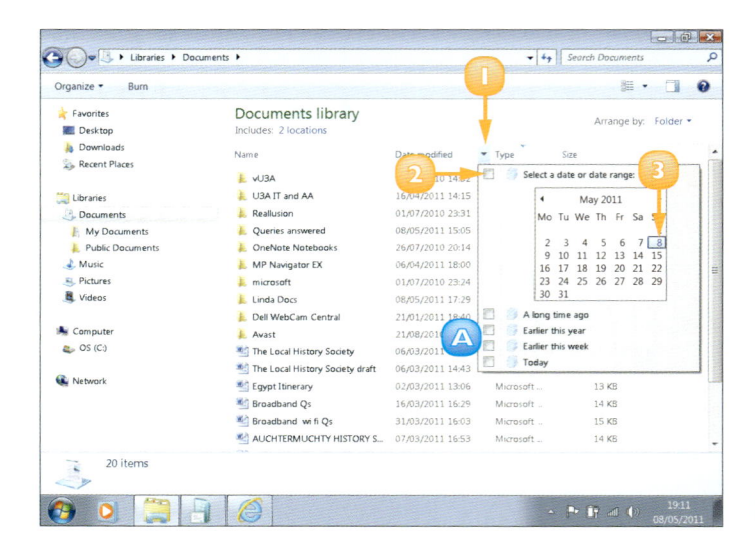

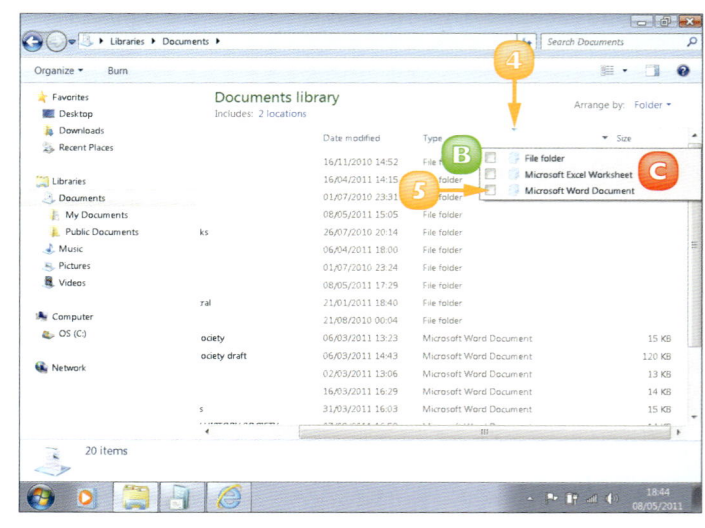

Search for Documents

1. Double-click **Documents**.

2. Type the name or part of the name of the document you are looking for in the **Search Documents** box.

   The results are listed.

3. Click in the Search box to add a filter.

4. Add a search filter to find a document by **Type**.

   A *You can also add a filter for author name.*

   B *You can also add a filter for date modified.*

   The results are listed.

Note: *You can double-click a document name to open it.*

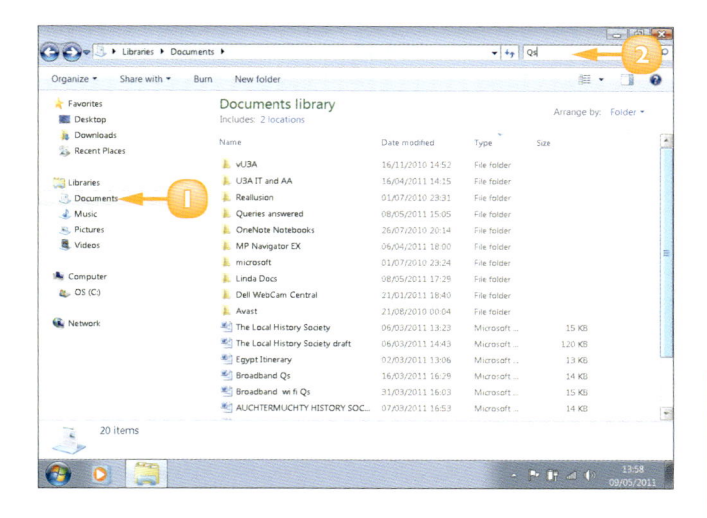

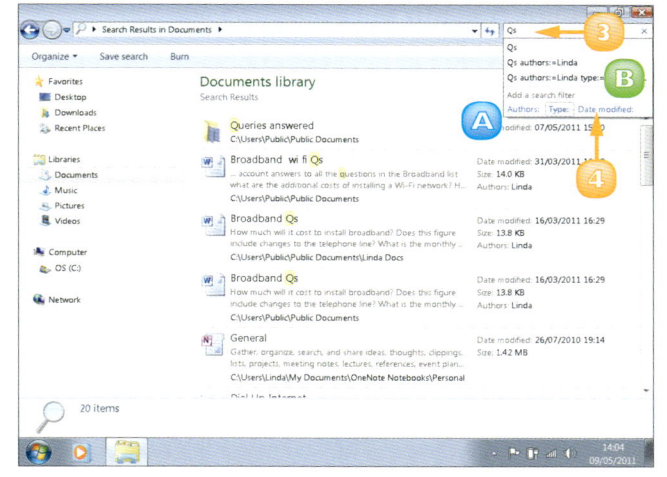

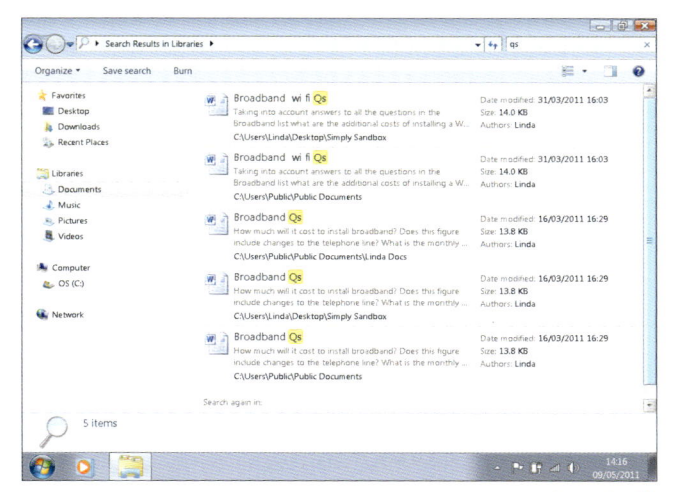

continued →

CHAPTER 13 ORGANISING FILES AND FOLDERS

FIND FILES AND FOLDERS (continued)

You can direct Windows Explorer to search for files in a specific location.

Search in a Specific Location

1. Click **Libraries** under the **Search again in** heading to look for the document in any of the libraries.

2. Click **Custom** to choose where to look for the document.

3. Click the check boxes next to the specific folders in which you want Windows Explorer to look.

4. Click **OK**.

   The results are listed.

> ✓ *Click **Libraries** on the left to return to Windows Explorer from the search results.*

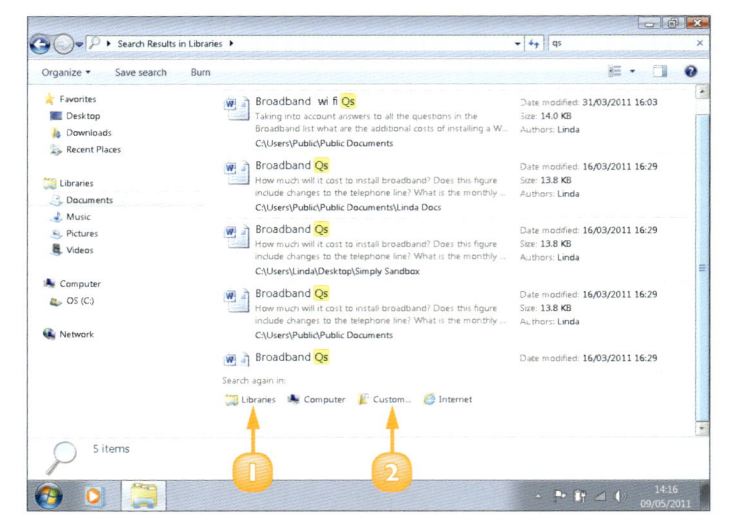

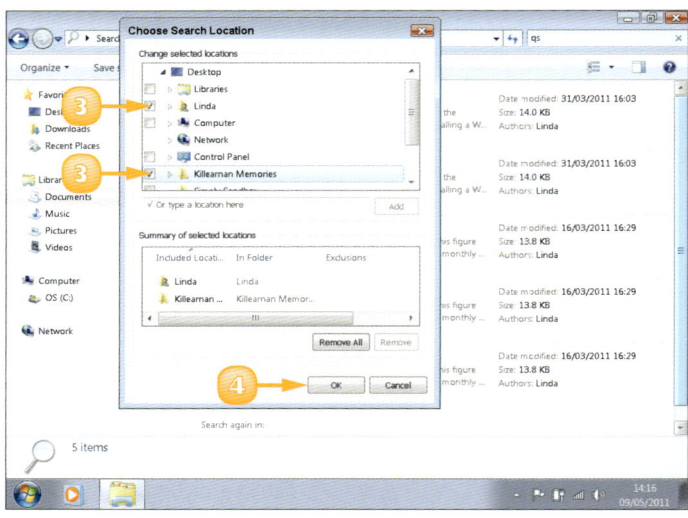

CHAPTER 13 ORGANISING FILES AND FOLDERS

RENAME A FILE OR FOLDER

You can change the name of a file or folder in Windows Explorer.

1. Point to the document or folder to be renamed.
2. Click the right mouse button.

   A menu appears.
3. Click **Rename**.

   The file is highlighted.
4. Type in a new name.
5. Press **Enter**.

   The name is changed.

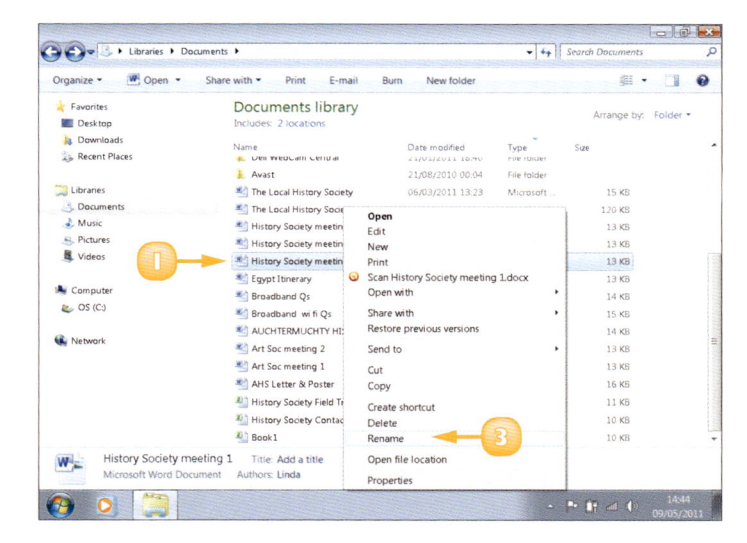

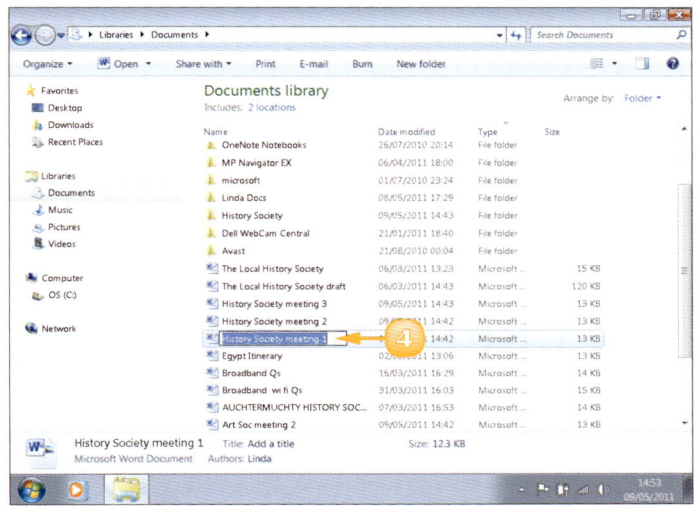

CHAPTER 13 ORGANISING FILES AND FOLDERS

CREATE FOLDERS

You can keep all your documents in the My Documents folder but you can also create other folders. This allows you to keep track more easily of all the documents that are related to a particular topic. In Windows Explorer, folders in the left pane with ▷ have more folders hidden inside the one you are looking at. Folders with ◢ contain no hidden folders.

Create a New Folder

1. Double-click the **Documents library**.

2. Click **New folder**.

   A new folder appears with the name box highlighted.

3. Type in a name for the folder.

4. Press `Enter`.

   A new folder is created with the name you gave it.

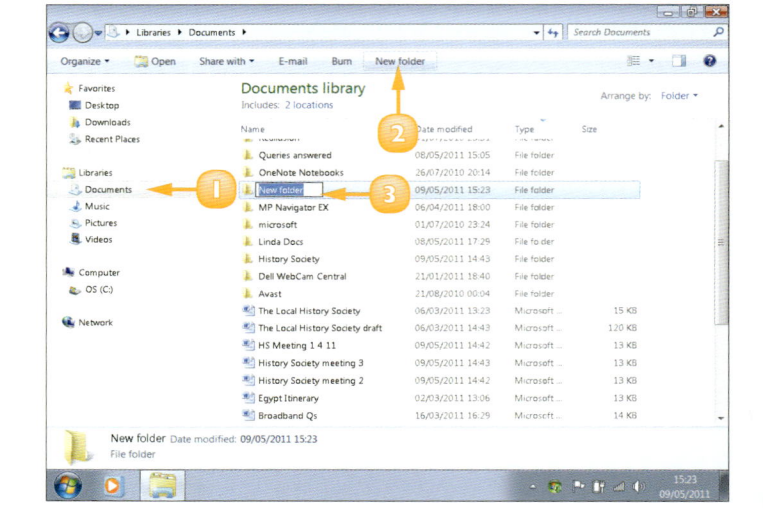

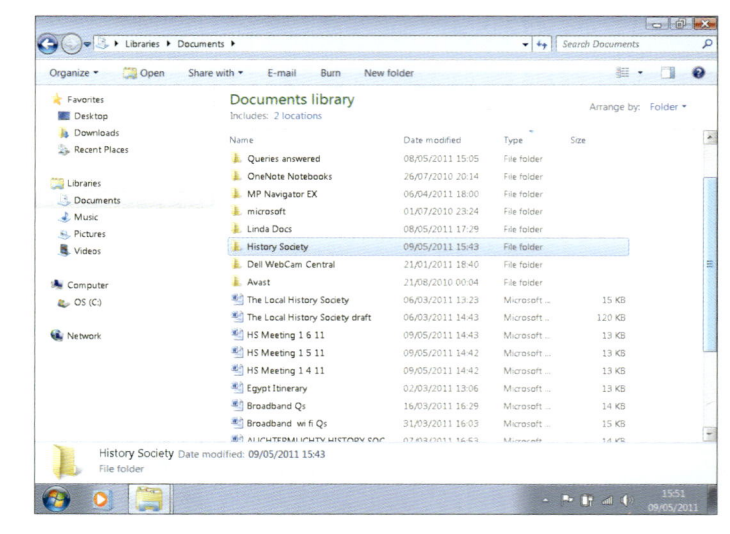

✓ *You can create a folder within any other folder in a similar fashion.*

CHAPTER 13 ORGANISING FILES AND FOLDERS

View Folders

1. Click **Documents**.
2. Click **My Documents**.
3. Click the folder you created.

Note: You may also need to click **Public Documents**.

- A. As you click each folder, its subfolders are displayed in the left pane.
- B. As you click each folder, its folders and documents are displayed in the right pane.

4. Click ◢ to close the folders on view.

Change the View

1. Click the **Arrange by** ▾ to change the order.
2. Click **Author** to order by author name.

- A. You can click **Clear changes** to remove all order changes.

Note: You can click Folder, Date modified, Tag, Type or Name to order by that item.

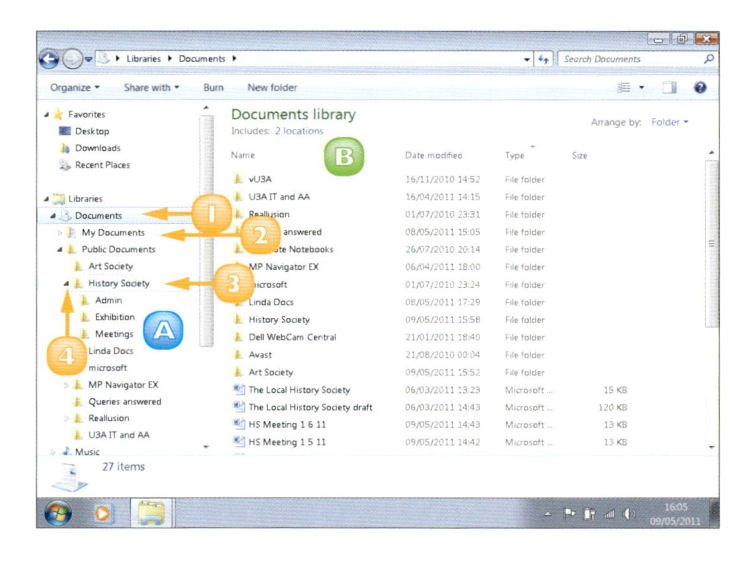

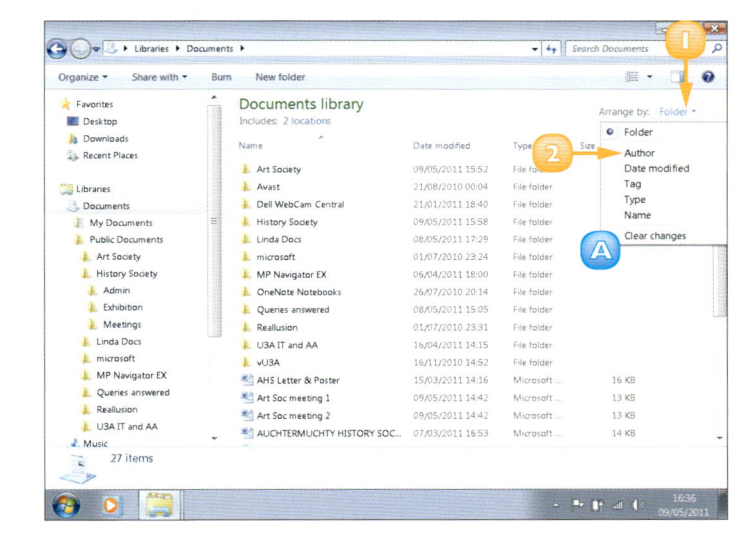

✓ *Use the scroll bars to move up and down in the two panes.*

CHAPTER 13 ORGANISING FILES AND FOLDERS

MOVE AND COPY FILES

Now that you have created folders, it is time to put some files into them. You can move or copy files from one folder to another. There are three ways to do this: the Organise menu, the right-click menu or by dragging and dropping.

Move a File Using the Organise Menu

1. Click the file to be moved.
2. Click **Organize**.
3. Click **Cut**.

4. Click the destination folder.

   The folder opens.

5. Click **Paste**.

   The file is pasted into the folder and is deleted from its original place.

✓ *If you use Copy in Step 3, the file will be in both folders.*

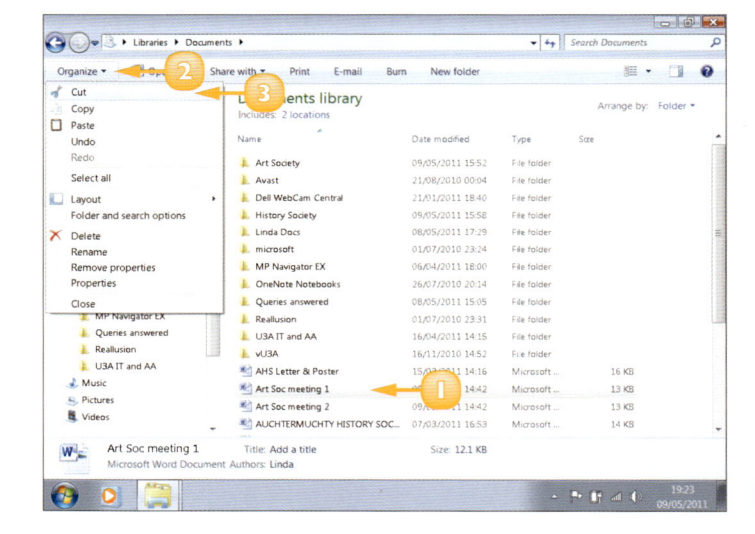

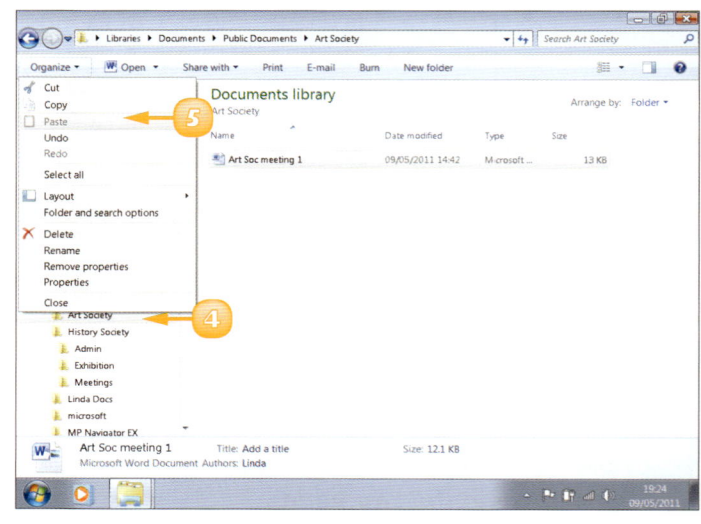

CHAPTER 13 ORGANISING FILES AND FOLDERS

Copy Files Using the Right-Click Menu

① Right-click the file to be moved.

② Click **Copy**.

③ Right-click the destination folder in the left pane.

④ Click **Paste** in the menu.

The file is copied into the folder.

Note: *The file is now in both folders.*

✓ *If you use **Cut** in Step 2, the file is deleted from the original folder.*

Move a File Using Drag and Drop

① Click the file to be moved.

② Hold down the left mouse button.

③ Drag the file to be moved to the destination folder.

④ Release the mouse button.

The file is moved to the folder.

Note: *To copy (rather than move) the file, hold down* Ctrl *from Steps 2 to 4.*

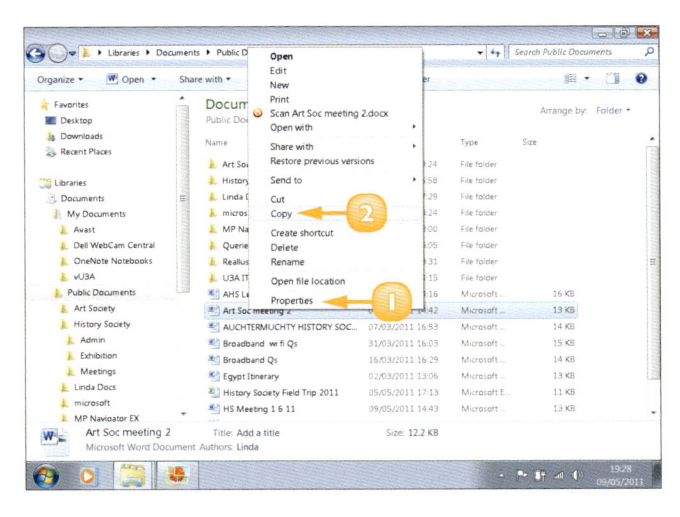

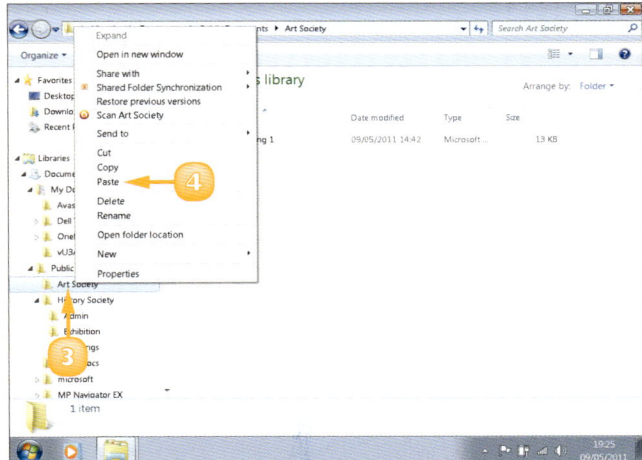

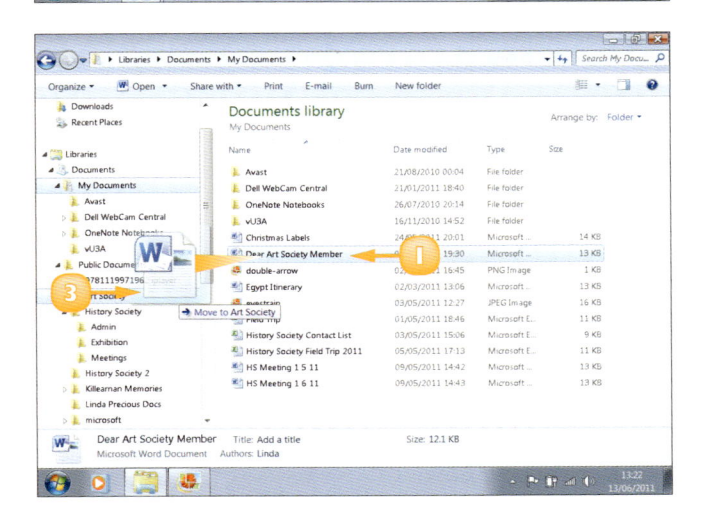

CHAPTER 13 ORGANISING FILES AND FOLDERS

183

DELETE AND RECOVER FILES

You may need to tidy up your libraries of documents and pictures at some point. In Windows Explorer, it is easy to delete files that you no longer need.

We all make mistakes. At some point, to our horror, we discover that we have deleted something important by mistake. It could be a folder of photographs or a file containing information that should have been kept. In tidying up your libraries, it is easily done but, fortunately, it is also quite straightforward to retrieve them.

Delete Several Files

1. Click on the first file to be deleted.
2. Hold down **Ctrl**.
3. Click the other files to be deleted.
4. Release the **Ctrl** key.
5. Click **Organize**.
6. Click **Delete**.

The Delete dialog appears.

7. Click **Yes**.

The files are deleted.

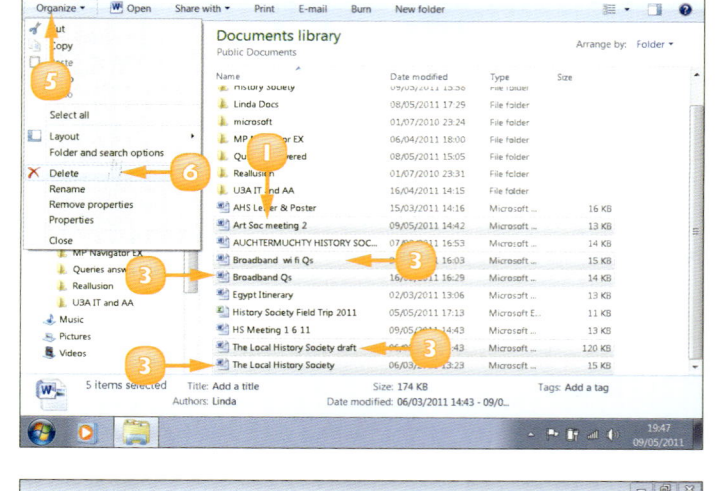

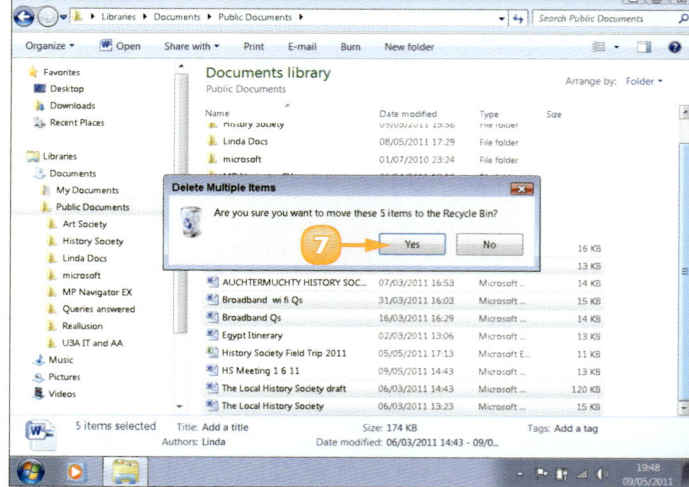

✓ *You can also press* **Del** *after selecting files.*

CHAPTER 13 ORGANISING FILES AND FOLDERS

Undo a Deletion

1. Click **Organize**.
2. Click **Undo** to retrieve the files.

The Recycle Bin

1. Click the **Recycle Bin** on the Desktop.

   The Recycle Bin opens, showing all the files that have been deleted.

2. Click a column heading to re-order the files.

3. Click the file or files you want to restore.
4. Click **Restore selected items**.

   The files are restored to their original location.

✓ *To select multiple files, hold down* Ctrl *while you click.*

✓ *Click **Empty the Recycle Bin** occasionally to free up space.*

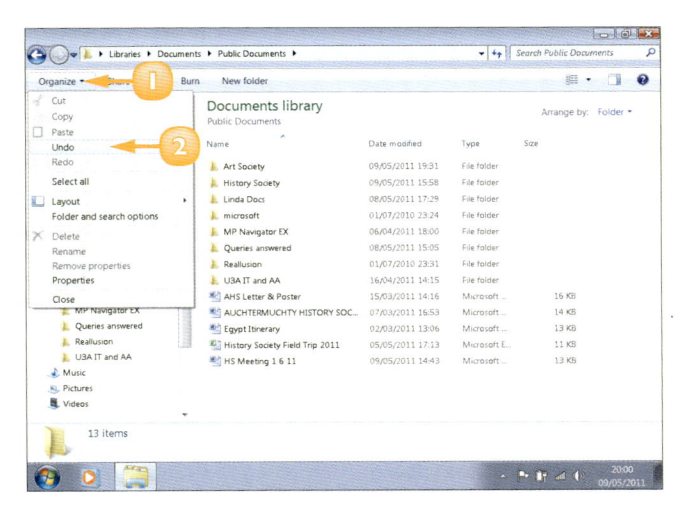

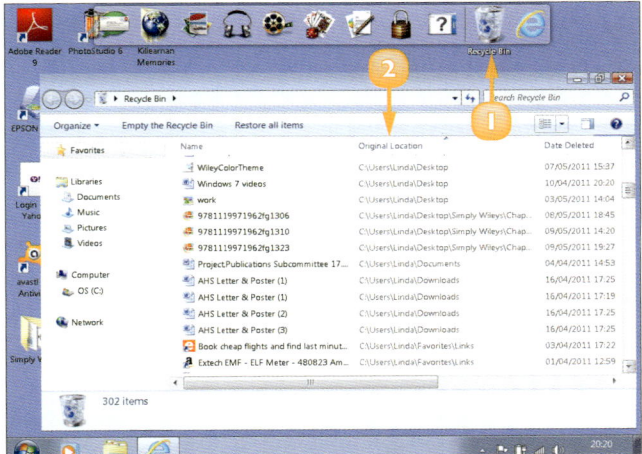

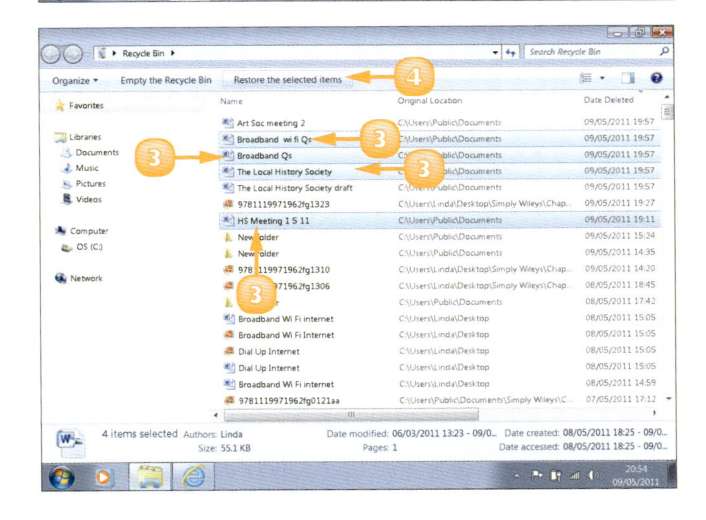

CHAPTER 13 ORGANISING FILES AND FOLDERS

KEEP COPIES OF FILES

In Chapter 11, we considered keeping copies of pictures using Windows Live Photo Gallery. It is just as important to keep backup copies of files and folders so that, if your computer fails, you do not lose all your records. For example, you may be keen on family history and have been recording information on past generations of your family. If your computer disk crashes, a backup copy of the data kept separately will ensure that you still have the precious data that you spent hours inputting. This method can also be used for copying pictures.

Format a CD

1. Open Windows Explorer.
2. Click on the folder (or file) to be copied to the CD.
3. Click **Burn**.

   The Burn to disc dialog appears.

4. Insert a CD-RW disc into the drive.
5. Click **Like a USB Flash Drive**.
6. Click **Next**. If asked if you wish to continue, click **Yes**.

   The formatting progress window opens. When the formatting is complete the disc is ejected.

✓ *You can also use a DVD-RW disc.*

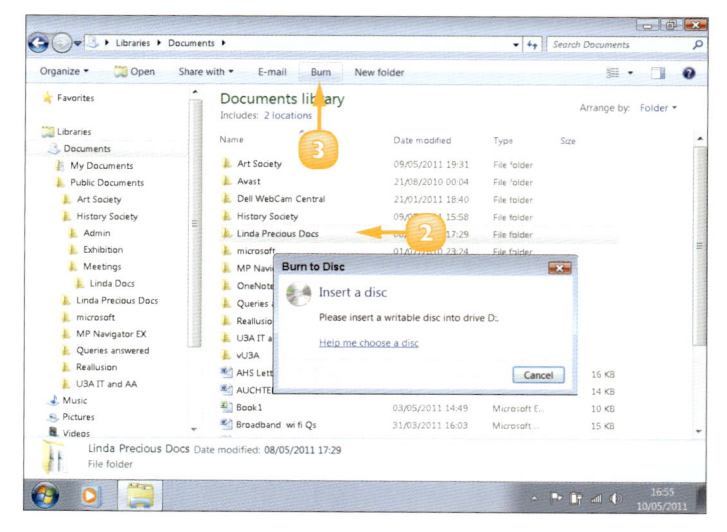

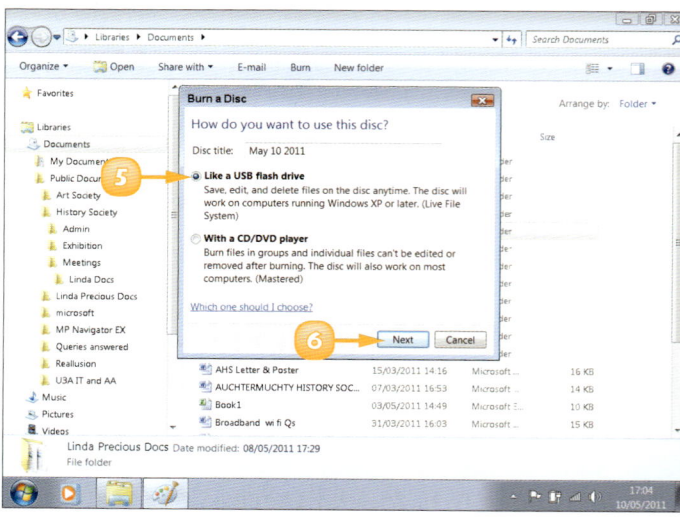

CHAPTER 13 ORGANISING FILES AND FOLDERS

Copy a folder to a CD

1. Insert the disc back into the CD or DVD drive.
2. Wait for the AutoPlay menu to appear.
3. Click **Open folder to view files**.

4. Click the folder to be copied.
5. Hold down the left mouse button and drag to the right pane.
6. Release the mouse button.

   The folder is copied to the disc.

Note: *You can also use the Organize menu to copy folders.*

Remove a CD

1. Click **Eject** in the File Menu.

   The disc is ejected and you are returned to the desktop.

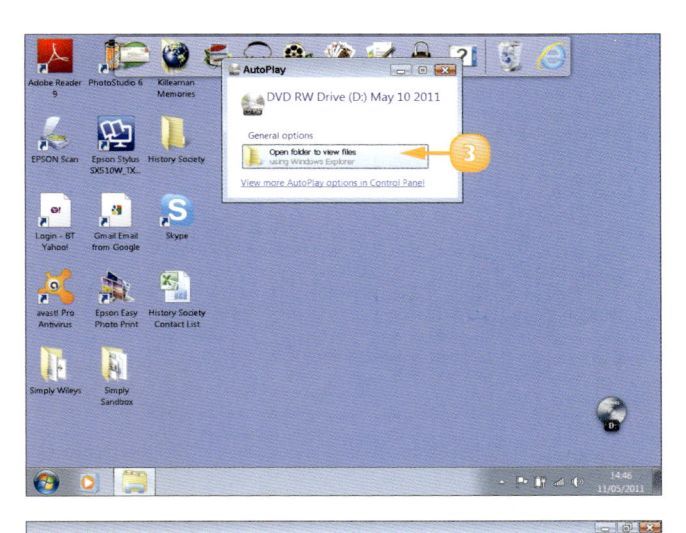

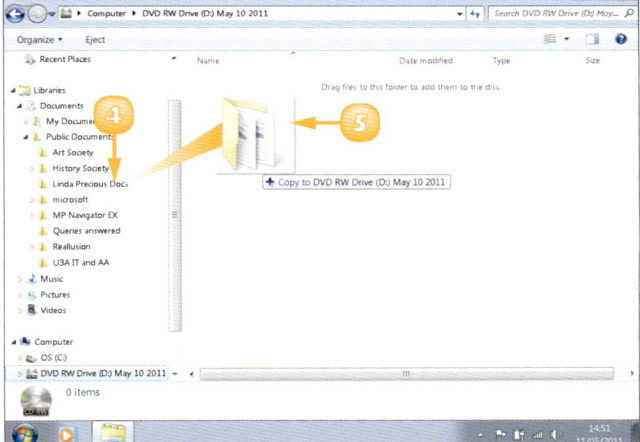

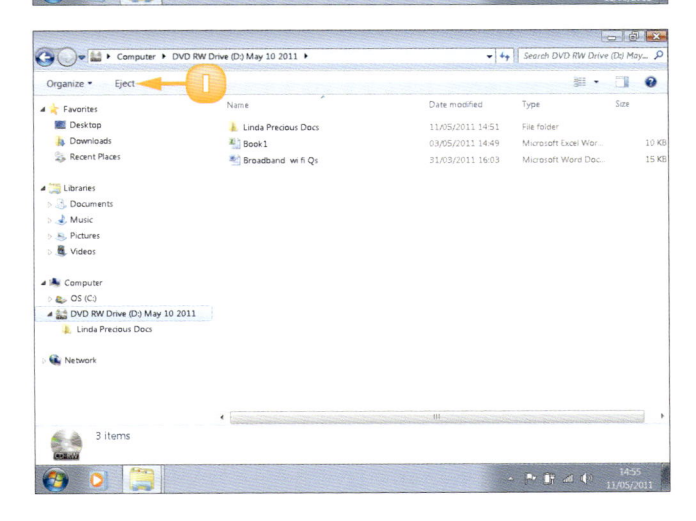

CHAPTER 13 ORGANISING FILES AND FOLDERS

CONTENTS

190 Play a Game
192 Watch a Film
194 Watch TV
196 Listen to Music
198 Use Playlists
200 Download Music
203 Listen to Internet Radio

14

ENTERTAINMENT

Taking a break or just enjoying the opportunities provided by your new computer, you will find that there are a lot of things to do. You can listen to music, play games, watch films and catch up on the last episode of your favourite programme with Windows 7 Media Player and Media Center and software downloaded from the Internet. How well these programs run varies depending on the specifications of your computer and your broadband speed.

PLAY A GAME

The basic principle with games is the same: you need to download them to your computer. There are vast amounts of games to choose from, ones you need to pay for and free ones. All games have detailed instructions on how to play and keep a record of how good or bad you are at the game. You need to choose whether you want to play alone or not, whether you are a beginner or an expert player and, occasionally, how fast you want to play. With most games, you need to click an icon to activate the game or start the clock.

Windows 7 Games

1. Click **Start**.

2. Type **games** into the search box.

3. Click **Games Explorer**.

4. Scroll slowly down the list.

    A. A short description of the game is displayed.

Note: Any games with Internet in the title take you online to find a partner to play with.

5. Click the name of a game.

    B. You can click **Ratings** to see the age rating for the game.

    C. You can click **Performance** to find out how well your computer will run the game.

    D. You can click **Statistics** to choose the level at which to play the game.

6. Double-click a game to open it.

✓ You can click 🗖 to play the game using the full screen.

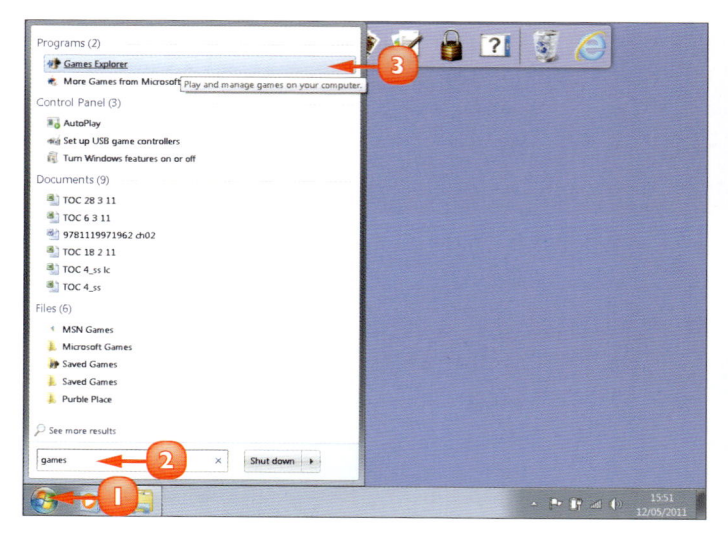

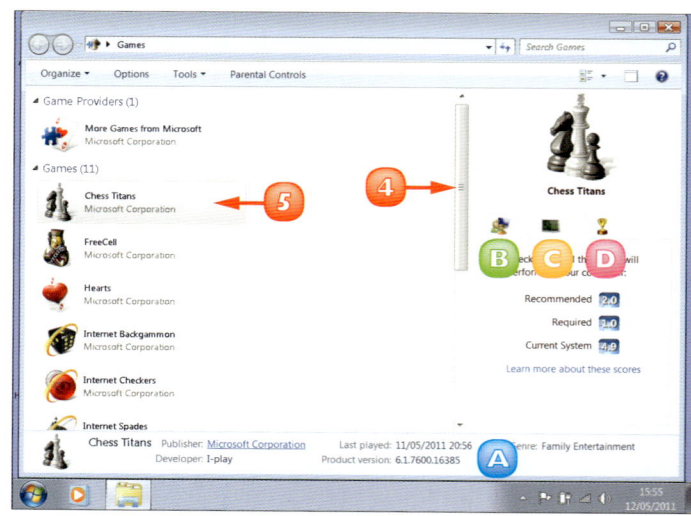

CHAPTER 14 ENTERTAINMENT

Play a Game

1 Click **Game**.

Note: Not all games have these options but many do.

2 Click **New game against computer**.

Ⓐ If you make a mistake when playing, click Undo.

Ⓑ You click ❌ to exit the game. You are asked if you wish to save it or not.

3 Click **Help**.

A drop-down menu appears.

4 Click **View Help**.

Help on how to play is displayed.

5 Click 📇 to close **Help**.

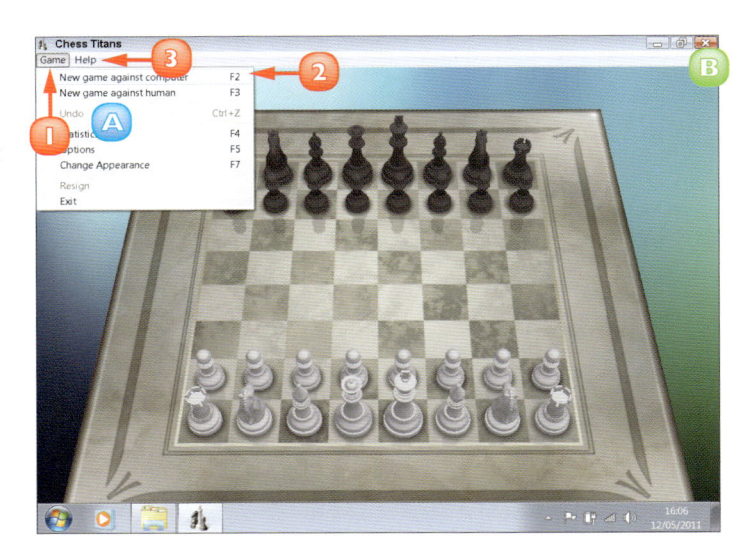

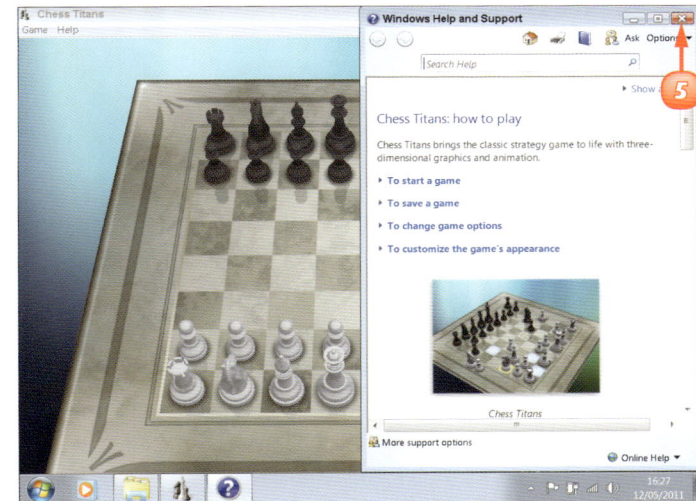

✅ *You can change the appearance of the board and chess pieces and make other choices in the Game menu.*

✅ *Go to chrome.angrybirds.com to see what everybody is playing just now. It's free and compulsive!*

CHAPTER 14 ENTERTAINMENT

WATCH A FILM

You can play normal film DVDs in the DVD drive of your computer. You can also find films online and play them directly.

Play a DVD

1. Insert the DVD into the DVD drive.

   Windows Media Player loads and plays through to the menu.

2. Click **Play All Projects**.

   A You can choose a specific episode.

3. Move the mouse and a control panel appears on the screen.

   B You can drag to adjust the volume.

   C You can move forward through the DVD.

   D You can move backward through the DVD.

   E You can pause the DVD.

   F You can stop the DVD.

4. When the DVD ends, click [X].

5. Click ▲ on the disc icon.

6. Click **Eject**.

   The DVD is ejected.

© Teaching Art Ltd and its respective contributors, 2005–2011

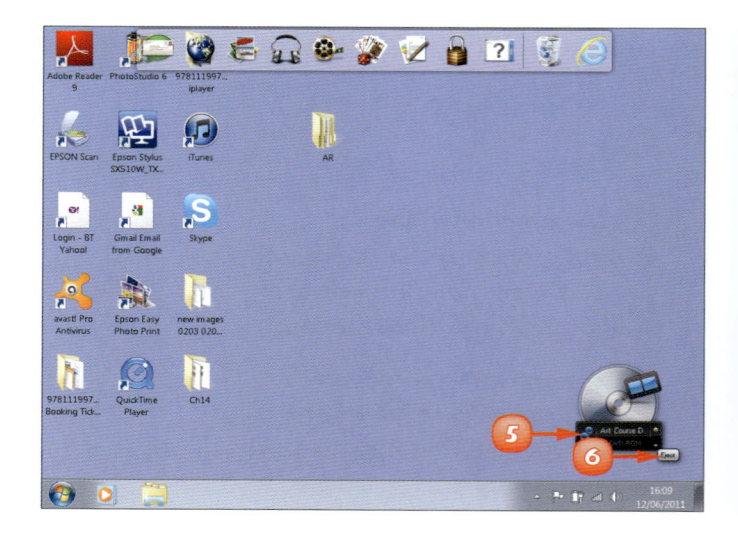

CHAPTER 14 ENTERTAINMENT

Watch a Video Online

1. Open Internet Explorer.
2. Type **youtube.com** into the address bar.
3. Type **adrian arnold** into the search box.
4. Click **Search**.

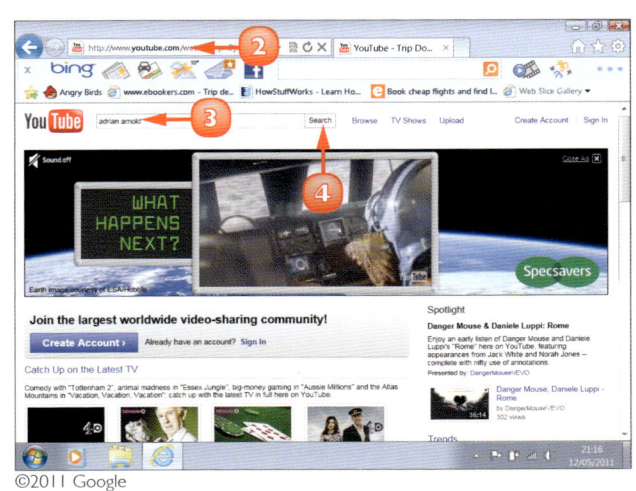

- Ⓐ You can change the order in which the results appear.
- Ⓑ You can see the length of each video.

5. Click **Top 5 Tips for staying safe online**.

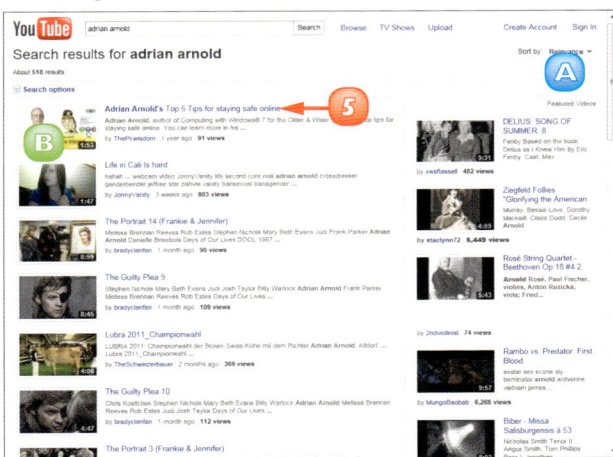

The video loads and plays.

- Ⓐ You can pause the video.
- Ⓑ You can adjust the volume.
- Ⓒ You can expand the screen.
- Ⓓ You can view the video using the full screen.

©2011 Google.

©2011 Google. *PC Wisdom* Copyright © 2000–2011 by John Wiley & Sons, Inc. or related companies. All rights reserved.

©2011 Google. *PC Wisdom* Copyright © 2000–2011 by John Wiley & Sons, Inc. or related companies. All rights reserved.

CHAPTER 14 ENTERTAINMENT

WATCH TV

Various websites allow you to watch television programmes on your computer. For some, you need to be a subscriber or pay to view programmes; others are free. You can also watch TV from around the world.

You can sometimes watch programmes as they are broadcast (you still need a TV licence in the UK) or you can catch up with programmes that you have missed.

1. Open Internet Explorer and type **uk.msn.com**.
2. Click **TV**.
3. Click **Watch full TV shows**.

The MSN video player opens.

4. Click **DOCUMENTARY**.

A menu of programmes is displayed.

- **A** You can click **Browse All TV** to see an alphabetical list of programmes.
- **B** You can also click to access **Comedy**, **Drama** or **Entertainment** programmes.
- **C** You can roll over these tabs to see programmes in the categories.

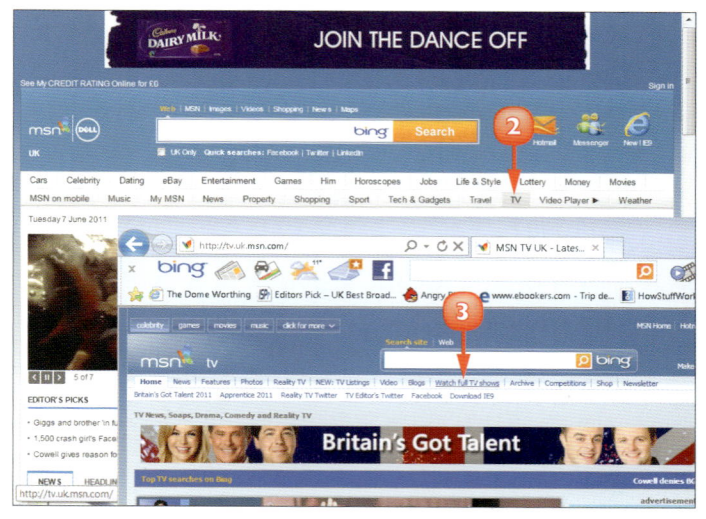

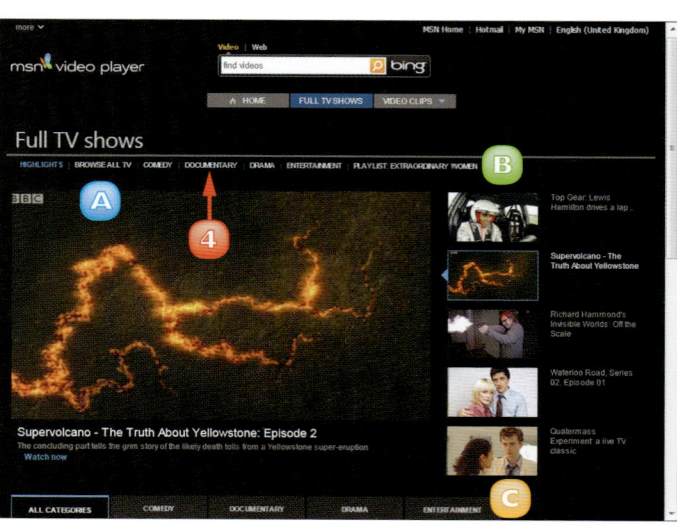

CHAPTER 14 ENTERTAINMENT

⑤ Scroll through the list and click to choose a programme.

Wait for the programme to load and run.

⑥ Hover on the picture just above the lower frame.

The menu appears.

⑦ Click **Full Screen**.

The picture fills the screen.

⑧ Press `Esc` to exit full screen mode.

⑨ Click to access a slider to increase or decrease the volume.

⑩ Click to pause the video.

Ⓐ You can click to share the video.

Ⓑ You can click to darken the area around the video player.

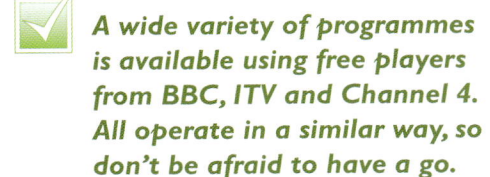

✓ *A wide variety of programmes is available using free players from BBC, ITV and Channel 4. All operate in a similar way, so don't be afraid to have a go.*

STOP *How well TV players work will depend on the speed of your broadband connection and the technical specification of your computer.*

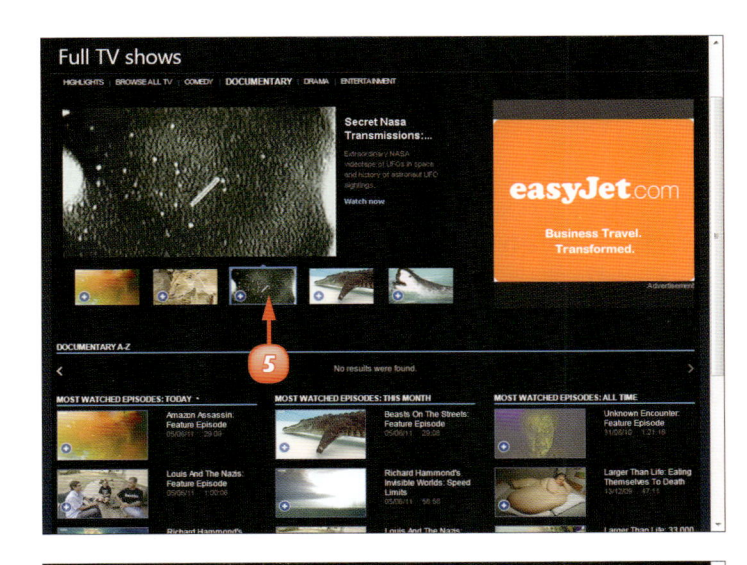

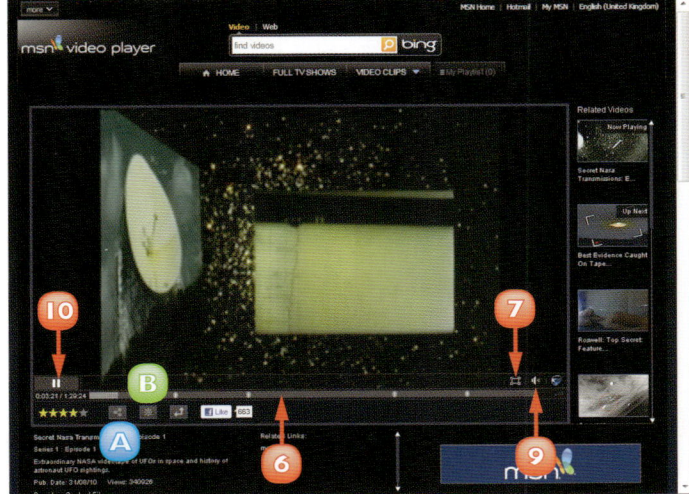

CHAPTER 14 ENTERTAINMENT

LISTEN TO MUSIC

Windows Media Player allows you to listen to music, make playlists, burn a CD or copy music to a flash drive.

Play Music

1. Click the **Windows Media Player** icon.

   Windows Media Player opens and displays the albums.

2. Double-click one of the album icons.

   The music plays.

3. Use the menu bar to control the playback.

   A You can play or pause the track.

   B You can adjust the volume.

   C You can move forward or backward a track.

   D You can shuffle the tracks.

   E You can repeat a track.

4. Click ⁞⁞ to switch to **Now Playing**.

5. Click ▣ to view the image in the full screen.

6. Click ▦ to return to the music library.

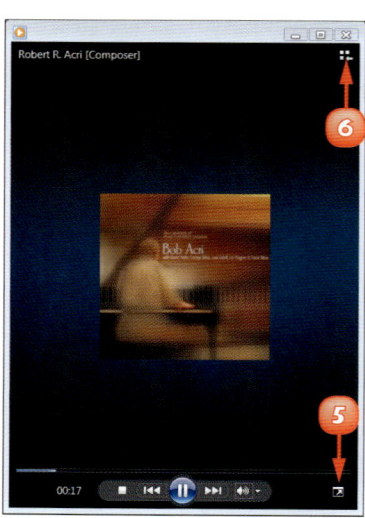

CHAPTER 14 ENTERTAINMENT

Copy Music to a CD

1. Click **Burn**.
2. Insert a blank CD into the CD or DVD drive.

   The AutoPlay menu appears.
3. Click **Burn an audio CD**.

4. Click a music track.
5. Drag it into the **Burn list**.
6. Click **Start burn** and wait for the burn to be completed.

   The CD is ejected.

Copy (Rip) Music from a CD

1. Insert a music CD into the CD or DVD drive.
2. Right-click the **CD icon**.
3. Click **Rip CD to library**.

   Wait for the rip to be completed.

   The CD is ejected.

> *Windows Media Center provides access to your music, pictures and videos from one place.*

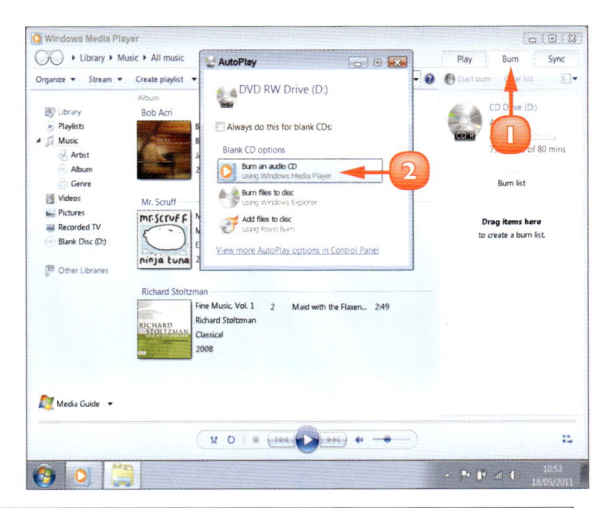

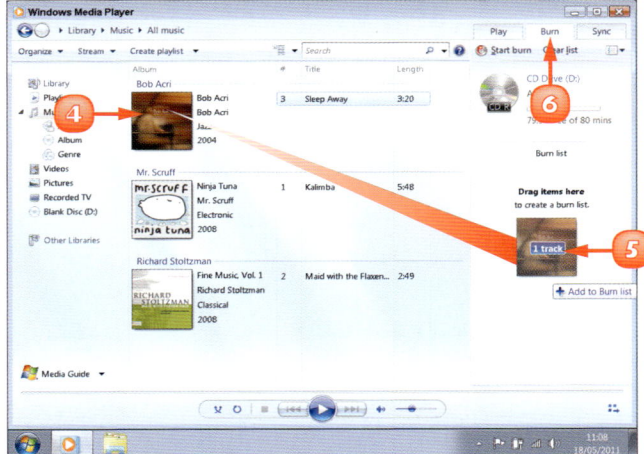

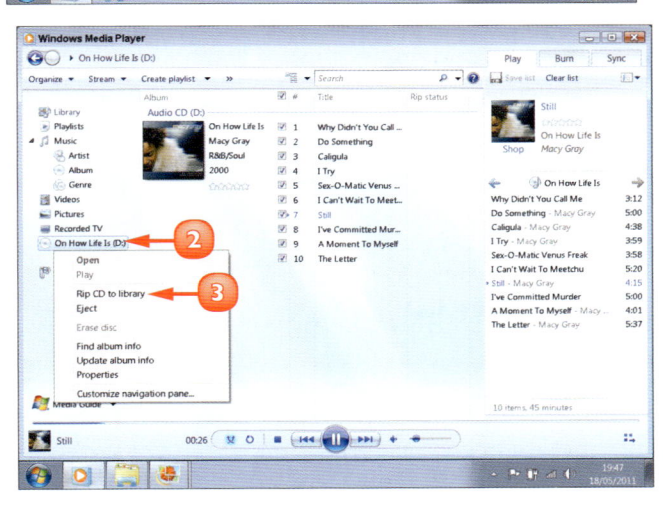

CHAPTER 14 ENTERTAINMENT

USE PLAYLISTS

A playlist lets you put together your favourite music from different singers and musicians which can then be transferred to a CD or an MP3 player.

You may wish to copy or sync playlists to your MP3 player to take with you on holiday or on a car or train trip.

Create a Playlist

1. Click **Music**.
2. Click **Play**.
3. Click a track.
4. Drag it to the playlist.
5. Repeat Steps 3–4 to complete the playlist.

6. Right-click a track in the playlist.

   A. You can play the track.

   B. You can remove the track from list.

   C. You can move the track up or down the list.

7. Click **Save list**.
8. Type a name for the list and click **Save list**.

   D. You can click **Clear list** to start a new list.

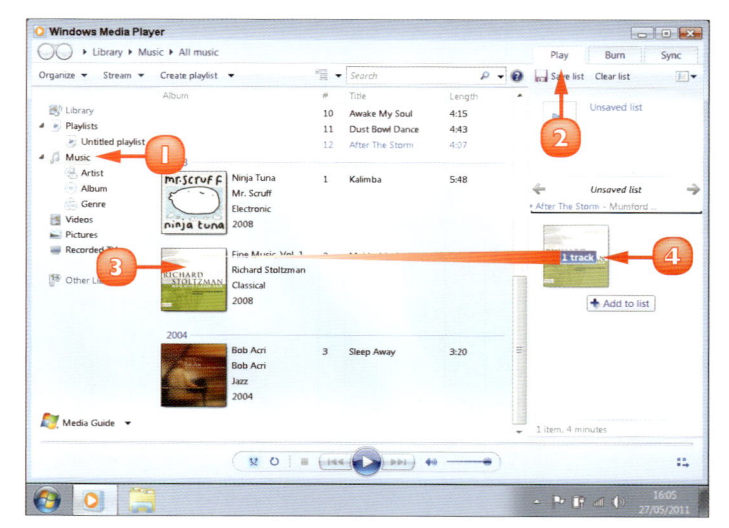

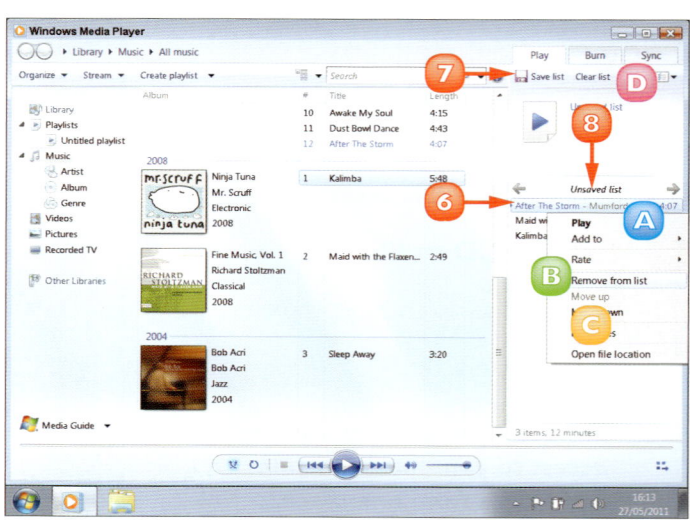

CHAPTER 14 ENTERTAINMENT

Sync a Playlist to an MP3 Player

1. Click **Playlists**.
2. Plug your MP3 player into the computer.
3. Click **Sync**.
4. Drag a playlist or individual tracks to the Sync list.
5. Click **Start sync**.

   A progress bar shows the syncing process.
6. Click **Click here** to check the sync results.
7. Click ▲.
8. Click **Eject Media**.
9. Click **Eject**.
10. Unplug the player when the "Safe to Remove Hardware" message appears.

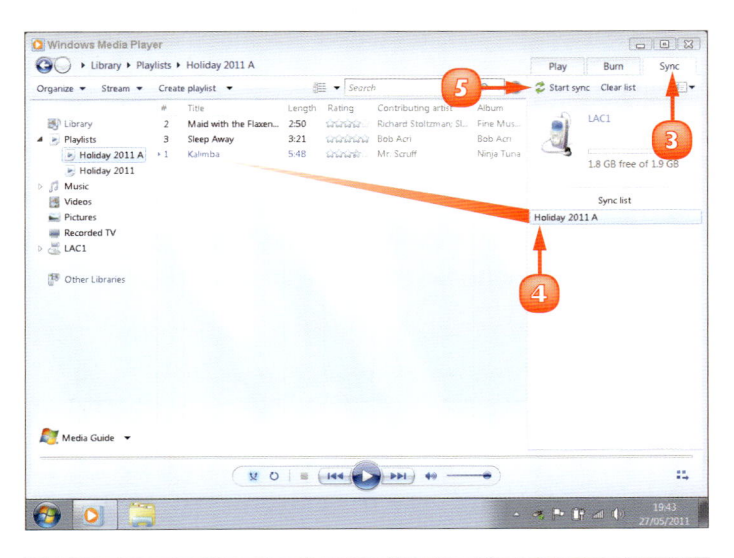

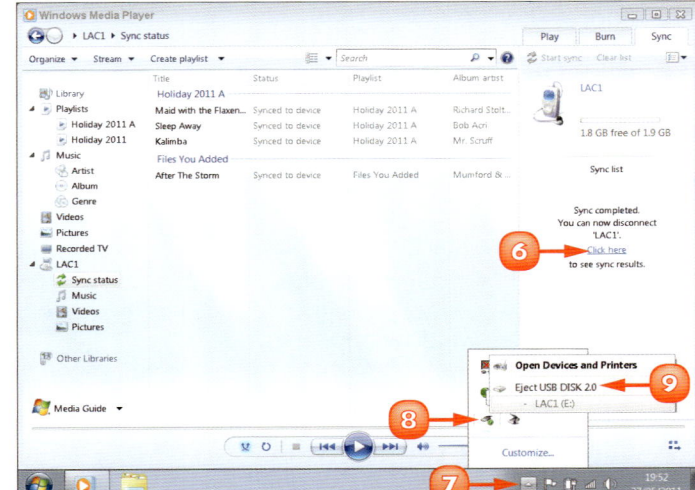

CHAPTER 14 ENTERTAINMENT

DOWNLOAD MUSIC

In order to download music from iTunes, you need to download the software. You must register as a subscriber to download music.

Once you have downloaded music, you can play it on your computer and copy it to a CD, a flash drive or another device, such as an iPod or other MP3 player.

Install the iTunes Software

1. Open Internet Explorer and type **apple.com/itunes** into the address bar.

2. Click **Download iTunes**.

   You are asked to Run or Save.

3. Click **Run**.

   The software starts to download. This could take a few minutes.

   The Installer window appears.

4. Click **Next**.

5. Click **I accept the terms in the licence agreement** and click **Next**.

6. Click **Use iTunes as the default player for audio files** to uncheck it and click **Yes**.

7. Click **Install.**

   The software starts to install. This could take a few minutes.

8. Click **Finish**.

CHAPTER 14 ENTERTAINMENT

Buy Music

1. Double-click 🎵.
2. Click **iTunes Store**.

   The iTunes Store opens.
3. Type the name of an artist or album in the **Search box**.

4. Click **Buy** next to an album.

   Ⓐ You can click **Buy** next to an individual item.

5. Click to create a new account.

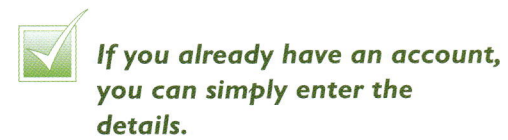

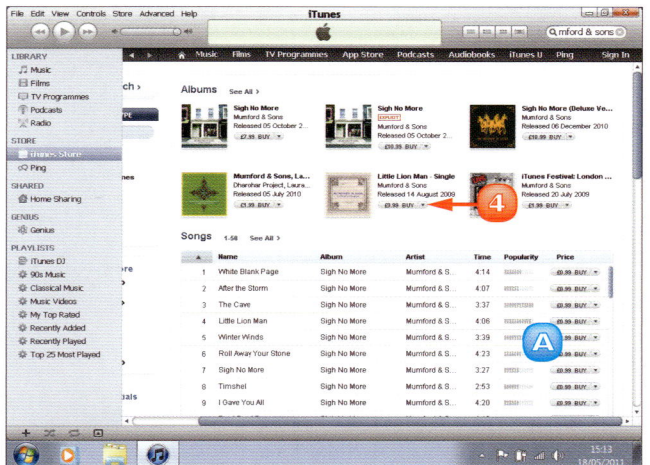

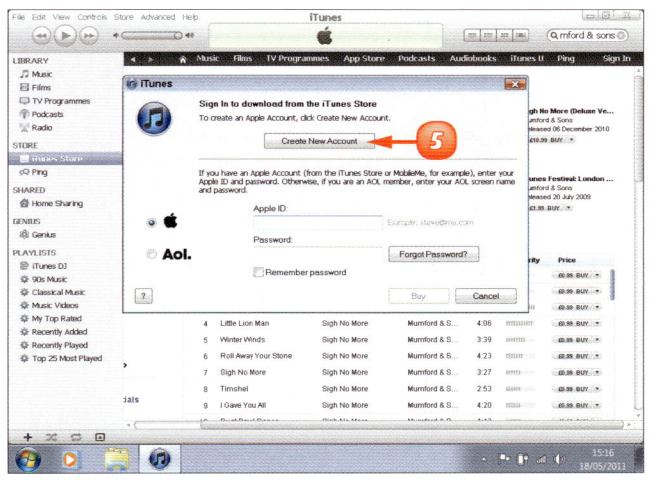

   ✓ *If you already have an account, you can simply enter the details.*

continued ➡

CHAPTER 14 ENTERTAINMENT

DOWNLOAD MUSIC (continued)

Online help is available for iTunes.

iTunes Help

1. Click **Help**.
2. Click **iTunes Tutorials**.

3. Click a topic.
4. Click **Click to Play**.

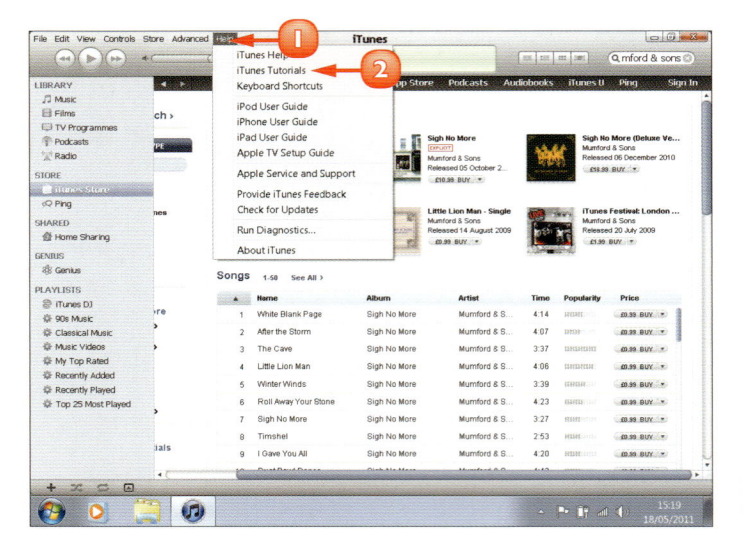

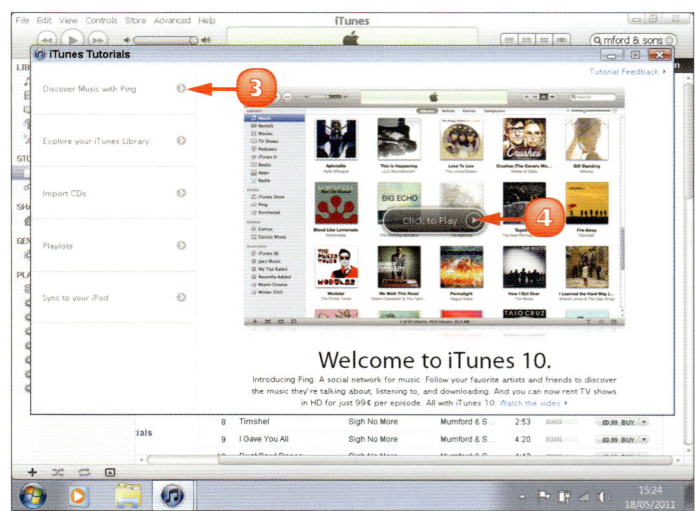

CHAPTER 14 ENTERTAINMENT

LISTEN TO INTERNET RADIO

With Windows Media Player, you can listen to radio stations across the world.

1. Open **Windows Media Player**.
2. Click **Media Guide**.
3. Click the link or type **windowsmedia.com** into the Internet Explorer address bar.

   The Guide appears.
4. Click an icon to select a station.

   The station starts to play.
5. Click **Search** to find a specific station.
6. Scroll down the list and choose a station.
7. Click [ ] to minimise Windows Media Player and listen while continuing with another task.

   A *You can click [X] to close Windows Media Player.*

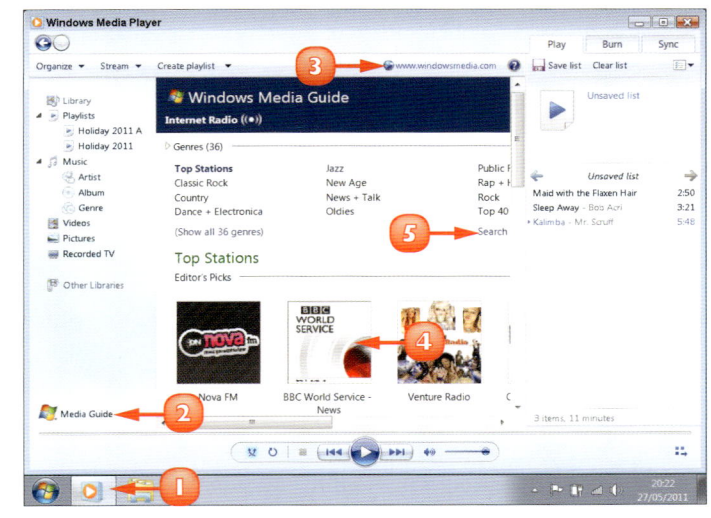

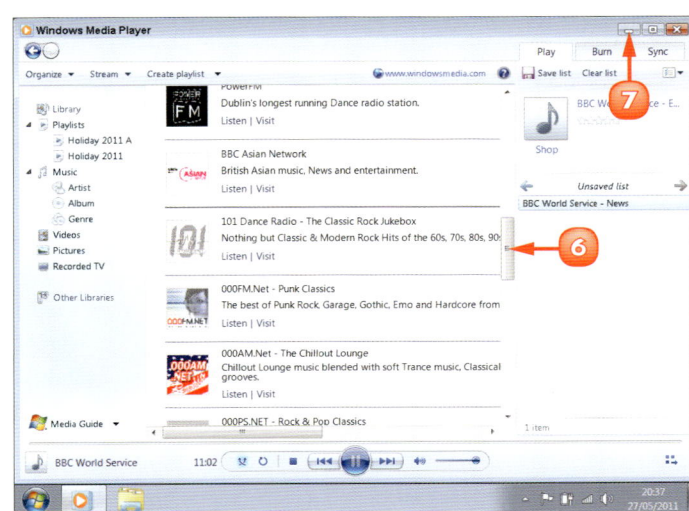

CHAPTER 14 ENTERTAINMENT

INDEX

A

accessing
    Accessories tools, 29
    contact lists, 140
    email accounts, 120–121
    files, 30–31
    Picture Tools, 57
accessories, 28–29
accounts. *See* email
Accounts Spreadsheets. *See also* Excel 2010 (Microsoft)
    adding lines to cells, 170
    creating, 166
    creating Final Total, 169
    entering figures and formulae, 168
    formatting cells for currency, 169
    improving layout, 167
    saving, 166
Action Center, 78
adding
    bullet points in Word 2010, 55
    contacts in Skype, 114
    descriptive tags to pictures, 149
    favourites, 92–93
    information in Excel 2010, 164–165
    lines to cells in Excel 2010, 170
    numbering in Word 2010, 55
    people to contact list, 138–139
    pictures in Word 2010, 57
    Skype to computers, 113
    text in Word 2010, 51
Address bar (Internet Explorer), 86, 140
adjusting
    cell styles in Excel 2010, 163
    column size in Excel 2010, 162
    contact lists, 139
    desktop appearance, 12–13

exposure in pictures, 151
file order, 175
folder view, 181
fonts in Word 2010, 52, 53
home page, 88–89
margins in Word 2010, 56
page size in Word 2010, 56
pictures in Word 2010, 58–59
print settings, 65
printer properties, 64
Quick Access Toolbar, 34–35
row size in Excel 2010, 163
text effects in Word 2010, 53
text size in Word 2010, 53
Windows Explorer view, 174–175
advertisements (email), 123
Aero Peek feature, 31
Aero Shake feature, 25, 31
air travel, booking, 105
aligning paragraphs in Word 2010, 54
antivirus software, 79
appearance (desktop), 12–13
arrow keys, 7, 36
attachments
    opening, 130–131
    removing, 135
    saving, 132–133
    sending, 134–135
auto adjusting pictures, 151

B

background (desktop), 13
Backspace key, 7
banking, online, 110–112
Bing Tools (Internet Explorer), 87
booking tickets and holidays, 106–107
broadband, 74, 87

browser (Web), 77
bullet points (Word 2010), 55
burning pictures to CDs, 152
buying
    books online, 102–103
    on eBay, 108–109
    music, 201

C

Calculator feature, 29
camera, connecting to computer, 144–145
Caps Lock key, 7
CDs
    burning pictures to, 152
    copying folders to, 187
    copying music from/to, 197
    formatting, 186
    removing, 187
cells (Excel 2010)
    adding lines to, 170
    changing styles, 163
    formatting for currency, 169
changing
    cell styles in Excel 2010, 163
    column size in Excel 2010, 162
    contact lists, 139
    desktop appearance, 12–13
    exposure in pictures, 151
    file order, 175
    folder view, 181
    fonts in Word 2010, 52, 53
    home page, 88–89
    margins in Word 2010, 56
    page size in Word 2010, 56
    pictures in Word 2010, 58–59
    print settings, 65
    printer properties, 64
    Quick Access Toolbar, 34–35
    row size in Excel 2010, 163
    text effects in Word 2010, 53
    text size in Word 2010, 53
    Windows Explorer view, 174–175

checking
    bank balances, 111
    sound settings in Skype, 115
    video settings in Skype, 115
choosing
    email accounts, 118–119
    ISPs, 74
    screen savers, 13
    themes, 12
chrome.angrybirds.com (website), 191
closing
    documents, 41
    programs, 20
    windows, 25
columns (Excel 2010)
    changing size, 162
    inserting, 164
Compatibility mode button (Internet Explorer), 86
computer, connecting camera to, 144–145
connections. **See** Internet
contact lists
    adding people to, 138–139
    creating, 160–161
    finding people in, 140–141
contacts (Skype), 114
copying
    documents, 68–69
    folders to CDs, 187
    music to/from CDs, 197
    pictures, 68–69, 153
correcting mistakes, 37, 161
creating
    Accounts Spreadsheets, 166
    contact lists, 160–161
    documents in Word 2010, 50
    email folders, 136
    email messages, 124
    Final Total in Excel 2010, 169
    folders, 180–181
    labels, 44–47
    passwords, 14–15
    playlists, 198

credit card bookings, 107
cropping pictures, 58, 150
cursor, 10, 36

D

date, 11
deleting
    emails, 126
    files, 184
    pictures, 145, 147
    text, 37
    websites from Favorites Bar, 93
desktop
    about, 10
    changing appearance, 12–13
    rearranging icons on, 24
dial-up access, 74
disconnecting
    cameras, 145
    flash drives, 153
documents
    closing, 41
    copying, 68–69
    creating in Word 2010, 50
    opening attachments in email, 130
    opening saved, 42–43
    previewing, 62
    printing, 64–65
    saving, 40, 132
    saving Web pictures to, 97
    saving Web text to, 96
    scanning, 70–71, 80–81
    searching for, 177
    sending, 134
    starting, 36
    zooming, 65
double-clicking, 8, 9
downloading music, 200–202
drafts (email), 125
drag and drop, 9, 183
dragging emails to folders, 137
DVDs, playing, 192

E

eBay, 108–109
email
    accessing accounts, 120–121
    adding people to contact list, 138–139
    choosing and setting up accounts, 118–119
    deleting, 126
    finding people in contact list, 140–141
    junk, 127
    opening attachments, 130–131
    reading and responding to, 122–123
    saving attachments, 132–133
    sending attachments, 134–135
    storing in folders, 136–137
    writing and sending, 124–125
enhancing text in Excel 2010, 165
Enter key, 6
entering figures and formulae in Excel 2010, 168
entertainment
    downloading music, 200–202
    listening to Internet Radio, 203
    listening to music, 196–197
    playing games, 190–191
    using playlists, 198–199
    watching films, 192–193
    watching TV, 194–195
ergonomics, 17
Escape key, 7
Excel 2010 (Microsoft)
    Accounts Spreadsheets, 166–170
    correcting mistakes, 161
    creating contact lists, 160–161
    enhancing text, 165
    help, 27
    inserting columns, 164
    inserting rows, 165
    opening existing spreadsheets, 164
    previewing, 171
    printing, 171
    saving spreadsheets, 161
    setting up columns and rows, 162–163
    starting, 158–159
eyesight, checking, 17

F

F1 key, 7
Facebook, 82
Favorites Bar, 93
favourites, 92–93
figures (Excel 2010), 168
File Tab (Excel 2010), 159
files and folders
    accessing files, 30–31
    changing folder view, 181
    changing order of files, 175
    copying files, 183
    copying folders to CDs, 187
    creating folders, 180–181
    creating in Word 2010, 50
    deleting files, 184
    email folders, 136–137
    finding, 176–178
    JPEG files, 97
    moving files, 182–183
    recovering files, 185
    Recycle Bin, 185
    renaming, 179
    saving copies of files, 186–187
    storing email in, 136–137
    Windows Explorer, 174–175
films, watching, 192–193
finding. **See** searching
Firefox (Mozilla), 77
folders. **See** files and folders
fonts (Word 2010)
    adding bullet points and numbering, 55
    adding pictures, 57
    aligning paragraphs, 54
    changing, 52
    changing font colour and text effects, 53
    changing margins, 56
    changing page size, 56
    changing text size, 53
    modifying pictures, 58–59
formatting
    CDs, 186
    cells for currency in Excel 2010, 169
formulae (Excel 2010), 168

G

games, playing, 190–191
getting started
    desktop appearance, 12–13
    health and safety, 17
    keyboard, 6–7
    locking computer, 16
    mouse, 8–9
    password protection, 14–15
    shut down, 5
    start up, 4
    touchpad, 9
    unlocking computer, 16
    Windows 7 screen, 10–11
Google, 118
grammar check, 36
gridlines, printing in Excel 2010, 171

H

hardware, 21
health and safety, 17
help
    Excel 2010, 27
    iTunes, 202
    Windows 7, 26–27
Help Button (Excel 2010), 159
highlighting text in Word 2010, 55
History (Internet Explorer), 86
Home icon, 91
home page, 88–89
Hotmail, 118, 120–121

I

icons, 10, 24
importing pictures, 144–145
inserting
    columns in Excel 2010, 164
    rows in Excel 2010, 165
installing iTunes software, 200
International payments, with online banking, 111
Internet. **See also** email
    booking tickets and holidays, 106–107
    broadband, 74, 87
    changing home pages, 88–89

Internet *(continued)*
    choosing ISPs, 74
    connection types, 75
    eBay, 108–109
    getting started, 76–77
    Internet Explorer, 86–87
    online banking, 110–112
    online shopping, 100–103
    printing Web pages, 94–95
    safety, 78–79
    saving favourite pages, 92–93
    saving text and pictures, 96–97
    searching Internet, 90–91
    sharing pictures on, 154–155
    Skype, 113–115
    social networking, 82–83
    travel sites, 104–105
    Windows Live Essentials, 80–81
Internet Explorer (Microsoft), 76, 77, 86–87
Internet Radio, 203
ISPs, 74
iTunes, 200, 202

J
JPEG files, 97
Jump List feature, 30
junk mail, 127

K
keyboard, 6–7
keypad, 68

L
labels, 44–7
left handed mouse, 9
Let Windows Suggest Settings option, 23
letter keys, 6
listening
    to Internet Radio, 203
    to music, 196–197
locking computer, 16
logging in to SkyDrive, 155

M
Magnifier feature, 28
Main Window (Internet Explorer), 87
managing email folders, 137
maps, printing, 94–95
margins (Word 2010), 56
maximising
    screen space, 93
    windows, 25
media
    downloading music, 200–202
    listening to Internet Radio, 203
    listening to music, 196–197
    playing games, 190–191
    using playlists, 198–199
    watching films, 192–193
    watching TV, 194–195
Microsoft Internet Explorer, 76, 77, 86–87
Microsoft Messenger, 82
Microsoft Office. **See** Excel 2010 (Microsoft); Word 2010 (Microsoft)
Microsoft Windows 7. **See** Windows 7 (Microsoft)
minimising windows, 25
mistakes, correcting, 37
mouse, 8–9
Mouse Properties dialog box, 9
moving
    blocks of text, 37
    between documents, 65
    email folders, 137
    files, 182–183
    pictures in Word 2010, 59
Mozilla Firefox, 77
MP3 players, syncing playlists to, 199
mums (website), 82
music
    buying, 201
    copying from/to CDs, 197
    downloading, 200–202
    listening to, 196–197
    playing, 196
    playlists, 198–199

N

navigating Word 2010 documents, 36
Navigation tools (Internet Explorer), 86
Notification Area, 11
number keys, 6
numbering (Word 2010), 55

O

online banking, 110–112
online shopping, 100–103
opening
    attachments, 130–131
    pictures, 146
    programs, 8, 22
    saved documents, 42–43
    spreadsheets, 164
    Windows Explorer, 174
optimising visual displays, 23
Organise Menu, 182

P

page size (Word 2010), 56
paragraphs, aligning in Word 2010, 54
password protection, 14–15
passwords
    email, 118–119
    hint, 4, 16
payments, making with online banking, 110
PayPal, 109
phone calls (Skype), 115
Picture Tools, 57
pictures
    adding in Word 2010, 57
    adjusting exposure, 151
    auto adjusting, 151
    burning to CD, 152
    copying, 68–69, 153
    cropping, 58, 150
    deleting, 145, 147
    modifying in Word 2010, 58–59
    opening, 146
    opening attachments in email, 131
    previewing, 63
    printing, 66–67
    saving, 133
    saving to flash drives, 152–153
    scanning, 70–71
    searching, 149
    sending, 135
    sharing on Internet, 154–155
    straightening, 151
    tagging, 148–149
    transferring from camera to computer, 144–145
    viewing, 147
    Web, saving to documents, 97
Pictures Tools, 97
playing
    DVDs, 192
    games, 190–191
    music, 196
playlists, 198–199
previewing
    documents, 62
    panes in Windows Explorer, 175
    pictures, 63
    spreadsheets, 171
Print dialog box, 95
Print Preview, 62–63
printing and scanning
    copying documents and pictures, 68–69
    Print Preview, 62–63
    printing documents, 64–65
    printing gridlines, 171
    printing maps, 94–95
    printing pictures, 66–67
    printing spreadsheets, 171
    printing Web pages, 94–95
    scanning documents and pictures, 70–71, 80–81
programs
    closing, 20
    opening, 8, 22
    windows, 22

Q

Quick Access Toolbar, 34–35, 159
Quick Link Tabs (Internet Explorer), 87

R

reading emails, 122
rearranging icons, 24
Recently Contacted List, 141
recovering files, 185
Recycle Bin, 147, 185
Refresh button (Internet Explorer), 86
registering
    on eBay, 108
    for online banking, 110
removing
    advertisements in emails, 123
    attachments, 135
    CDs, 187
renaming files and folders, 179
resizing pictures in Word 2010, 58
responding to emails, 123
restarting, 5
retrieving
    deleted emails, 126
    messages from Junk folder, 127
Ribbon (Excel 2010), 159
Ribbon Minimise Button (Excel 2010), 159
Right-Click Menu, 183
right-clicking, 9
ripping music from CDs, 197
rows (Excel 2010)
    changing size, 163
    inserting, 165

S

safety (Internet), 78–79
saving
    Accounts Spreadsheets, 166
    attachments, 132–133
    documents, 40, 132
    emails as drafts, 125
    favourite pages, 92–93
    pictures to CDs/flash drives, 152–153
    spreadsheets, 161
    Web pictures to documents, 97
    Web text to documents, 96
scanning. **See** printing and scanning

screen (Windows 7), 7, 10–11, 22–23
screen savers, 13
scroll bar
    navigating Word 2010 pages with, 36
    in panes, 181
Scroll Bar (Internet Explorer), 87
Search Box (Internet Explorer), 87
searching
    for books online, 100–101
    for contacts, 141
    for documents, 177
    files and folders, 176–178
    Internet, 90–91
    people in contact list, 140–141
    pictures, 149
    in specific locations, 178
security, 78–79
selecting
    email accounts, 118–119
    ISPs, 74
    screen savers, 13
    themes, 12
selling on eBay, 109
sending
    attachments, 134–135
    emails, 125
    messages to Junk folder, 127
seniors (website), 82
setting up
    email accounts, 118–119
    group email, 139
    home pages, 89
sharing pictures on Internet, 154–155
Shift keys, 7
shopping online, 100–103
shut down, 5
signing in to email accounts, 120–121
signing out of email accounts, 121
SkyDrive (Windows), 154–155
Skype, 113–115
Snap feature, 25, 31
Snipping Tool feature, 29
social networking, 82–83

software
  antivirus, 79
  copying with, 69
  defined, 21
  iTunes, 200
sound settings (Skype), 115
Space bar, 6
spell check, 38–39, 124
spreadsheets
  opening, 164
  previewing, 171
  printing, 171
  saving, 161
standing orders, in online banking, 112
Start button, 10
Start menu, 20–21, 26, 30
start up, 4
starting
  documents, 36
  Excel 2010, 158
  Word 2010, 34
Status Bar (Excel 2010), 159
Sticky Notes feature, 28
Stop button (Internet Explorer), 86
storing email in folders, 136–137
straightening pictures, 151
symbol keys, 6
syncing playlists to MP3 players, 199

T

Tab key, 6
tagging pictures, 148–149
taskbar
  about, 11
  Jump List on, 30
  rearranging icons on, 24
Taskbar icons, 11
text
  adding in Word 2010, 51
  changing effects in Word 2010, 53
  changing size in Word 2010, 53
  deleting, 37
  enhancing in Excel 2010, 165
  highlighting in Word 2010, 55
  moving blocks of, 37
  Web, saving to documents, 96
Text Search feature, 149
themes, selecting, 12
Thesaurus feature, 39
thetrainline.com (website), 104
time, 11
Title Bar (Excel 2010), 159
Title Bar (Internet Explorer), 86
title bar icons, 25
To: box, accessing contact list from, 140
Toolbar (Internet Explorer), 86
tools
  Accessories, 29
  Picture, 57
touchpad, 9
travel websites, 104–105
Twitter, 82

U

UK train travel, 104
unlocking computer, 16
uploading to Windows SkyDrive, 154–155

V

video settings (Skype), 115
videos, watching online, 193
viewing
  contact list, 141
  folders, 181
  pictures, 147
visual displays, optimising, 23

W

watching
  films, 192–193
  TV, 194–195
  videos online, 193
Web browser, 77
Web pages, printing, 94–95
Web pictures, saving to documents, 97
Web text, saving to documents, 96

Window Controls (Excel 2010), 159
windows (program), 22, 25
windows (Windows 7), 24
Windows 7 (Microsoft)
    accessing files, 30–31
    accessories, 28–29
    games, 190
    help, 26–27
    icons, 24
    screen, 10–11, 22–23
    Start menu, 20–21
    startup, 4
    windows, 25
Windows Explorer, 174–175
Windows Live Essentials, 80–81
Windows Media Player, 203
Windows SkyDrive, 154–155
wireless broadband access, 74
Word 2010 (Microsoft)
    adding bullet points and numbering, 55
    adding pictures, 57
    adding text to documents, 51
    closing documents, 41
    correcting mistakes, 37
    creating documents, 50
    creating labels, 44–7
    fonts, 52, 53
    Help, 27
    modifying Quick Access Toolbar, 34–35
    navigating, 36
    opening saved documents, 42–43
    saving documents, 40
    spelling and grammar check, 38–39
    starting, 34
    starting documents, 36
Workbook Window Controls (Excel 2010), 159
Worksheet (Excel 2010), 159
writing emails, 124

Y

YouTube, 82

Z

zooming, 65

SIMPLY
the easiest way to tackle technology...

- ✓ Step-by-step introduction to technology
- ✓ Concise, jargon-free information
- ✓ Packed with full-colour screenshots

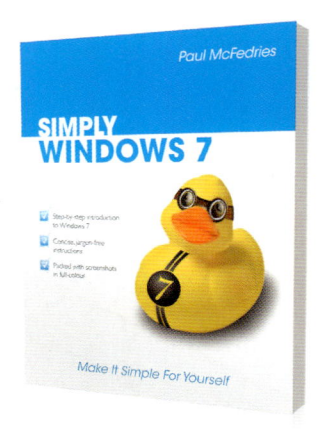

SIMPLY WINDOWS 7 — Paul McFedries
ISBN 978-0-470-71133-0
£10.99

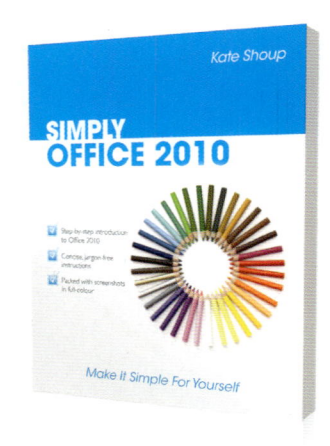

SIMPLY OFFICE 2010 — Kate Shoup
ISBN 978-0-470-71129-3
£10.99

Available from all good bookshops

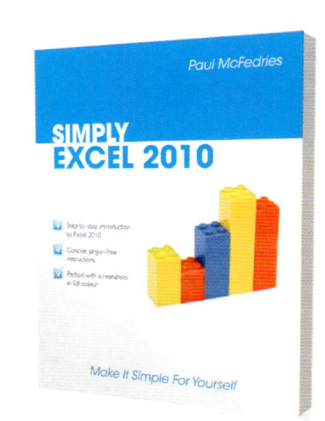

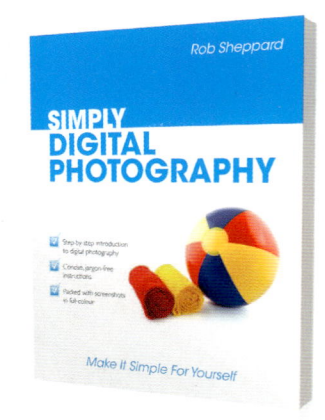

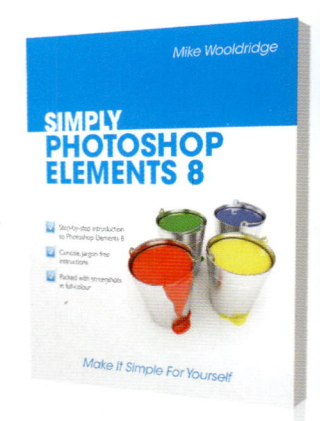

SIMPLY EXCEL 2010 — Paul McFedries
ISBN 978-0-470-71131-6
£10.99

SIMPLY DIGITAL PHOTOGRAPHY — Rob Sheppard
ISBN 978-0-470-71132-3
£10.99

SIMPLY PHOTOSHOP ELEMENTS 8 — Mike Wooldridge
ISBN 978-0-470-71128-6
£10.99

WILEY
wiley.com